DINNER TONIGHT

For Zach and Henry

ABOUT THE AUTHOR

Lindsey Bareham started to cook seriously when she was asked to edit the restaurant section of *Time Out* and has built a reputation for recipes that always work, taste good and are easy to achieve, even by the most inexperienced cook. She wrote a daily after-work recipe for the *Evening Standard* for eight years and currently writes the much-loved *Dinner Tonight* daily column for *The Times*. She is the author of over a dozen cookery books including *In Praise of the Potato, A Celebration of Soup, Dinner in a Dash, The Fish Store, The Trifle Bowl and Other Tales* and *Just One Pot*. She also wrote *The Prawn Cocktail Years* with Simon Hopkinson and helped him write *Roast Chicken and Other Stories*, which has been voted the Most Useful Cookery Book Ever by chefs and food writers.

Also by Lindsey Bareham
In Praise of the Potato
A Celebration of Soup
Onions Without Tears
The Little Book of Big Soups
The Big Red Book of Tomatoes
Supper Won't Take Long
A Wolf in the Kitchen
Just One Pot
Dinner in a Dash
Hungry?
The Fish Store
Pasties
The Trifle Bowl and Other Tales
One Pot Wonders

With Simon Hopkinson
Roast Chicken and Other Stories
The Prawn Cocktail Years

An Hachette UK Company
www.hachette.co.uk

First published in Great Britain in 2016 by Mitchell Beazley, a division of Octopus Publishing Group Ltd, Carmelite House, 50 Victoria Embankment, London EC4Y 0DZ
www.octopusbooks.co.uk

The recipes in this book were previously published in *The Times' Dinner Tonight* column.

Design and layout copyright © Octopus Publishing Group 2016
Text copyright © Home Cook Limited 2016

ISBN 978-1-78472-111-4

A CIP catalogue record for this book is available from the British Library.

Printed and bound in China.

10 9 8 7 6 5 4 3 2 1

Publisher's notes
- Standard level spoon measurements are used in all recipes.

  1 tablespoon = one 15 ml spoon
  1 teaspoon = one 5 ml spoon
- Eggs should be medium unless otherwise stated.
- Milk should be whole or semi-skimmed unless otherwise stated.

DINNER TONIGHT

200 DISHES YOU CAN COOK IN MINUTES

Lindsey Bareham

Illustrations by Lucinda Rogers

MITCHELL BEAZLEY

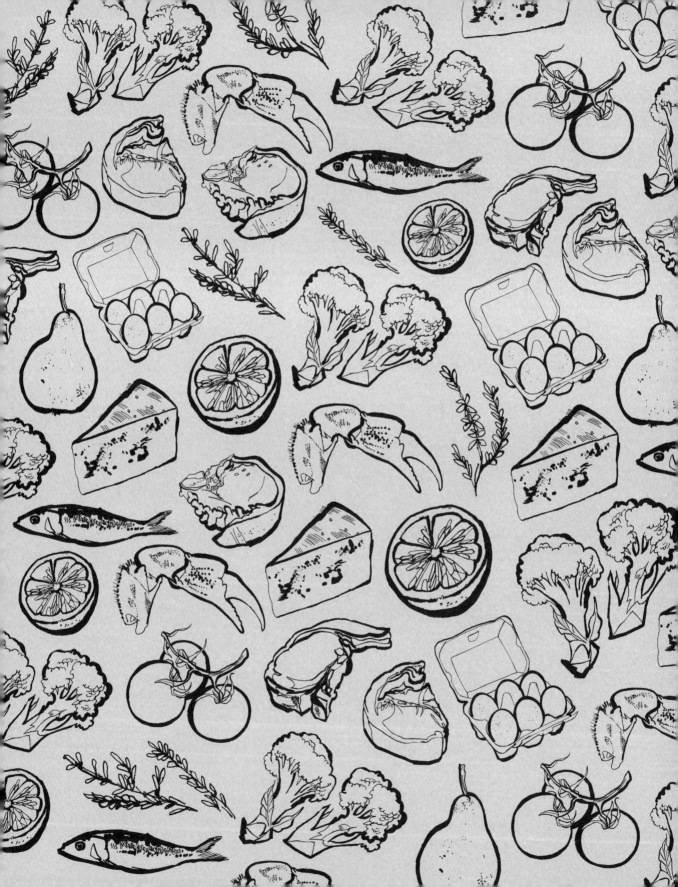

CONTENTS

INTRODUCTION

It's 6.30pm, the working day is over and I'm in my kitchen peering into the fridge and wondering what I am going to cook for dinner. It's particularly well stocked today because I've just done a supermarket shop, yesterday was farmers' market day and this morning there were bargains aplenty at my favourite fruit and veg stall on the high road. It's not always like this. I am not an organized shopper and often face self-imposed gluts and run out of basics like onions and canned tomatoes. But I like putting myself on the spot when it comes to deciding what's for dinner tonight. Not for me a handful of weekly regular favourites; my job is creating something fresh and interesting that anyone can cook for supper when they get home from work.

Tonight the fridge is fit to burst with a huge cauliflower taking up most of one shelf. Maybe I'll turn it into risotto or a chunky soup with lemon zest, basil and Parmesan. Perhaps I'll fry it with Indian spices. There are fillets of sole that need eating up, so maybe it'll be fish fingers with cheesy cauliflower purée. But there are tomatoes in a bowl on the table that beg to be turned into pasta sauce, I have leeks and minced lamb, two fat glistening aubergines, and peas in the freezer. Ideas are whizzing round my head, but I have a vegetarian friend coming to dinner tonight, so I'd better concentrate on that thought.

Inspiration for my *Dinner Tonight* column in *The Times* comes from anywhere and everywhere. People always ask where I get my ideas and it could be a chance remark, a pub menu, something I heard on the radio or the changing seasons. I go through crazes. It might be the discovery of an ingredient like giant couscous, known as maftoul in Palestine and fregola in Italy, or a smart new way of cooking fish or using an unfamiliar seasoning. Always, though, the recipes are healthy and don't rely on a load of arcane or expensive ingredients. The recipes don't depend on a big supermarket shop either; in fact they tend to be easy to shop for on the way home from work. Often, it's likely that much of what is required is already in the fridge, freezer or food cupboard.

The recipes are a mixture to encompass all our after-work eating moods and needs. There are quick and easy pasta dishes and simple yet stylish ways of cooking and serving familiar fish like cod but also lesser-known, cheaper varieties such as gurnard, Cornish sole (megrim) and sardines. There are dishes that show how to use the remains of the Sunday lunch with stylish aplomb and how to afford a mid-week steak dinner. There are plenty of ways of cooking chicken, of using minced meats and of cooking with inexpensive cuts like belly pork and daunting offal such as lambs' liver and kidneys. When the cupboard is bare and inspiration lacking, there are ideas for making a feast from a fridge clear-out or a scrounge at the back of the food cupboard.

Seasonality rings through the book, incorporating recipes for seasonal gluts, like cauliflower, tomatoes, strawberries, asparagus and courgettes. Often an unexpected extra, it could be something from the fruit bowl, or chilli, saffron or ginger, or fresh herbs like mint or dill that will take flavours in a surprising direction. Economy and value for money are built into the recipes, but when something is worth splashing out on, it is put into context. Conversely, *Dinner Tonight* is not a food snob, so some of the super-quick recipes incorporate useful storecupboard standbys like piquillo peppers in a jar, Spanish diced onions wilted in olive oil in a can, ready-made gnocchi or pre-cooked lentils.

There are comfort dishes, dishes using leftovers and clever ways of using very ordinary ingredients like frozen peas and canned beans, with appetizing spins on familiar dishes such as bangers and mash and cauliflower cheese. There are dishes without meat and many that use a small amount to good effect. There are big salmagundi salads and hearty main-dish soups using storecupboard staples such as tinned chickpeas, lentils, beans, quinoa and gnocchi as well as seasonal foods. There are dishes for one or two, dishes for four and more, and puddings for people who think they haven't the time to make puddings. Although most of the recipes are aimed at speedy gratification, there are also dishes to make now and eat later, and dishes that could be made today for tomorrow.

This is the book I have been longing to write for many years and it's a response to the endless requests I receive from *The Times* readers wanting a book of *Dinner Tonight* recipes. The column has a touchingly loyal following that generates appreciative letters with stories of when particular recipes were used for particular occasions. Many readers cut out and stick the recipes on kitchen pin boards or the fridge. Others have a ring binder ordered by key ingredient and that is how this book is organized, as in, *'I have some chicken/salmon/ sausages in the fridge in need of using up'*, or *'How can I turn a mountain of tomatoes/ aubergine/cauliflower into supper for four?'* These are the sorts of questions I am regularly asked. I once saw an extremely unwieldy collection of laminated *Dinner Tonight* recipes that spilled across its own work surface.

Above all, this is a book that understands the demands of a working person with a home to run who wants to eat healthily and well. Recipes are written in my trademark style of *real time*, with the preparations done in the order they really happen in rather than sliced onions or tablespoons of chopped parsley being shunted into the ingredients list. This means that anyone can follow the recipes; you don't have to be an experienced cook to get results. There are canny tips for time-saving. If, for example, boiling water is required for a recipe, I will suggest putting on the kettle rather than a pan. Kettles boil faster than open pans – a tip from Edouard de Pomiane in *Cooking in Ten Minutes*, which was first published in 1948.

So, whatever you decide to make – be it a completely new recipe or an update on an old favourite – I do hope that you enjoy cooking, eating and sharing my recipes as much as I do.

Eggs and Cheese

Eggs and cheese are perfect storecupboard standbys for quick, easy meals. I'm a stickler for buying the best available eggs, by which I mean fresh, organic and free-range. It pays to open the box and check over the eggs to ensure there are no cracks.

Learning to cook eggs well is a basic but important skill. I once saw Albert Roux (then three-Michelin-starred chef of Le Gavroche, now run by his son Michel) fry an egg, treating it like the finest fillet steak. The magical properties of eggs mean that they combine with other modest ingredients, like onions, to make stupendous tarts; a godsend for feeding a crowd.

Grating hard cheeses or crumbling soft cheeses over salad, baked potatoes or pasta is a gift for fast, lazy meals. Melting blue cheese to make sauces for pasta or salads is another useful trick and so is grilling feta and halloumi. Both look and taste delicious with peppery salad leaves and lime and chilli vinaigrette.

EGGS

If you have eggs in the fridge, you won't go hungry. Variations on a breakfast fry-up are the easy option, but an omelette or scramble, adding cheese or torn ham, chopped tomatoes or herbs, is easy enough. A poached egg will turn soup or salad, dahl or a baked potato into supper.

SALAD AUVERGNATE

SERVES 2 | **PREP** 20 MINUTES | **COOK** 20 MINUTES

The name of this salad gives little away, although aficionados might expect Cantal cheese and potatoes, two favourites in the cooking of the Auvergne. Here the creamy, firm cheese is sliced thinly in big pieces and layered with green beans, tomato wedges, frilly leaves and country ham. The whole lot is hidden under a dramatically fried egg, the yolk soft and the white spread super-thin and the size of a plate. The garnish is thin slices of potato, quickly fried and arranged around the edge of the dish, with chives giving an oniony finish. A triumphant take on ham, egg and chips.

150g green beans
2 vine tomatoes
100g Cantal or Ossau-Iraty
  cheese
1 small oak leaf or other frilly
  green lettuce or 80g bag
  mixed salad leaves
2 Charlotte or other large
  new potatoes
small bunch of chives
6 slices of cured ham such as
  Serrano or Parma
2 tablespoons sunflower oil
2 eggs
crusty bread and butter,
  to serve

For the vinaigrette
1 teaspoon smooth Dijon
  mustard
1 tablespoon red wine vinegar
3 tablespoons sunflower oil
salt and freshly ground
  black pepper

Top and tail the beans, snap in half and boil in salted water for 2 minutes. Drain, then splash with cold water to cool and arrest cooking.

Cut the core from the tomatoes in a pointed plug shape and cut into quarters. Slice the cheese into large thin slices approximately 7 × 4cm × 2mm thick.

Next make the vinaigrette. Put everything in a jam jar with a lid and give it a good shake or whisk thoroughly until smooth.

Separate the lettuce leaves, rinse and shake dry. Peel the potatoes, slice as if making thick chips and cut in half into bite-sized pieces. Finely slice 1 tablespoon chives.

Assemble the salad on 2 dinner plates, layering lettuce, tomatoes, beans, a few chives, cheese and ham. Heat the oil in a spacious (preferably) non-stick frying pan and quickly fry the potatoes in batches until just cooked through and lightly golden. Transfer to kitchen paper to drain as you go.

Spoon the vinaigrette over the salad. Quickly fry the eggs in the frying pan, one after another, aiming to spread the white by swirling the pan. Top each salad with an egg and edge with potato slices. Scatter with the remaining chives and serve with crusty bread and butter.

SCRAMBLED EGGS ON TOAST WITH SMOKED SALMON AND HERBS

SERVES 2 | **PREP** 15 MINUTES | **COOK** 15 MINUTES

This simple dish, cooked by a friend for brunch one Christmas Day, was the hit of the holiday. I make it often, for supper, using relatively inexpensive smoked salmon trimmings and serve it on buttered toast with a dill or chive garnish to sharpen the flavours. Instead of smoked salmon, try crisp-fried chorizo slices or batons of smoked streaky bacon. It's also good with roasted red pepper or skinned, deseeded and diced tomato instead of salmon, chorizo or bacon.

100g smoked salmon trimmings

6 eggs

40g butter

1 tablespoon thick cream, optional

2 thick slices of sourdough bread

1 tablespoon finely snipped chives or dill

salt and freshly ground black pepper

Snip the salmon into bite-sized pieces. Whisk the eggs and season lightly with salt, generously with pepper.

Melt most of the butter – the rest is for buttering the toast – in a non-stick medium pan over a medium–low heat and add the eggs. Stir constantly with a wooden spoon, from the sides to the middle, keeping the eggs on the move to avoid them sticking, adjusting the heat as necessary, continuing until beginning to set.

Pop the bread in the toaster now.

If you're going for the luxury version, stir the cream into the eggs, then the smoked salmon. The smoked salmon should barely change colour and the eggs should remain soft and creamy.

Butter the toast, top with the egg and salmon mix and sprinkle over the chives or dill.

PEA AND PARMESAN FRITTATA

SERVES 4 | **PREP** 5 MINUTES | **COOK** 25 MINUTES

I often buy bread from Carluccio's, and one day as I waited in line, the person ahead of me ordered a slice from a lovely-looking pea frittata. It was the inspiration for this big fat omelette. I like it served cold, in thin slices as a snack (good in the lunch box) with a dribble of sweet chilli dipping sauce, or over crisp salad with lime and chilli vinaigrette.

150g frozen petits pois
6 eggs
2 tablespoons mascarpone
　or crème fraîche, optional
50g Parmesan cheese
knob of butter
salt and freshly ground
　black pepper
asparagus or lettuce salad,
　to serve

Cook the peas in plenty of salted water until tender. Drain and set aside.
　Preheat the oven to 200°C, Gas Mark 6.
　Separate the eggs. Use a fork to mix the yolks with the mascarpone or crème fraîche, if using, and grate most of the Parmesan over the top. Season and add the peas. Give a final stir. Whisk the egg whites until they form soft peaks. Use a metal spoon to stir a couple of tablespoons into the yolks, then fold the rest in as if making a soufflé, which you are, sort of.
　Melt the butter in a deep, heavy-based, 20cm non-stick frying pan with an ovenproof handle, swirling it round the sides but not allowing it to brown. Add the eggs. Place on a middle shelf in the oven and cook for 15–20 minutes or until the top is souffléd and just set.
　Serve hot, warm or cold. Grate the remaining Parmesan over, before serving in wedges with asparagus, or lettuce salad.

ROAST PEPPER EGGS

SERVES 2 | **PREP** 15 MINUTES | **COOK** 35 MINUTES

A quick and easy eggs-on-toast supper inspired by Piperade, a Basque dish of scrambled egg with roast peppers.

2 Romano red peppers
6 eggs
50g butter plus extra for
　the toast
1 tablespoon snipped chives
4 rashers smoked streaky
　bacon
2 thick slices of sourdough
　bread
salt and freshly ground
　black pepper

Preheat the oven to 200°C, Gas Mark 6.
　Lay the peppers on a small baking tin. As soon as the oven comes up to temperature, pop in the peppers and cook for 15 minutes. Turn the peppers and cook for 5–10 more minutes, no more.
　Transfer the peppers to a plate. Cover with a tight stretch of clingfilm. Leave for 10 minutes, then rip off the skin. Remove the stalks, pulling away as many seeds as possible, then split the floppy peppers lengthways and scrape away the remaining seeds. Re-cover to keep warm. Preheat the grill to high.
　Crack the eggs into a mixing bowl. Scramble with a fork, seasoning with salt and pepper. Melt half the butter in a small – ideally non-stick – saucepan and stir in the eggs. Stir constantly, adjusting the heat, so that the eggs cook gently and evenly. When they are slightly under-cooked, stir in the remaining 25g butter and the snipped chives. Turn off the heat.
　Meanwhile, grill the bacon until very crisp. Toast and butter the bread. Pile the eggs over the toast, drape with peppers and garnish with bacon criss-cross.

ALSACE ONION TART

SERVES 4 | **PREP** 30 MINUTES | **COOK** 1¼ HOURS

The classic onion tart of Alsace with its crisp pastry base and succulent filling turns a few egg yolks, a carton of cream and a humongous amount of onions into a luxurious treat. The onion must be cooked slowly, turning into sweet, buttery softness. This can take up to an hour, but it's undemanding work that fills the house with wonderful aromas. The tart reheats perfectly; either in portions or the whole thing.

The leftover egg whites could be whisked into meringue (50g caster sugar to each egg white, added 1 tablespoon at a time to the whisked eggs piped onto a baking parchment-lined baking sheet and baked in a preheated oven at 150°C, Gas Mark 2 for 1½ hours).

125g butter plus extra
   for greasing
100g plain flour plus extra
   for dusting
5 egg yolks
4 Spanish onions
300ml double cream
salt

Dice 50g of the butter and quickly rub it into the flour. Add 1 egg yolk, a pinch of salt and enough cold water to form a firm dough. Knead into a ball, pop in a plastic bag and chill for 30 minutes.

Meanwhile, halve, peel and finely slice the onions. Melt the remaining butter in a spacious, lidded pan over a low heat. Add the onions and ½ teaspoon salt. Stew very gently, covered, stirring occasionally, for about 25 minutes until soft, sloppy and hardly coloured. Remove the lid and continue cooking until the liquid has evaporated. Set aside to cool.

Preheat the oven to 180°C, Gas Mark 4. Butter a 20cm loose-based flan tin, dust with flour and shake out the excess. Roll out the pastry, on a flour-dusted surface, as thinly as possible and use it to line the tin. Cover the pastry with foil or baking parchment and fill with baking beans or raw rice. Blind bake the pastry case for 15 minutes. Remove the foil or parchment and return to the oven for 5 minutes until straw-coloured. Place on a baking sheet. Using a fork, mix the remaining egg yolks and cream into the cooled onions. Tip into the pastry case, filling to the rim. Bake for 30 minutes or until set and lightly browned.

Cool slightly, then stand the flan tin on a can to remove the collar.

CHEESE

I try never to run out of cheese because I am addicted to cheese on toast. When you break out of the Cheddar and mustard rut, there are so many ways of ringing the changes. Apart from the flavour and melting qualities of different cheeses, the bread and complementary add-ons transform this great British standby.

In an ideal world I always have a big chunk of Parmesan, a block of feta and another of mature Cheddar or something similar in my fridge. I am also rarely without blue cheese. I use feta constantly. Its gently assertive flavour and creamy yet crumbly texture give instant interest to so many things, from omelettes to salad, pastries and tarts. And it goes with figs and other soft fruit. Feta grills beautifully, softening like blancmange with a thin golden crust. Try it on toast, with caramelized onion underneath surrounded by salad. Always buy Greek feta, which will be made with goats' or sheep's milk, and try aged feta, which is richer and denser. I buy both from a Greek importer at my local farmers' market (www.thefoodmarketchiswick.com). He is also worth a special journey for other Greek cheeses, honey and olive oil. The best way to keep feta is covered in water in a plastic box in the fridge, which is how he sells it. All recipes that specify feta could be made with soft goats' cheese instead.

PASTA WITH FETA, WALNUTS AND DILL
SERVES 2 | **PREP** 15 MINUTES | **COOK** 15 MINUTES

The paucity of the ingredients belies the deliciousness of this simple pasta dish.

12 walnut halves
2 garlic cloves
10g dill
about 8 mint or basil leaves
200g pappardelle
4 tablespoons Greek or other
 fruity olive oil
100g Greek feta cheese
salt
rocket salad, to serve

Roast the walnut halves in a heavy frying pan, tossing them around for a couple of minutes until aromatic and slightly darkened in colour. This intensifies their flavour. Cool slightly and break into chunky pieces.

Crack open the garlic cloves, flake away the skin, chop finely, then crush to a paste with the flat of a knife. Tear the fronds off the dill stalks and chop. Shred the mint or basil leaves.

Cook the pasta according to the packet instructions in plenty of salted water. Drain. Add 2 tablespoons olive oil and the garlic to the pasta pan. Cook, stirring constantly, for a couple of minutes until aromatic.

Return the pasta to the pan and stir to mix. Add the walnuts, dill and mint or basil. Crumble the feta over the top and combine. Serve drizzled with the remaining olive oil and accompanied by rocket salad.

LETTUCE HEARTS WITH ROQUEFORT SAUCE

SERVES 6 | **PREP** 15 MINUTES | **COOK** 5 MINUTES

I can't pretend this is a low-cal salad but it's such a delicious one, guaranteed to become a favourite. And so simple. It is useful in all sorts of ways. Try it as a starter, alone, or with Parma or Serrano ham, or with a grilled cherry tomato salad made by grilling them with 1 part balsamic vinegar to 4 parts olive oil for 5–8 minutes until the tomatoes pop but before they collapse. Scoop the tomatoes into a serving dish, then crush a clove of garlic and stir it into the oil mix before pouring it over the top of the tomatoes. Leave to cool before adding a few torn basil leaves.

This is great as a side dish, too, with barbecued meats or as an all-in-one cheese and salad course before pud. It could also be made with other blue cheese; at Christmas try Stilton.

200g Roquefort cheese
4 tablespoons crème fraîche
6 Little Gem lettuce hearts
(as small as possible)

Break the cheese into pieces into a small saucepan. Add the crème fraîche and gently cook together over a low heat, stirring occasionally, until melted. Remove from the heat and leave to cool.

Wash the whole lettuce hearts and shake dry. Trim the stalk and remove any damaged outer leaves. Halve small lettuce hearts lengthways and quarter larger ones, ensuring to cut through the stalk-cum-core so that most of the leaves stay attached. Arrange, cut-side uppermost, on a serving platter, nudging the pieces close together. Pour over the cooled sauce, making sure it dribbles through the layers. Yum.

GORGONZOLA DOLCE AND POLENTA GRATIN

SERVES 2, GENEROUSLY | **PREP** 15 MINUTES | **COOK** 25 MINUTES

There are two types of Gorgonzola, the protected blue cows' milk cheese made by 30-odd producers in a designated area around Milan. *Dolce* is mild, squidgy and very creamy, while *piccante* resembles Stilton. I chose the former to make this luscious gratin and used plenty of it layered between molten polenta, the dish buttered first and liberally coated with grated Parmesan. The Parmesan forms an all-round thin crust and the Gorgonzola becomes Vesuvial as it oozes between the soft polenta. Eat it in chunky slices hot from the oven with extra Parmesan.

A few roasted red peppers cooked in the oven at the same time or a thick, smooth tomato sauce go well with this. Slices fry up beautifully, so it's a useful make-ahead dish and could be served as a starter with a walnut and chicory salad.

50g butter

3 tablespoons freshly grated Parmesan cheese plus extra to serve

200g dolce Gorgonzola cheese

150g quick-cook (1-minute) polenta

salt and freshly ground black pepper

Boil the kettle. Use some of the butter to liberally grease a 1-litre, 4cm-deep gratin dish. Use some of the Parmesan to coat the sides and base of the dish. Cut the rind off the Gorgonzola (it is edible but will spoil the texture of this dish).

Measure 600ml boiling water from the kettle into a deep saucepan. Bring to the boil and add the polenta, immediately stirring with a wooden spoon. Keep stirring for a minute or until the polenta is thick and coming away from the sides of the pan. Stir in the remaining butter and season to taste.

Pour one third of the polenta into the prepared dish, then slice half the Gorgonzola over the top. Make another layer of polenta and cheese, then finish with polenta. Dredge the top with the remaining Parmesan. Bake for 25 minutes or until the Parmesan has formed a thin crust. Serve immediately, cut into thick slabs dusted with extra Parmesan.

GOATS' CHEESE RAREBIT WITH BACON

SERVES 2 | **PREP** 15 MINUTES | **COOK** 10 MINUTES

There's a Roy Lichtenstein card called Mustard on White perched on my kitchen windowsill and it looks remarkably like this scratch supper. I use Dijon mustard for this subtle take on Welsh rarebit with mature Cheddar-style goats' cheese, a splash of white wine and an egg, the yolk stirred into the hot mix and the stiffly whisked white folded in at the last minute. The thick, creamy cheese is spooned over hot toast, then flashed under the grill where it puffs and turns golden very quickly.

4 tablespoons white wine
150g mature hard goats'
　cheese
2 teaspoons Dijon mustard
1 egg
2 large slices of sourdough
　or country bread
4 rashers pancetta or thin-cut
　rindless streaky bacon
salad leaves, to serve

Pour the wine into a small pan and simmer briskly over a medium heat to reduce by half. Take care, as this happens quickly. Grate the cheese on the large hole of a box grater or using the appropriate food processor attachment.

Reduce the heat to low under the pan and stir the mustard and cheese into the hot wine, stirring constantly until melted into a thick, creamy sauce. Remove from the heat. Separate the egg and stir the yolk into the hot sauce. Whisk the white until stiff while you toast the bread and preheat the grill to its highest setting.

Line the grill pan with foil – shiny side up – lay out the toast and edge with the pancetta or bacon. Fold the egg white evenly through the hot sauce and spoon over the toast, letting it go right up to the edges. Place under the grill and cook until the rarebit is puffy and golden and the bacon crisp. Serve immediately, surrounded by salad leaves.

FENNEL AND PARMESAN GRATIN

SERVES 2–4 | **PREP** 15 MINUTES | **COOK** 35 MINUTES

A pretty gratin made by blanching halved fennel, then covering it in grated Parmesan. It bakes to a crisp, making a golden shell over the soft, delicately aniseedy fennel. The gratin goes with most foods, particularly roasted tomatoes – pop tomato halves or cherry tomatoes (be sure to pierce them first to avoid bursting) in the oven at the same time. This simple but simply delicious gratin is also very good with fish or chicken.

4 fennel bulbs, about
　175g each
25g butter
75g Parmesan cheese
salt

Preheat the oven to 220°C, Gas Mark 7.

Boil the kettle. Half-fill a medium-sized pan with the water and bring back to the boil. Halve the fennel bulbs lengthways. Trim the ends and drop into the vigorously boiling water. Add ½ teaspoon salt. Establish a steady simmer, cover and cook for 6–12 minutes until tender with a hint of resistance to the point of a sharp knife. Scoop the bulbs into a colander to drain; it is worth saving the water for soup.

Use a knob of the butter to smear an oblong gratin dish that can hold the fennel snuggled up close in a single layer. Arrange the fennel in the dish, top-to-tail, reassembling loose layers as necessary. Add dots of the remaining butter and finely grate the Parmesan over. Bake for 20 minutes or until the Parmesan is crusty and golden. Serve immediately.

Vegetables

Most of the recipes in this section of the book are vegetarian but a few aren't, relying on a small amount of meat, fish, eggs or cheese to point up rather than dominate the vegetables. These demi-vegetarian recipes are increasingly my favourite; dishes like Tomato Tarts with Goats' Cheese and Basil, Black Cabbage Soup with Anchovy, and Mushroom, Chorizo and Chickpea Stew. I like to follow the seasons, shopping for vegetables in farmers' markets and street markets, as well as my local greengrocer and supermarkets. I'm lucky, though, to have several ethnic shops nearby, so often shop there for indigenous herbs and vegetables like Thai lemon grass and pink shallots, different-shaped aubergines and tomatoes, and big bunches of pungent coriander, flat leaf parsley, mint and dill. All the recipes prove that we are no longer a meat-and-two-veg nation – much of our most exciting and increasingly cross-cultural cooking is vegetarian.

ASPARAGUS

It's not difficult to buy imported asparagus all year round from Peru, Mexico or Spain, but the short English season, usually starting at the end of April, is the time to enjoy it at its freshest and best and most keenly priced.

I dumped my asparagus cooker years ago and now boil it briefly, loose, not in a bundle, in plenty of salted water. It can be steamed, but the colour fades and it's easy to over-cook. Griddle-cooking asparagus is a revelation of texture and flavour. The spears will pop, fidget and roll, but it's quick and exciting. Roasting takes longer, about 10 minutes.

The awkward question concerning asparagus is why it makes our wee smell funny. Don't give it a second thought as you tuck into another bundle of the first taste of summer. It's due to sulphur-containing amino acids in the spears that break down during digestion.

SIMPLE ASPARAGUS RISOTTO

SERVES 2, GENEROUSLY | **PREP** 20 MINUTES | **COOK** 35 MINUTES

I eat asparagus most days while the British asparagus season reigns. Risotto is a perfect way of turning it into a glorious mid-week treat. It's not an occasion to hold back on butter and one to use freshly grated Parmesan. Special stock is not necessary.

250g British asparagus
1 shallot
50g butter
200g Arborio rice
150ml Noilly Prat or dry
    white wine
4 tablespoons freshly grated
    Parmesan cheese plus extra
    for serving

Pour 1 litre water into a medium pan and bring to the boil. Snap off the asparagus woody ends, rinse and add to the pan, cover and cook for 10 minutes to flavour the cooking liquor. Scoop out of the pan and discard. Cut the rest of the stalks into 4cm lengths. Add to the pan and boil, uncovered, for 2 minutes. Scoop the asparagus into a sieve using a draining spoon, reserving the cooking liquor. Cover the pan with a lid to keep the liquor hot.

Meanwhile, soften the peeled, finely diced shallot in half the butter in a sauté pan. Stir in the rice, stir-frying until semi-translucent. Add the alcohol, stirring as it bubbles away into the rice. Add one third of the hot stock, stirring as it sizzles and then stirring regularly, until the rice has absorbed most of the liquid. Add another third of hot stock and cook as before, then add the final lot, continuing until the rice is almost tender with a firm centre and a creamy, porridge-like consistency. Allow about 20 minutes in total. Stir in the Parmesan, remaining butter and asparagus. Cover and leave for 5 minutes before giving a final stir and serving with extra Parmesan.

ASPARAGUS AND PROSCIUTTO ROLLS

MAKES 28 | **PREP** 20 MINUTES | **COOK** 16 MINUTES

This recipe comes via Sydney, cooked for me by my sister's boyfriend when a visit coincided with our asparagus season. Crusty with grated Parmesan and wrapped in prosciutto, the asparagus rolls are so moreish it is hard to stop eating them.

Serve as part of a tapas feast in the garden or turn into a main dish with minted new potatoes and peas or broad beans. They are good, too, as a starter before lightly cooked salmon with mayo and buttered new potatoes with chives.

28 British asparagus spears
2 × 7-slice packs prosciutto
100g butter plus extra
    for greasing
100g Parmesan cheese
salt

Preheat the oven to 200°C, Gas Mark 6. Butter a couple of baking trays.

Boil the kettle. Trim the woody ends of the asparagus and cut the spears in half. Pour the boiled water into a medium pan, add a pinch of salt and cook the asparagus for 1 minute. Drain and cool.

Cut the prosciutto slices in half widthways. Melt the butter. Finely grate the Parmesan, reserving some for sprinkling. Get a production line going: first brush the asparagus with melted butter, then sprinkle with the Parmesan, then wrap 2 spear halves in each piece of prosciutto. No need to be too neat about this.

The parcels are then ready to be lined up in a single layer on the trays. Sprinkle with the reserved Parmesan and bake for 10–15 minutes until the Parmesan is crusty and golden. Cool slightly so that the ham crisps, separate and serve.

ASPARAGUS AND GOATS' CHEESE TARTS

SERVES 6 | **PREP** 15 MINUTES | **COOK** 25 MINUTES

This is a quick, uncomplicated way of turning a few asparagus spears into quiche-style tarts. I wish I could share the smell of them baking and you could hear the flaky crunch as my knife cuts through the pastry. Please make them and devour with or without potatoes, salad etc.

knob of butter for greasing
8 British asparagus spears
320g ready-rolled puff pastry
100g Greek feta or soft
    goats' cheese
2 eggs
150g double cream
2 tablespoons freshly grated
    Parmesan cheese plus a
    few curls
salt and freshly ground
    black pepper

Boil the kettle. Preheat the oven to 220°C, Gas Mark 7. Lightly butter a non-stick, 6-hole muffin tin.

Pour the boiling water into a medium pan and cook the asparagus for 2 minutes. Scoop onto a fold of kitchen paper to drain. Cut off the tips, approximately 6cm, to fit the top of the tarts, and slice the rest of the stalks into 5mm-thick pieces.

Lightly roll the puff pastry sheet to increase its size, then cut out 6 × 10cm pastry circles (re-rolling may be necessary). Fit the circles into the tin, snuggling and patting to fit. Pierce all over with a fork. Scatter the chopped asparagus in the base and add a crumble of feta. Whisk the eggs and cream together until smooth and season with salt and pepper. Pour the custard over the filling, going almost to the lip of the pastry. Arrange the reserved tips across the tarts; 2 will get 2 tips. Dust the tops of the tarts lightly with grated Parmesan and cover the asparagus tips with Parmesan curls to protect them from the fierce heat. Bake for 20 minutes until puffed and golden.

GRIDDLED ASPARAGUS ON TOAST

SERVES 2 | **PREP** 15 MINUTES | **COOK** 15 MINUTES

Don't be put off by the multi-tasking or cookery juggling required to make this delicious asparagus snack supper. I love the moreish combination of textures and flavours so much that I've been known to make it two nights running. The very slightly woody ends of the asparagus are snapped off and cooked with peas, then puréed with a hint of bottled mint sauce and a spoonful of crème fraîche. This gorgeous thick and luscious purée is piled onto griddled toast, then topped with smoky griddled asparagus nudged alongside folds of Serrano or Parma ham. A swirl of your best olive oil and splash of thick aged balsamic vinegar, or balsamic syrup, pulls everything together and the icing on the cake is a soft-poached egg. Believe me, this is very good indeed.

250g British asparagus
½ teaspoon salt
100g frozen petits pois
1 tablespoon crème fraîche
1 teaspoon mint sauce
3 tablespoons olive oil
2 thick slices of sourdough
    bread
splash of white wine vinegar
2 eggs
4, or more, slices of Serrano
    or Parma ham

To garnish
2 tablespoons best olive oil
aged balsamic vinegar or
    balsamic syrup

Boil the kettle. Snap the ends off the asparagus – the spears will break naturally at the right place, about 3cm from the end. Place a griddle pan over a high heat and leave for a few minutes to get very hot.

Pour two thirds of the boiling water from the kettle into a medium pan and add the asparagus ends. Boil for a couple of minutes, then add the salt and peas. Boil under tender. Drain and tip into the bowl of a food processor with the crème fraîche and mint sauce. Blitz until smooth and keep warm by keeping the lid on the food processor.

Smear the asparagus spears with a little of the measured olive oil and lay out on the griddle. Cook, turning often, for about 3 minutes in total until seared yet al dente.

Brush the bread with the remaining olive oil and cook on the griddle until crusty and toasty. Simultaneously, half-fill a small pan with water from the kettle and re-boil with the vinegar. Crack one egg at a time into a cup and slip, one after the other, into the simmering water. Cook for 1–2 minutes until the white has set but the yolk remains soft. Scoop onto a fold of kitchen paper to drain.

To assemble, divide the pea purée between the slices of toast, top with the asparagus, nudge folds of ham alongside, garnish with a swirl of best olive oil and a dribble of balsamic and top with an egg.

AUBERGINE

If you don't eat meat, or want a night off, aubergine is a very good option. It needs thorough cooking to become buttery soft but is good hot or cold and goes with most carbs from couscous to pasta, even boiled potatoes. It loves tomatoes and red peppers, Middle Eastern flavours like cumin and coriander, chilli and saffron and goes exceptionally well with lamb. It suits being served with yoghurt, white cheese or soft-poached eggs.

Under its glossy purple black skin, aubergine is very absorbent, so salting first or dusting the slices with flour helps stop it drinking up the oil you'll need to fry or roast it.

LINGUINE WITH AUBERGINE, MINT AND RICOTTA

SERVES 4 | **PREP** 20 MINUTES | **COOK** 35 MINUTES

Here's a great pasta sauce to have on standby in the fridge. It's inspired by something similar a friend described eating in Paris. Slippery chunks of aubergine in a thick tomato sauce, with fresh mint, a hint of chilli and salty white cheese.

1 aubergine, about 300g
1 Spanish onion
1 celery stick
2 tablespoons olive oil
2 garlic cloves
400g can chopped tomatoes
pinch of dried chilli flakes
¼ teaspoon sugar
400g linguine
150g ricotta, Greek feta
  or other salty, creamy
  white cheese
handful of chopped mint
salt

Trim and quarter the aubergine lengthways. Chop it into sugar-lump-sized pieces. Dissolve 1 tablespoon salt in a mixing bowl with sufficient water to cover the aubergine. Use a lid or plate to keep it immersed for at least 20 minutes.

Next, peel and finely chop the onion and celery. Soften both, covered, in a spacious, lidded sauté pan in half the olive oil with a pinch of salt, stirring occasionally. Peel and finely chop the garlic. Stir it into the soft, lightly coloured onion, cook for a couple of minutes, then stir in the tomatoes, chilli and sugar. Cook briskly, stirring, for 5 minutes. Tip into a bowl and set aside.

Bring a large pan of salted water to the boil and cook the pasta according to the packet instructions until al dente.

Add the remaining oil to the sauté pan. Rinse, drain and pat the aubergine dry, then toss regularly in the hot oil until damp-looking, soft and shrunken. Return the tomato mixture to the pan, reheat and stir in the cheese and chopped mint just before serving, ragu-style, over the drained pasta.

ROAST AUBERGINE AND TOMATO COUSCOUS

SERVES 2, GENEROUSLY | **PREP** 20 MINUTES | **COOK** 30 MINUTES

This lazy, mid-week supper is lo-cal, vegetarian and easy to shop for. Diced aubergine is tossed with smoky cumin, then roasted with tomato halves and piled over saffron couscous enlivened with toasted pine nuts, lemon and coriander. A dollop of creamy, garlicky yoghurt unites the dish.

400g aubergine
3½ tablespoons olive oil
   plus extra for greasing
1 teaspoon ground cumin
250g small vine tomatoes,
   about 20g each
¼ vegetable stock cube
pinch of saffron threads
150g couscous
2 tablespoons lemon juice
25g toasted pine nuts
10g coriander
1 garlic clove
300g sheep's milk or other
   thick yoghurt
salt and freshly ground
   black pepper

Preheat the oven to 220°C, Gas Mark 7. Lightly oil a shallow roasting tin.

Trim and quarter the aubergine lengthways, halve the quarters lengthways and chop into kebab-sized pieces. Toss with 1 tablespoon of the olive oil. Add the cumin and toss again. Spread out on the oiled tin. Edge with the halved tomatoes. Smear their cut surface with ½ tablespoon of the oil. Season all with salt and pepper. Roast for 30 minutes or until the aubergine and tomatoes are very soft.

Meanwhile, stir the stock cube and saffron into 225ml boiling water. Add the couscous, 1 tablespoon of the olive oil and 1 tablespoon of the lemon juice, stir, cover and leave for 10 minutes to hydrate. Fork up, then mix in the pine nuts and chopped coriander.

Peel the garlic, chop and crush to a paste, then beat into the yoghurt with the remaining lemon juice and oil.

Scoop the roasted veg over the couscous and top with a dollop of yoghurt.

RED WINE AUBERGINE STEW

SERVES 2 | **PREP** 15 MINUTES | **COOK** 35 MINUTES

The remains of a bottle of red wine and a plump aubergine glistening next to it turned out to be a great combination. This is very good with lamb but makes a terrific mid-week supper piled over garlicky bruschetta with a soft-poached egg or slices of feta quickly burnished under the grill.

1 medium onion
2 tablespoons olive oil
1 aubergine, about 300g
1 tablespoon plain flour
200ml red wine
salt and freshly ground
   black pepper

Halve, peel and chop the onion. Heat the oil in a large, lidded pan. Stir in the onion with a good pinch of salt. Stir-fry over a medium heat for a few minutes, then reduce the heat, cover and cook for 10–15 minutes, stirring occasionally.

Trim the aubergine, halve lengthways, then cut into chunky dice. Place in a mixing bowl, add the flour and toss repeatedly to thoroughly coat. By now the onion will be sloppy and juicy. Increase the heat, stir in the aubergine and keep stirring to seal. The pan will go quite dry, so reduce the heat, add a pinch more salt, stir, then cover and cook for 10–15 minutes until the pieces wilt, soften and look juicy.

Add the wine, stirring briskly to thicken. Cover and cook gently until the aubergine is creamy and very soft. Check the seasoning and serve.

AUBERGINE CANNELLONI WITH CREAMED SPINACH AND MUSHROOMS

SERVES 2 | **PREP** 25 MINUTES | **COOK** 1 HOUR

If you have a stash of roasted aubergine slices in the fridge, use them to furl with spinach, creamy goats' cheese and lemony fried mushrooms. Lined up in a gratin dish, the bundles are baked under tomato sauce and grated Gruyère. Comfort food *par excellence*.

2 aubergines, about
   300g each
3 tablespoons olive oil
200g frozen spinach
400g can tomatoes
¼ teaspoon sugar
15g butter
150g mushrooms
1 garlic clove
pinch of dried chilli flakes
1 tablespoon lemon juice
150g soft goats' cheese
whole nutmeg for grating
2 tablespoons double cream
4 tablespoons grated Gruyère
   or Emmental cheese
salt

Preheat the oven to 200°C, Gas Mark 6.

Trim and slice each aubergine lengthways into 5 equal slices. Using a sharp knife, score the skin of the end slices with a lattice. Smear a shallow roasting tin with oil and lay out the aubergine slices. Smear the tops with some oil. Bake for 15 minutes, turn, add a final smear of oil and bake for a further 10–15 minutes or until buttery soft.

Meanwhile, defrost the spinach – I do this over a low heat in a dry pan. Coarsely chop, then place in a mixing bowl.

Blitz the tomatoes in a food processor until smooth, then transfer to a small pan and simmer steadily, stirring occasionally, with a pinch of salt and the sugar for about 15 minutes until reduced and very thick. Beat in the butter.

Wipe and chunky chop the mushrooms. Briefly stir-fry in a medium frying pan with the remaining oil, crushed garlic and chilli until juicy and dark. Add the lemon juice and bubble up, then add to the spinach. Add the goats' cheese and stir. Add a generous grating of nutmeg.

Divide the mushroom mix between the aubergine slices, roll up and nestle in a 24 × 18 × 4cm gratin dish. Spoon over the tomato sauce and top with the cream and grated cheese. Bake for 25–30 minutes until golden and crusty.

CAPONATA

SERVES 4 | **PREP** 30 MINUTES | **COOK** 50 MINUTES

Creamy green olives and sharp, tangy capers muddle amongst this thick tomato and aubergine stew with its hint of sweet-sour back taste. I like to eat it cold with a soft-poached egg but it also works with simply cooked fish, roast chicken or lamb, or team with pasta, gnocchi or polenta. It reheats perfectly and is also delicious served lukewarm with creamy Italian burrata cheese.

1 aubergine, about 400g
1 large red onion
2 garlic cloves
5 tablespoons olive oil
1 tablespoon sugar
2 tablespoons red wine
  vinegar
400g can chopped tomatoes
12 pitted green olives
2 tablespoons capers in
  brine, drained
salt and freshly ground
  black pepper

Dissolve 1 tablespoon salt in a mixing bowl of cold water. Trim and cut the aubergine into kebab-sized pieces. Use a lid or plate to keep it immersed in the water for 30 minutes.

Halve, peel and finely chop the onion. Peel the garlic and slice into thin rounds. Heat 2 tablespoons of the oil in a spacious, heavy-based, lidded pan over a medium heat. Stir in the onion and garlic with a generous pinch of salt. Stir-fry for a few minutes, reduce the heat, cover and cook, stirring occasionally, for about 15 minutes until sloppy. Add the sugar and vinegar, stirring as the sugar melts, and cook until juicy rather than wet. Add the tomatoes. Simmer gently while you finish the aubergine.

Rinse and pat the aubergine dry. Heat the remaining oil in a wok or spacious frying pan over a medium–high heat. Add the aubergine and toss constantly to seal, reduce the heat to medium and keep tossing for about 20 minutes. There will come a point when the aubergine gives back the oil and begins to seriously soften. Don't slack on this – it must be squidgy. Tip the aubergine into the tomatoes with the olives and capers, adding a little water if dry. Heat through, season to taste and serve now or later.

BEETROOT

I love beetroot and buy it raw or boiled but never in vinegar. It is surprisingly versatile, surprisingly satisfying and good hot or cold. Tomatoes, lemon and lime and balsamic vinegar balance its natural sweetness, and it loves chilli, creamy white cheeses, yoghurt and eggs. It goes particularly well with earthy Puy lentils, with strong-flavoured fish and in Middle Eastern and Asian curries. Roasting concentrates its flavour and donning rubber gloves is the best way to rub off the skin, root and trimmed stalks, revealing its immaculate, glossy surface.

BEETROOT AND HORSERADISH TARTS

SERVES 4 | **PREP** 15 MINUTES | **COOK** 5–8 MINUTES

Creamed horseradish offsets the earthy sweetness of beetroot, while lemon and a twist of salt point up the flavours. A generous garnish of chives lends its onion note and everything is unified with a spoonful of a creamy yoghurt sauce with a hint of garlic. For the pastry bases, I use flaky puff pastry, but don't allow it to rise – they should end up almost biscuity. Tomatoes go well with this; diced and tumbled over the tarts before you add the chives looks very pretty.

flour for dusting
200g puff pastry
knob of butter
350g medium–small boiled beetroot (but not the type preserved in vinegar)
½ lemon
1 small garlic clove
150g natural yoghurt (I like sheep's milk yoghurt)
1 tablespoon olive oil
4 tablespoons creamed horseradish
1 tablespoon snipped chives
salt

Preheat the oven to 220°C, Gas Mark 7.

Dust a work surface with flour. Cut the pastry into four equal pieces and roll into 15cm circles. Prick the pastry bases all over with a fork, going right through. Smear a baking sheet with butter to secure the baking parchment and smear the surface with more. Carefully transfer the pastry circles. Bake in the middle of the oven for 8 minutes, checking after 5; you want the pastries crisp and golden. Slip onto a wire rack to cool.

Cut the peeled beetroot into chunky slices. Squeeze a little lemon juice over the slices and season with salt.

To make the sauce, peel, chop and crush the garlic with a pinch of salt. Scoop into a suitable bowl. Add the yoghurt and beat with 1 tablespoon lemon juice and the olive oil. Spread the pastry thickly with creamed horseradish and cover with beetroot. Dribble attractively with sauce, garnish with the chives and serve.

BEETROOT MASH WITH LEMON COD AND WATERCRESS SALSA VERDE

SERVES 4 | **PREP** 25 MINUTES | **COOK** 35 MINUTES

Stunning to look at, vibrant to eat, healthy, easy to shop for and quick to make; what's not to love? The combination of creamy beetroot mash, big flakes of lemony cod and a thick, peppery, salty watercress green sauce goes extremely well with baked sweet potatoes popped in the oven before you start on the other preparations.

4 sweet potatoes, about 200g each
750g boiled beetroot
1 tablespoon balsamic vinegar
2 tablespoons olive oil
1 lemon
4 thick cod fillets, skin on
salt and freshly ground black pepper

For the salsa verde
65g watercress, with stalks
2 teaspoons capers in brine, drained
1 garlic clove
2 teaspoons Dijon mustard
3 anchovy fillets in olive oil, drained
100ml olive oil

Preheat the oven to 200°C, Gas Mark 6.

Place the sweet potatoes on a foil-lined baking sheet. Pierce a few times with a fork. Bake for 35 minutes or until tender.

Meanwhile, peel, chop and blitz the beetroot with the vinegar and 1 tablespoon of the olive oil until smooth. Transfer to a pan and season to taste with salt, pepper and a squeeze of lemon. Simmer gently, stirring often, for 2–3 minutes until thick and fluffy. Keep warm.

Smear the cod fillets with the remaining tablespoon of oil and place, skin-side up, on a small foil-lined roasting tin. Add a squeeze of lemon. The fish needs 10–15 minutes in the oven depending on thickness of the fillets, so co-ordinate the cooking or wait until the potatoes are done.

To make the salsa verde, place the watercress, capers, crushed peeled garlic, mustard, anchovies and 1 tablespoon of the olive oil in the bowl of a food processor. Blitz, scraping down the inside wall as necessary, then, with the motor running, add the remaining oil in a trickle until thick and bumpy.

Ease off the fish skin and serve the fish with the beetroot mash and a spoonful of salsa verde plus a baked potato, slashed open to reveal its orange flesh, on the side.

BORSCHT RISOTTO

SERVES 4 | **PREP** 20 MINUTES | **COOK** 30 MINUTES

Beautiful beetroot needs plenty of seasoning to work well in risotto. Here it gets garlic, chilli and lemon. If ham stock is available, it's the best choice. The risotto is served, borscht-style, with a dollop of soured cream or crème fraîche with a top-knot of chives, dill, flat leaf parsley or mint.

2 shallots
60g unsalted butter
4 beetroot, about 700g
1 garlic clove
generous pinch of dried
    chilli flakes
350g Arborio rice
1 lemon
1.2 litres ham, chicken or
    vegetable stock
4 tablespoons soured cream
    or crème fraîche
few sprigs soft herbs

Peel and finely chop the shallots. Melt 50g of the butter in a large sauté pan or similarly wide-based pan and gently soften the shallots.

Peel, wash and grate the beets; there will seem an awful lot. Finely chop the peeled garlic. Stir the beets and garlic into the shallot, tossing for several minutes until wilted. Add the chilli flakes.

Add the rice, stirring until glistening. Add juice from the lemon.

Heat the stock to boiling. Add 500ml to the pan and simmer briskly, stirring occasionally, until the rice is swollen. Stir in another 500ml stock and continue cooking as before, for a further 15 minutes or so, until the liquid is absorbed and the rice tender with a slight bite in the centre. Add extra liquid if needed. Stir in the remaining butter, remove from the heat, cover and leave for 5 minutes.

Serve the risotto with a dollop of soured cream or crème fraîche and the chopped soft herbs.

RED FLANNEL HASH WITH PEAS

SERVES 2 | **PREP** 15 MINUTES | **COOK** 30 MINUTES

Leftover cooked steak, a new jar of creamed horseradish and freshly boiled beetroot brought this intriguingly named fry-up to mind. Instead of steak, leftover roast beef or smoked mackerel are good alternatives. Beaten egg binds the ingredients, but don't expect a neat dish.

2 medium red onions
25g butter
300g cooked steak, roast beef
    or smoked mackerel fillet
300g waxy or new potatoes
300g boiled beetroot
1 egg
1 tablespoon milk
2 tablespoons creamed
    horseradish
1 tablespoon olive oil
150g frozen petits pois, boiled
salt and freshly ground
    black pepper

Halve, peel and finely chop the onions. Melt the butter in a large, lidded, non-stick frying pan and gently soften the onions, stirring often.

Meanwhile, cut the meat into 2mm thick × 3cm strips. If using mackerel, flake it off the skin in bite-sized pieces.

Peel and chop the potatoes into 1cm dice. Rinse and boil in salted water until tender. Drain. Peel and dice the beets similarly.

Crack the egg into a mixing bowl, beat with the milk and horseradish and stir in the meat or fish, potato and beetroot. Season generously with salt and pepper and stir in the very soft onion.

Pour half the oil into the frying pan over a medium heat, and when hot, spread the mixture evenly in the pan. Cook without fiddling for 10–15 minutes or until cake-like and forming a crusty base. Loosen with a spatula. Cover with a lid or large plate, invert, add the remaining oil, swirl it round the pan and slip the hash back. Add the cooked peas, cover and cook for 5 minutes.

BEETROOT AND HORSERADISH PURÉE WITH STRIP STEAK

SERVES 4 | **PREP** 20 MINUTES | **COOK** 45 MINUTES

Here's a very simple but immensely versatile way of preparing beetroot that is good hot or cold and a useful sauce-cum-purée-cum-mash to have on standby in the fridge. Sometimes when I came home starving, desperate for something quick and easy, I pile the fluffy purée onto garlicky bruschetta topped with a fried egg. It is unbelievably good. Instead of the egg, try a different sort of cheese on toast with slices of feta, halloumi or mozzarella, the bruschetta flashed under the grill until the cheese softens and burnishes. Try it, too, with grilled sardines or mackerel, or steak. Once rested the steak is sliced across its width. Watercress and/or grilled tomato halves go well with this, but so do chips or skinny fries.

For the beetroot purée
400g similar-sized beetroot
2 tablespoons creamed
    horseradish
1 lemon
splash of Tabasco sauce
salt

For the steak
4 sirloin steaks
2 tablespoons groundnut or
    sunflower oil
bunch of watercress
1 lemon
freshly ground black pepper

Begin with the beetroot purée, which will keep, covered, in the fridge for 48 hours. Wash the beets and trim any stalks but leave the root. Boil, covered, in plenty of salted water for about 30 minutes, more if large, until tender to the point of a knife. Drain and rub away the skin – easy wearing rubber gloves. Coarsely chop and transfer to the bowl of a food processor. Add the creamed horseradish, 1½ tablespoons lemon juice, 1 tablespoon hot water, a splash of Tabasco and a generous seasoning of salt. Blitz for several minutes to purée. Taste and adjust the seasoning with more lemon, salt and Tabasco.

Smear the steaks with oil and set aside while you heat a griddle pan over a medium–high heat. When very hot, season the steaks with salt and pepper and cook, 2 at a time, for 2 minutes on each side for rare, 2–3 minutes on each side for medium–rare or 5 minutes on each side for well done. Transfer to a chopping board to rest while you cook the second batch. Rest the meat for 5 minutes before slicing.

Trim away the fat collar on one side of the steaks and slice thickly across the width, transferring to a hot platter for sharing. Add any resultant cooking juices, the watercress and lemon, cut into wedges. Serve the cold or hot beetroot purée (it can be quickly reheated in a small saucepan over a low heat, stirring continuously) in a separate bowl.

SUPER-QUICK BORSCHT WITH MUSHROOM PIROSHKI

SERVES 2 | **PREP** SOUP: 10 MINUTES; DUMPLINGS: 20 MINUTES | **COOK** SOUP: 10 MINUTES;
DUMPLINGS: 10 MINUTES

The soup stock is flavoured with lemon juice and garlic, fine-tuned with Tabasco, salt and pepper and served with a classic dollop of soured cream and dill. The traditional accompaniment is tiny dumpling-cum-pasties stuffed with trimmings from the ingredients used to make the soup stock. I usually use puff pastry, but Chinese dumpling skins are a liberating alternative; the 10cm thin pastry discs (from oriental stores) are stuffed with minced mushrooms. Keep leftover skins in the freezer.

For the soup
500ml vegetable stock
350g boiled, peeled beetroot
1 large garlic clove
½ lemon
Tabasco sauce, to taste
2 tablespoons soured cream
small bunch of dill or chives
salt and freshly ground
   black pepper

For the piroshki
150g medium closed-cap or
   chestnut mushrooms
1 tablespoon flat leaf
   parsley leaves
1 garlic clove
2 tablespoons sunflower oil
1 tablespoon fresh white
   breadcrumbs
10 dumpling (gyoza)
   skins

Heat the stock to boiling. Chop the beets and blitz in a food processor until smooth with the boiling stock, crushed garlic and a squeeze of lemon juice. Simmer for 5 minutes, then taste and adjust the seasoning with salt, pepper, lemon juice and Tabasco. Preheat the oven to 200°C, Gas Mark 6.

Wipe the mushrooms and blitz briefly in the food processor with the parsley and chopped garlic to make a paste. Stir-fry in ½ tablespoon of the oil for 2–3 minutes until juicy, stir in the breadcrumbs and spread on a plate to cool.

Brush a small roasting tin with a little oil. Lay a pastry disc on one hand, smear a 1cm border with water, add a heaped teaspoon of the mushroom mixture, fold over and press the edges to seal. Arrange in the oiled tin, smear the tops with oil and bake for 8–10 minutes until the edges are crusty and golden. If preferred, poach for 2 minutes in simmering water, drain and quickly fry, potsticker dumpling-style, on one side.

Serve the soup with a dollop of soured cream and small sprigs of dill or finely snipped chives, with the dumplings on the side.

BEETROOT AND TOMATO SALAD WITH EGG MAYO

SERVES 6 | **PREP** 20 MINUTES | **COOK** 10 MINUTES

The sweetness of beetroot is very good with the acidity and fresh zing of ripe tomatoes and in this colourful salad they combine deliciously well with quickly pickled cucumber and peppery rocket. Lemon juice and olive oil is all that is needed in the way of vinaigrette. The salad, ready plated for portion control, becomes a meal served with halved hard-boiled eggs topped with mayonnaise, finely grated hard cheese and a salty anchovy cross. This is perfect summer food and very satisfying served with crusty bread and a humongous fruit salad to follow.

6 eggs
½ cucumber
pinch of sugar
2 tablespoons wine vinegar
750g boiled beetroot
1 large lemon
2 large handfuls of
  wild rocket
5 large vine tomatoes
splash of olive oil
2 tablespoons mayonnaise
6 anchovy fillets in olive oil,
  drained
3 tablespoons finely grated
  hard cheese
2 tablespoons chopped
  flat leaf parsley or basil
Maldon sea salt

Place the eggs in a pan and cover with cold water. Boil for 7 minutes. Drain under cold running water, crack the shells and then carefully peel the eggs.

Peel the cucumber, halve lengthways, scrape out the seeds with a teaspoon and slice thinly. Dissolve the sugar in the vinegar and stir into the cucumber.

If necessary, peel the beets. Cut into chunky bite-sized pieces onto a large plate. Squeeze over juice from half the lemon and season with salt. Divide the rocket between 6 dinner plates. Top with beets, then cucumber, finishing with chunkily cut pieces of tomato. Squeeze the remaining lemon over the top and splash with olive oil.

Halve the eggs lengthways. Arrange on a plate and top with the mayo. Split the anchovies lengthways and make a cross over the mayo. Finish with the grated cheese. Garnish the salad with parsley or basil and serve with the eggs.

BUTTERNUT SQUASH AND PUMPKIN

Butternut squash is a useful standby. It keeps for ages, doesn't need fridge space and children love it. So do I. I often buy a couple with no particular end in view, and when inspiration fails, I might roast it with a splash of olive oil and a small bundle of aromatic herbs. I like it with roast tomatoes and a crumble of feta, but slices or chunks cooked alongside a mid-week roast chicken make a great alternative to potatoes. It's also a good addition to a quick, simple chicken curry and will thicken the juices. Like potatoes, which it often replaces, it has the ability to soak up flavours without being dominated by them.

Pumpkin, too, can sit around for ages. It is associated with Halloween and you'll find recipes here for putting it to good use when the celebrations are over. The skin of butternut squash is edible, but remove the skin of other thick-skinned squash and pumpkins.

BUTTERNUT AND CHICKEN KORMA WITH BASMATI

SERVES 2 | **PREP** 15 MINUTES | **COOK** 30 MINUTES

This looks and tastes like a sophisticated curry but is a bit of a cheat. It's made with curry powder instead of ground spices, yet lemon juice and ground almonds, with the sweetness of butternut in a thick coconut sauce gives the dish layers of flavour.

1 medium onion
1 tablespoon unflavoured
   oil such as groundnut
   or sunflower
½ butternut squash,
   about 300g
4 skinned chicken thigh fillets
½ chicken stock cube
3 teaspoons mild curry
   powder
200g basmati rice
160ml can coconut cream
1 tablespoon ground almonds
½ lemon
10g coriander
salt
mango chutney, to serve

Halve, peel and finely chop the onion. Heat the oil in a medium, heavy-based pan and stir in the onion. Cook gently, stirring occasionally, until limp.

Meanwhile, chop the deseeded squash into bite-sized chunks. Slice the chicken into similar-sized pieces. Dissolve the stock cube in 250ml boiling water.

Stir the curry powder into the limp onions, cooking for 30 seconds before adding the chicken, adjusting the heat and turning the pieces to seal. Add the stock and squash. Bring to a simmer, stirring to loosen any bits stuck to the bottom of the pan, reduce the heat slightly, cover and cook for 15 minutes.

While the curry simmers, rinse the rice and place in a pan with 300ml water. Bring to the boil, then immediately turn very low, cover and cook for 10 minutes. Turn off the heat and leave, covered, for 10 minutes.

Finish the curry by adding the coconut cream and ground almonds. Stir thoroughly, taste and adjust the seasoning with salt and lemon juice. Cook for a further 5–10 minutes until the squash is tender. Coarsely chop the coriander, stir into the korma and serve over the forked-up rice with mango chutney.

BUTTERNUT IN ORANGE TOMATO SAUCE

SERVES 2 | **PREP** 15 MINUTES | **COOK** 30 MINUTES

Orange and tomato is a time-honoured combination in many Spanish recipes, but it was Ping Coombes on *MasterChef* who added butternut squash, inspiring this recipe. For an easy mid-week veggie meal, pile this on sourdough toast with a poached egg. Try it, too, with pasta or asparagus.

1 medium onion
1 tablespoon olive oil
2 garlic cloves
350g butternut squash
3 vine tomatoes, about 300g
3 juicing oranges
pinch of dried chilli flakes
squeeze of lemon
salt

Boil the kettle. Halve, peel and finely chop the onion. Soften gently in the olive oil in a medium lidded pan.

Crack the garlic with something heavy, flake away the skin, chop, then crush to a paste with a pinch of salt. Chop the deseeded butternut into dice no larger than the size of a sugar lump.

Pour boiling water from the kettle over the tomatoes, count to 30, drain, quarter and scrape the seeds into a sieve placed over a bowl whilst wiping away the skin, reserving the tomato flesh. Crush the seeds to extract maximum juice. Squeeze the oranges through the sieve.

Stir the garlic into the onions and stir-fry for 1 minute. Add the butternut, chilli, tomato and orange juice. Simmer, covered, over a medium heat for 10 minutes. Dice the tomato flesh and add to the pan. Cook, covered, stirring a few times, for 10 minutes until the butternut is tender, the tomato melted and the mix juicy. Season to taste with salt and lemon juice.

BUTTERNUT AND RED PEPPER THAI CURRY

SERVES 2–3 | **PREP** 20 MINUTES | **COOK** 45 MINUTES

Ribbons of roasted Romano peppers, saintly sweet and luscious, slide over the chunks of squash in this curry, with slivers of ginger and slippery-soft strands of red onion all held in searingly hot coconut gravy. Lemon grass and lime juice lend a sharp edge, and fresh coriander consolidates the Thai flavours.

2 Romano red peppers
600g butternut squash
2 tablespoons groundnut oil
2 medium red onions
1 tablespoon grated ginger
1 garlic clove
25g Thai green curry paste
160ml can coconut cream
300ml vegetable stock
2 lemon grass stalks
1 lime
10g coriander
salt
boiled basmati rice, to serve

Preheat the oven to 200°C, Gas Mark 6. Place the peppers in a small roasting tin and bake on the top shelf for 15 minutes. Turn and move to a lower shelf for 15 minutes. Transfer to a plate, cover with clingfilm and leave to cool for 15 minutes. Remove the skin, discard the seeds and slice the flesh into ribbons.

Cut the squash into kebab-sized pieces. Toss with 1 tablespoon oil, spread in a roasting tin and roast for 30 minutes along with the peppers. Increase the heat to 220°C, Gas Mark 7, and cook for a further 8 minutes.

Halve, finely slice and soften the onions in the remaining oil in a spacious pan. Stir in the ginger and garlic and cook for 2 minutes, then scoop out of the pan. Add the curry paste, coconut cream, stock and lightly crushed lemon grass. Stir well and simmer for 5 minutes.

Stir in the lime juice, squash, onion mixture and the pepper ribbons. Simmer for 5 minutes, season with salt to taste, stir in the chopped coriander and serve with the rice.

ROAST PUMPKIN PASTA WITH LIME

SERVES 4 | **PREP** 25 MINUTES | **COOK** 35 MINUTES

Once the Halloween ghosties and ghoulies have gone to bed, here's a lovely way of cooking the inevitable discarded pumpkin. Big chunks are roasted, then stirred into short, chunky pasta like penne or radiatore and tossed with green beans, toasted pine nuts and chunks of feta. A splash of olive oil and squeeze of lime point up the flavours.

700g pumpkin or butternut
  squash
2 tablespoons olive oil
300g green beans
350g penne or similar pasta
3 tablespoons best olive oil
50g pine nuts
200g Greek feta cheese
2 limes
salt

Preheat the oven to 220°C, Gas Mark 7. Peel the pumpkin, if using. Deseed and cut the pumpkin or butternut squash into large kebab-type chunks. Smear with most of the 2 tablespoons olive oil and spread out on a baking sheet. Bake for 25–35 minutes until tender with crusty edges.

Top and tail the beans, snap in half and cook in boiling salted water for 2 minutes. Drain.

Co-ordinate the vegetable cooking with cooking the pasta – in plenty of boiling salted water – then drain and return to the pan with a splash of the best olive oil and about 2 tablespoons pasta cooking water.

Quickly stir-fry the pine nuts in the remaining olive oil until golden. Tip onto a fold of kitchen paper to drain.

Tip all the cooked ingredients into a warmed serving bowl, crumble the feta over the top, add the remaining best olive oil and toss before serving with the limes, cut into wedges, to squeeze over the top.

SAUSAGE, SAGE LENTILS AND ROAST PUMPKIN

SERVES 4 | **PREP** 20 MINUTES | **COOK** 45 MINUTES

Pumpkins are piled high in the shops leading up to Halloween, tempting our carving technique rather than palate, but let me recommend giving it a good roasting. For this forgiving supper, wedges are roasted at the same time as sausages while dark green Puy lentils simmer. Everything comes together to make the perfect autumnal fork supper. Good with garlic bread.

500g piece of pumpkin
4 tablespoons olive oil
16 meaty chipolata sausages
1 medium onion
2 garlic cloves
generous pinch of dried
    chilli flakes
¼ teaspoon chopped sage
350g Puy lentils
½ chicken stock cube
1 lemon
10g flat leaf parsley
salt and freshly ground
    black pepper

Preheat the oven to 220°C, Gas Mark 7. Peel the pumpkin, deseed and cut into large kebab-type chunks. Smear lightly with olive oil and spread out on a baking sheet. Repeat with the sausages, placing in their own roasting tin. Bake for 25–35 minutes until both are crusty and tender.

Meanwhile, peel and finely chop the onion and garlic, then soften in 1 tablespoon oil in a lidded pan that can accommodate the lentils. Stir in the chilli flakes, sage, lentils, 750ml water and crumbled stock cube. Bring to the boil, stirring to dissolve the cube, reduce the heat, cover and simmer for 30 minutes or until tender and most of the liquid has been absorbed.

Leave, covered, for 5 minutes, then season to taste with salt, pepper, lemon juice and the remaining olive oil. Halve the sausages on the slant and stir them through the sloppy lentils, adding the pumpkin. Reheat and serve now or later, with the chopped parsley leaves.

CABBAGE, CHARD AND SPINACH

It's funny to think of vegetables as fashion victims, but the cabbage family, particularly inky black cavolo nero, crinkly kale and rainbow-coloured chard, is having its moment. Chard is possibly my favourite, the wide stalks good enough to serve like asparagus, the big ruched leaves sometimes boiled with garlic and blitzed to purée. I am a recent convert to red cabbage, discovering that coleslaw can be a feast and stewed red cabbage an unsung hero. Young spinach leaves, as opposed to a big bunch of flourishing leaves with thick stems, is the veg we all fling in the shopping trolley. If I am anything to go by, it often turns slimy before it comes up on the cooking radar. To be on the safe side, because I love spinach, I've taken to keeping a bag of frozen spinach alongside the peas for emergency greens.

BLACK CABBAGE SOUP WITH ANCHOVY
SERVES 4 | **PREP** 20 MINUTES | **COOK** 30 MINUTES

It always seems a shame to chop cavolo nero's elegant long black leaves that remind me of crushed velvet. The dense texture takes ages to soften, so it's perfect in big chunky vegetable soups like this. As suits the cabbage family, it is served with salty anchovy pounded with garlic, olive oil and lemon. A poached egg and grated Parmesan are good extras.

1 medium red onion
1 tablespoon olive oil
1 trimmed leek, about 125g
2 medium carrots, about 125g
3 celery sticks, about 125g
5cm rosemary sprig
1 lemon
2 medium potatoes,
    about 165g
1 small head cavolo nero,
    about 125g
1 litre chicken or vegetable
    stock
50g can anchovy fillets in
    olive oil
1 large garlic clove
salt and freshly ground
    black pepper

Halve, peel and dice the onion and stir-fry in the oil for 5 minutes on a high temperature in a spacious, lidded pan while you slice the leek into 1cm rings, rinse and shake dry.

Reduce the heat and stir the leek into the onion with a generous seasoning of salt and pepper. Stir, cover and cook for 5 minutes while you peel and slice the carrots and dice the celery. Add both to the pan with the rosemary and a 5cm strip of lemon zest. Stir, cover and cook for a further 5 minutes.

Peel, dice and rinse the potatoes, and slice the cabbage 3cm thick. Add the stock to the pan, increase the heat to boil, stir in the cabbage and potato and simmer, partially covered, for 10 minutes or until potato and cabbage are tender.

Check the seasoning and serve the soup with the chopped anchovies mixed with the crushed garlic, 1 tablespoon lemon juice and 1 tablespoon oil from the anchovies.

RED SLAW

SERVES 6, GENEROUSLY | **PREP** 40 MINUTES

This is coleslaw for people like me who think they don't like it. It's made with red cabbage, onion, carrot and celery for crunch, tomatoes and apple for sweetness and a different kind of juiciness. Finely chopped gherkin is a surprisingly good extra. The mayonnaise that binds the salad gets extra verve with lemon juice and Dijon mustard. This feast of healthiness is great on its own but goes with everything, from pesto or anchovy bruschetta to cold cuts, and is perfect barbecue background food. It keeps well and could be laced with grated strong Cheddar or tuna from a can, turning it into perfect al desko or picnic food.

½ red cabbage
2 carrots
2 celery sticks
1 large red onion
2 vine tomatoes
1 gherkin
1 lemon
1 apple
3–5 tablespoons Hellmann's
    mayonnaise
1 dessertspoon Dijon mustard
salt and freshly ground
    black pepper

Cut the dense core out of the cabbage, slice finely and then chop into small pieces. Scrape then grate the carrots on the large hole of a cheese grater. Trim, rinse and very finely slice the celery. Halve, peel and finely dice the onion. Core and chop the tomatoes. Dice the gherkin into small pieces. Squeeze half the lemon into a mixing bowl. Quarter, core, peel and slice the apple into the lemon. Toss, then add all the prepared ingredients.

Add 3 tablespoons of mayo, the mustard and a generous seasoning of salt and pepper. Toss thoroughly, taste and adjust the seasoning with salt, pepper and lemon juice, adding more mayo if you think it needs it.

MERDA DE CAN

SERVES 4 | **PREP** 30 MINUTES | **COOK** 30 MINUTES

Not Quite Nice, a ripping yarn by Celia Imrie, was the perfect bedfellow as I fought off flu with little interest in food. Gradually, though, as I came across recipes for watercress soup and tomato tarte Tatin, my appetite began to stir. I know they love chard in Nice, but I'd never heard of this vividly named sausage-shaped gnocchi recipe. It is introduced to hilarious effect in the book and will definitely be a talking point around the dinner table. It's a bit of a faff to make but really worth it.

900g even-sized potatoes
350g chard or mature
   spinach, roughly chopped
   if large
2 egg yolks
100–150g plain flour
20g butter
8 sage leaves
whole nutmeg for grating
salt
freshly grated Parmesan
   cheese, to serve

Boil the unpeeled potatoes in salted water until tender. Drain, remove the skins, then pass through a mouli-legume or ricer, or mash super-smooth. Place the potato in a mixing bowl to cool.

Meanwhile, boil the chard or spinach; if the stalks are very large, cook them for 5 minutes before adding the leaves and cooking both for a further 3–5 minutes or until the stalks are tender. Scoop into a colander to drain and cool. Squeeze out the excess liquid, chop finely, return to a sieve and press out as much liquid as possible, then wrap in kitchen paper to dry thoroughly.

Use a fork to mix the egg yolks, then the greens into the potato. Sift spoonfuls of flour over the top, use a fork to disperse, then knead to mix; continue until no longer sticky. I used 100g flour; you may need more or less depending on the type of potato. Form into a ball, dust with flour, cover and chill for 30 minutes.

Divide the mixture into 4 equal pieces. On a floured surface, roll each quarter into a chipolata-thick sausage. Cut each into 8 pieces and halve again to make cocktail sausage-sized, or smaller, fatter pieces.

Cook the gnocchi in 2–3 batches in vigorously boiling salted water. Scoop out of the pan as they rise to the surface. Briefly rest on kitchen paper and serve with the hot butter melted with the sage leaves, freshly grated nutmeg and masses of grated Parmesan. Also good with a chunky tomato sauce.

CHARD PENNE

SERVES 2 | **PREP** 15 MINUTES | **COOK** 15 MINUTES

My son Zach came up with this way of turning chard into a classy pasta supper. As a student he worked at the River Café and it was there he learnt to love chard and taught me their natty way of removing stalk from leaf. It's useful to know that chard can be prepared in advance and kept in the fridge for several days without spoiling, ready to spring into instant suppers like this. Good, too, on bruschetta with a soft-poached egg and splash of your best olive oil.

200g penne
250g chard
4 tablespoons extra virgin
   olive oil plus extra to serve
1 tablespoon Dijon mustard

Cook the pasta according to the packet instructions. Drain and return to the pan.

Meanwhile, fold the chard leaves in half and slice off the stalks, following through into the leaf as necessary. Chop the stalks into 2.5cm lengths. Boil the stalks in salted water, adding the shredded leaves after a couple of minutes. Boil for a further 2 minutes, drain, squeeze dry and finely chop.

4 tablespoons crème fraîche,
   mascarpone or thick cream
salt and freshly ground
   black pepper
freshly grated Parmesan
   cheese, to serve

Transfer the chard to a warmed serving bowl and stir in the extra virgin olive oil, Dijon and crème fraîche, mascarpone or cream. Season well.

Stir the pasta into the chard. Serve with a generous topping of grated Parmesan and a drizzle of extra olive oil.

GREEK SPINACH AND FETA PIE WITH DILL

SERVES 4–6 | **PREP** 30 MINUTES | **COOK** 55 MINUTES

Cheese or spinach, or both? That was the dilemma every day as we queued for breakfast pies at our favourite bakery on the Greek island of Limnos. Filo coils are a devil to reproduce, but a pie for sharing makes an awesome supper, something to remember for guests who don't eat meat. Serve with Greek salad or a thick tomato sauce. Another option is a grilled cherry tomato salad with black olives, and a crisp green salad (see page 15).

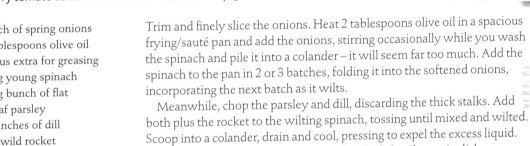

bunch of spring onions
6 tablespoons olive oil
   plus extra for greasing
500g young spinach
100g bunch of flat
   leaf parsley
2 bunches of dill
75g wild rocket
2 eggs
200g Greek feta cheese
260g filo pastry
salt and freshly ground
   black pepper

Trim and finely slice the onions. Heat 2 tablespoons olive oil in a spacious frying/sauté pan and add the onions, stirring occasionally while you wash the spinach and pile it into a colander – it will seem far too much. Add the spinach to the pan in 2 or 3 batches, folding it into the softened onions, incorporating the next batch as it wilts.

Meanwhile, chop the parsley and dill, discarding the thick stalks. Add both plus the rocket to the wilting spinach, tossing until mixed and wilted. Scoop into a colander, drain and cool, pressing to expel the excess liquid.

Preheat the oven to 200°C, Gas Mark 6. Lightly oil a gratin dish approximately 24 × 18 × 4cm.

Whisk the eggs in a mixing bowl. Crumble in the feta, season with salt and black pepper and stir in the spinach mixture. Working quickly, open out the filo and paint the top sheet with olive oil. Place it over the dish, pressing into the base and leaving a deep overhang. Repeat with half the filo. Fill with spinach, fold in the overhang and oil, then fold and top with the remaining filo. Oil the top sheet and use a sharp knife to etch a wide diagonal lattice. Bake for 40 minutes or until crusty and golden.

CAULIFLOWER AND BROCCOLI

Cauliflower is rising phoenix-like from its cauliflower cheese doldrums, proving itself immensely versatile. Now we cook it with Mediterranean and Middle Eastern flavours, fry and roast it as well as steaming and boiling the vegetable Mark Twain described as nothing but cabbage with a college education. I love it puréed with a smidgen of cream and sometimes cheese, to serve with crusty homemade fish fingers. Its siblings, broccoli, calabrese, purple sprouting and lanky tenderstem, go particularly well with anchovy and chilli.

RISOTTO-STYLE CAULIFLOWER CHEESE

SERVES 2–4 | **PREP** 20 MINUTES | **COOK** 20 MINUTES

A quick and gentle risotto-style cauli cheese with a tumble of chopped hard-boiled egg, crisp breadcrumbs and chives. Serve with salad or slow-roasted tomato halves.

1 large egg
1 medium cauliflower
35g butter
25g fresh white breadcrumbs
25g plain flour
1 dessertspoon Dijon mustard
200ml milk
1 tablespoon snipped chives
2 tablespoons freshly grated
   Parmesan cheese
salt and freshly ground
   black pepper

Boil the kettle. Place the egg in a small pan and cover with cold water. Boil for 9 minutes. Drain, crack and peel under cold running water.

Discard any green stalks and quarter the cauliflower. Cut each quarter into 4 or 5 pieces with a share of white stalk. Pour a 10cm depth of water from the kettle into a medium pan and return to the boil. Add 1 teaspoon salt and the cauliflower. Cover and boil for 5–8 minutes until tender to the point of a knife. Drain, reserving a cup of cooking water, return to the pan, cover and leave to keep warm.

Melt 10g of the butter in a frying pan and quickly stir in the breadcrumbs, stirring constantly, for 2–3 minutes until crusty and golden. Tip them onto kitchen paper.

Melt the remaining 25g butter in a milk pan. Stir in the flour until smooth, followed by the mustard, then the reserved water. Remove from the heat and gradually add the cold milk, stirring briskly until smooth. Return to the heat and cook, stirring constantly, for a few minutes to cook the flour. Season with salt and pepper and stir the sauce into the cauliflower.

Tip the cauliflower onto serving plates or a platter. Finely chop the egg over the top, followed by the breadcrumbs, chives and Parmesan.

ROAST CAULIFLOWER WITH GINGER, CUMIN AND SAFFRON

SERVES 2 | **PREP** 20 MINUTES | **COOK** 30 MINUTES

Indian cooks have always been clever with cauliflower and this exciting way of cooking it owes much to Reza Mahammad's inspiring *Reza's Indian Spice*. The cauli is sliced and fried with red onion, lots of ginger, cumin, chilli and saffron, ending up toasty yet lightly cooked with plump, sweet raisins and sultanas to balance the spicy seasoning. Serve it with hard-boiled eggs and mango chutney.

500g white cauliflower
2 pinches of saffron threads
3 tablespoons vegetable oil
1 medium red onion
25g fresh root ginger
½ teaspoon dried chilli flakes
½ teaspoon cumin seeds
2 tablespoons pine nuts
2 tablespoons jumbo raisins
    and sultanas
1 lime
few coriander sprigs
salt

Boil the kettle with minimum water. Slice the cauli into 3mm-thick pieces. Soften the saffron in 75ml boiling water.

Heat 1 tablespoon of the oil in a spacious frying/sauté pan over a medium heat and brown half the cauli on both sides. Move to the side and repeat with the rest.

Halve, peel and thinly slice the onion. Peel and thinly slice the ginger into small scraps.

Move all the cauli to the side, add the remaining 2 tablespoons oil and toss the onion in the oil, cooking for a couple of minutes before adding the ginger, chilli, lightly crushed cumin, saffron water and pine nuts. Stir-fry for a few minutes. When the onion wilts, fold in the cauli and raisins and sultanas. Stir-fry for a few minutes.

Turn off the heat, cover and leave for 5 minutes. Season with salt and a generous squeeze of lime. Chop the coriander, add and serve.

CAULIFLOWER AND LEMON RISOTTO WITH SCALLOPS

SERVES 4 | **PREP** 30 MINUTES | **COOK** 40 MINUTES

When cauliflower is piled high in the shops and prices fall to rock bottom, you can be sure autumn has arrived. In Cornwall, where they flourish, they are virtually given away at this time of year. Also in season at the same time and abundant in Cornish waters are scallops. One year I bought several dozen and this dish was a favourite combination – sweet, quickly burnished scallops with cabbagey cauli uplifted with flecks of lemon zest and creamy rice; a surprisingly good mix.

Don't waste the cauli stalk and leaves, as they are nutrient-rich and make the basis of the stock for the risotto. It is also worth salting the scallops briefly before they are fried. It makes them stand proud and plump as well as seasoning them perfectly.

1 large cauliflower
1 medium onion
few thyme sprigs
½ chicken or vegetable
  stock cube
2 large shallots
60g butter
pinch of dried chilli flakes
4–6 scallops per person,
  cleaned, corals intact
1 garlic clove
1 lemon
250g Arborio rice
1 teaspoon finely chopped
  flat leaf parsley
sunflower or groundnut oil
  for brushing
salt

Cut the outer leaves off the cauliflower. Quarter the cauli lengthways and cut the florets off the central stalk. Coarsely chop the leaves and large stalks and place in a large pan with 1 teaspoon salt, the chopped, unpeeled onion and 1 litre water to cover. Strip the thyme leaves off the stalks and add the stalks to the pan along with the crumbled stock cube. Simmer, semi-covered, for 20 minutes while you prepare everything else.

Cut the cauli into small florets, each with a bit of stalk. Peel and finely chop the shallots. Melt half the butter in a spacious, lidded sauté pan and stir in the shallots with the chilli flakes and thyme leaves. Cook gently, stirring often, for 5 minutes.

Salt the scallops lightly and leave for 10 minutes, then rinse and pat dry with kitchen paper.

Peel and finely chop the garlic. Remove the zest from half the lemon in shirt-button-sized scraps.

Stir the garlic and zest into the shallots, then stir in the rice and lemon juice. Let it bubble away into the rice, then stir in the cauli florets and add the strained hot stock gradually, a ladleful at a time, continuing until the rice is creamy with a slight bite at the centre; about 25 minutes. Remove from the heat, stir in the parsley and remaining butter and leave, covered, while you cook the scallops.

Brush the scallops with a little oil. Heat a dry, heavy frying pan or griddle pan until very hot and put the scallops in one by one. Leave for 2 minutes to brown, turn and cook for another 2 minutes. They should be burnished, just hot in the middle and very moist. Serve with the risotto.

PURPLE SPROUTING WITH PANGRATTATO

SERVES 2 | **PREP** 15 MINUTES | **COOK** 15 MINUTES

Pangrattato is a rough and ready-fried bread mix that brings crunch and zing to the simplest plain food but is particularly good with cabbagey purple sprouting broccoli. The bread is blitzed with anchovy and chilli so that the coarsely chopped crumbs end up salty and chilli-hot. The mix is fried in olive oil until crusty and golden, the chilli heat softening slightly in the frying. To get the chunky texture required, you really need sourdough or a similarly dense-crumbed bread. You do not want to end up with fine and even bread sauce-style crumbs.

2 thick slices of day-old
   sourdough bread
1 teaspoon dried chilli flakes
50g can anchovy fillets in
   olive oil
1 tablespoon olive oil
300g purple sprouting broccoli
salt
chunk of Parmesan cheese,
   to serve, optional

Begin by making the pangrattato. Tear the bread, crust-and-all, into pieces into the bowl of a food processor. Add the chilli and oil from the anchovies. Lift the anchovies out of the can, separate and tear or quickly chop and add to the mix. Pulse to chop and amalgamate, but don't decimate.

Heat the olive oil in a frying pan, add the crumbs and stir-fry, tossing constantly, until golden. Tip onto a plate.

Cook the broccoli in a large pan of boiling salted water for about 5 minutes until the stalks are just tender. Drain thoroughly.

Serve the broccoli topped with a handful of pangrattato. Parmesan, to grate over the top, is an optional extra.

SOY TENDERSTEM STIR-FRY WITH RICE NOODLES

SERVES 2 | **PREP** 20 MINUTES | **COOK** 15 MINUTES

The asparagus season ends and British tenderstem broccoli begins. Although quite different, they are interchangeable in many dishes but not in this stir-fry, with chilli, garlic, anchovy and soy sauce, a combination that complements the sweet cabbage flavour of tenderstem.

75g tagliatelle-style rice
   noodles
2 medium red onions
2 large garlic cloves
1 large red chilli
6 anchovy fillets in olive oil,
   drained
220g tenderstem broccoli
   spears
2 tablespoons vegetable oil
2 tablespoons soy sauce
1 tablespoon toasted sesame oil
1 tablespoon toasted sesame
   seeds
salt

Boil the kettle. Place the noodles in a large bowl and cover with boiling water. Leave until required.

Prepare the veg and anchovies, keeping them in separate piles: trim, halve and peel the onions, then slice the halves into chunky half-moons. Peel and slice the garlic into wafer-thin rounds. Split the chilli, scrape out the seeds and slice into skinny batons, then small dice. Chop the anchovies. Cut the broccoli into bite-sized pieces, keeping the florets and stalks separate.

Heat a wok over a high heat. Add the vegetable oil and swirl it round the wok. Add the onions, tossing constantly for a couple of minutes until it wilts slightly, then add the garlic and broccoli stalks. Season lightly with salt and stir-fry constantly for 2 minutes.

Add the broccoli florets, anchovies and chilli. Reduce the heat slightly and add the soy sauce and 2 tablespoons water. After 5–6 minutes of continuous tossing, drain the noodles in a sieve and add to the pan with the toasted sesame oil, then stir well. Sprinkle over the sesame seeds, toss and devour.

COURGETTES

I used to loathe courgettes, or zucchini as it's smart to call them (and how they are referred to in the US), but I've learnt how to cope with their mild flavour and tender flesh since I misguidedly sowed eight plants in a brand new allotment. My first success was soup (900g, grated, stirred into buttery softened onion, a diced potato, simmered for 5 minutes with 1.5 litres stock, then liquidized with 25g each of mint and flat leaf parsley), tapping into their love of mint. They are easy to griddle well, either small ones whole or cut into thick, long slices, and given a quick blast of heat, just enough to burnish the surface. I particularly like them piled with a crumble of feta and thyme, then given a generous splash of lemon juice and olive oil; this makes a delicious, gently flavoured base for lemon-grilled plaice.

The secret, I reckon, is minimal cooking, preferably not in water. Try them sliced in gratins with tomatoes or an eggy, cheesy sauce, or grated in pancakes with Parmesan, in a mixture thick enough to take a dusting of polenta so that they cook to a crisp. They are particularly good as well in individual filo pastry pies, Greek-style with feta cheese, egg and mint. They end up like a golden pillow, puffed and swollen with a gorgeously moist and creamy filling. I like them with a tomato relish made with balsamic vinegar, cooked shallots and masses of coriander.

My latest discovery is raw courgette, grated and salted, mixed with chilli and herbs, then packed into ramekins to turn out later and serve with a pretty salad of broad beans and watercress, or with a gooey stew of tomato and roasted red pepper.

Even if you aren't struggling to keep up with your own plants, courgettes at the peak of their summer season are definitely worth learning to love.

LINGUINE WITH LEMON COURGETTES

SERVES 2 | **PREP** 20 MINUTES | **COOK** 15 MINUTES

Once again, and it happens every year, I've germinated far too many courgette plants, so will soon be facing a glut of the vegetable I've learnt to love. This way of cooking it, briefly with tiny scraps of onion, is delicious with pasta in a lemony cream sauce. The icing on the cake, as it were, is lashings of freshly grated salty Parmesan. The dish manages to be all at once fresh, delicate, creamy and comforting. It's cheap, too, and very quick to make, so the perfect mid-week supper.

200g linguine or spaghetti
1 small onion
2 medium courgettes, about 250g
2 tablespoons olive oil
juice of ½ small lemon
3 tablespoons double cream
  or crème fraîche
salt and freshly ground
  black pepper
chunk of Parmesan cheese,
  to serve

Boil a full kettle. Use water from the kettle to cook the pasta al dente according to the packet instructions, likely to be 8–12 minutes. Drain.

While the pasta cooks, halve, peel and finely chop the onion. Trim and halve the courgettes, then slice into batons about ½cm thick × 4cm long.

Heat the oil in a spacious frying pan over a medium–low heat and stir in the onion. Stir-fry for a couple of minutes before adding the courgettes. Season with salt and pepper and stir-fry for 4–5 minutes until the courgettes and onion wilt and colour. Add the drained pasta, lemon juice and cream or crème fraîche. Stir thoroughly and serve with Parmesan to grate over the top.

COURGETTE AND TOMATO PARMESAN CRUMBLE

SERVES 4 | **PREP** 25 MINUTES | **COOK** 1 HOUR

If you are facing a courgette glut and most allotmenteers will, here's a lovely way of turning them into almost ratatouille with a cheesy crumble topping. Good with a crisp green salad or roast chicken, lamb or fish.

2 medium onions
3 tablespoons olive oil
2 tablespoons pine nuts
2 large garlic cloves
500g courgettes
750g ripe tomatoes
4 piquillo peppers from a jar
  or 1 small red pepper
1 bay leaf
4 thyme sprigs
1 rosemary sprig
75g butter
75g plain flour
75g Parmesan cheese
salt and freshly ground
  black pepper

Halve, peel and chop the onions. Heat 1 tablespoon of the oil in a spacious frying/sauté pan over a medium heat and quickly stir-fry the pine nuts until golden brown. Scoop onto kitchen paper. Add the remaining oil and stir in the onion with a pinch of salt. Stir occasionally.

Peel and chop the garlic; chop the courgettes into chunks. Pour boiling water over the tomatoes, count to 30, drain, peel, quarter, scrape out the seeds and chop the flesh. Drain and chop the piquillos or chop the pepper.

Stir the herbs into the softening onion with the garlic. Cook for a few minutes before adding the piquillos or pepper and courgettes. Stir-fry for 5 minutes, then add the tomatoes and a generous seasoning of pepper. Adjust the heat and cook, stirring often, for about 15 minutes until cooked. Tip into a 24 × 18 × 4cm gratin dish. Scatter over the pine nuts.

Preheat the oven to 200°C, Gas Mark 6.

Rub the chunked butter into the flour until it resembles breadcrumbs. Grate and mix in the Parmesan, then spoon over the vegetables. Bake for 30 minutes or until the crumble is crusty and golden.

COURGETTE SPAGHETTI WITH TOMATO CHICKEN

SERVES 2 | **PREP** 20 MINUTES | **COOK** 45 MINUTES

A chance remark by a friend prompted this recipe. Her description of a simple way of transforming the texture and flavour of leftover roast chicken harks back to a dish her husband remembers from a childhood in Belgrade. It begins with a chunky, well-seasoned tomato sauce, and once thick and creamy, torn chicken is added and cooked until shredded and very, very soft. A knob of butter and lots of chopped flat leaf parsley consolidate the dish, which is served piled over al dente courgette spaghetti.

1 medium–large onion
1 garlic clove
2 tablespoons olive oil
generous pinch of dried
  chilli flakes
6–8 tomatoes, about 800g
125g cooked chicken
  (prepared weight)
pinch of sugar

Halve, peel and finely chop the onion and garlic. Heat the olive oil in a spacious frying pan and soften the onion, stirring occasionally, over a medium heat. Stir in the garlic and chilli.

Meanwhile, place the tomatoes in a bowl and cover with boiling water, count to 30, drain, splash to cool, cut out the core in a pointed plug shape, quarter, peel and chop.

Shred the chicken into bite-sized pieces.

Stir what seems like an impossible amount of tomato into the onion, add the sugar, season with salt and pepper and cook, stirring often, until thick

knob of butter

25g flat leaf parsley

2 large courgettes, about
200–250g each

salt and freshly ground
black pepper

and sauce-like. Stir in the chicken, establish a steady simmer over a low heat and cook, stirring often, for about 30 minutes until very thick and creamy. Stir in the butter, season to taste and add the chopped parsley leaves.

About 10 minutes before the dish is ready, spiralize the courgettes or slice into ribbons, dust with 1 teaspoon salt and leave to drain. Rinse, boil for 1 minute, drain and serve topped with the sauce.

WATERCRESS AND PEA TART WITH BABY COURGETTES

SERVES 4 | **PREP** 20 MINUTES | **COOK** 20 MINUTES

This is a faux tart-cum-pizza, created from a thin sheet of puff pastry thickly spread with a soft, green cream made of watercress, peas and ricotta. The top is covered with quickly griddled baby courgettes flavoured with lemon and thyme. The tart looks stupendous and provides four generous wedges to serve with salad or roast tomatoes. Another good choice would be my super-quick baked potatoes made by halving them lengthways, cutting a deep surface lattice, adding a smear of oil and baking on shiny foil in a very hot oven. They will be perfect after about 30 minutes. Both the pastry base and cream can be prepared up to 24 hours in advance.

100g frozen petits pois

flour for dusting

150g puff pastry

butter for greasing

85g watercress

75g ricotta cheese

2 tablespoons soured cream
or crème fraîche

200g baby courgettes

1 tablespoon olive oil

½ lemon

1 teaspoon finely chopped
thyme

salt and freshly ground
black pepper

chunk of Parmesan cheese,
to serve

Preheat the oven to 220°C, Gas Mark 7.

Boil the peas in salted water until tender. Drain and leave to cool.

Dust a work surface with the flour and roll out the pastry until you can cut out a 28cm circle. Work the pastry with the tines of a fork to entirely cover with holes. Line a baking sheet with buttered baking parchment and carefully transfer the pastry. Bake in the middle of the oven for 8 minutes, checking after 5; you want it crisp and golden. Slip onto a wire rack to cool.

Place a griddle pan over a high heat. Blitz the peas, watercress, ricotta, salt and pepper and enough soured cream or crème fraîche in a food processor to make a thick, fairly stiff cream. Trim the courgettes, halve lengthways, smear with the oil and cook on the hot griddle for 2 minutes per side.

Spread the pastry with the cream. Toss the courgettes with the squeezed lemon juice and the thyme and arrange over the cream. Dredge with the grated Parmesan and serve.

MUSHROOMS

A punnet of mushrooms in the bottom of the fridge is a saviour for quick, easy dinners. A quick stir-fry in olive oil with a squeeze of lemon and maybe a hint of chilli is all they need. Try them piled over bruschetta or polenta, or mixed into pasta or gnocchi with grated Parmesan or a crumble of soft white cheese. A few dried mushrooms, porcini or Chinese black mushrooms will transform a noodle dish or stew.

BALSAMIC RED ONION AND MUSHROOM PASTA
SERVES 2 | **PREP** 15 MINUTES | **COOK** 35 MINUTES

Onions cooked in balsamic vinegar are transformed into a slippery, dark mess that goes with anything and everything. Try it on toast under grilled cheese or with chicken livers, or turn it into gravy to serve with sausages by adding a dusting of flour and a little stock.

In this robust sauce for pasta, balsamic onion makes a rich and spicy background for flat mushrooms cooked with garlic and chilli, then finished with wilted spinach. Other good additions would be a few slices of crisp-fried chorizo or a last-minute crumble of Greek feta cheese.

3 medium red onions
2 tablespoons olive oil
2 garlic cloves
3 large flat mushrooms, about 300g
½ teaspoon dried chilli flakes
1 tablespoon thick balsamic vinegar, such as Belazu
handful of young spinach, about 100g
200g casarecce, penne or other short or stumpy pasta
squeeze of lemon
salt

Halve and peel the onions, then slice them into thin wedges. Heat the oil in a spacious frying pan and stir in the onions with ½ teaspoon salt. Toss for a couple of minutes, turn down the heat, cover and cook gently for 10–15 minutes until melting.

Crack the garlic, flake away the skin and finely chop. Wipe the mushrooms clean, then cut into ½cm-thick slices.

Stir the garlic and chilli flakes into the onions and continue cooking, uncovered, for a couple of minutes before you add the mushrooms. Stir constantly until the mushrooms darken and turn juicy. Add the balsamic vinegar, stirring as it bubbles into the onions and mushrooms. Fold in the spinach and turn off the heat.

Cook the pasta in plenty of boiling water according to the packet instructions. Drain and add to the mushrooms, tossing to mix thoroughly. Add a squeeze of lemon, toss again and serve.

SKINNY MUSHROOM PIE

SERVES 4 | **PREP** 20 MINUTES | **COOK** 30 MINUTES

The buttery crunch of golden puff pastry filled with minced mushrooms softened with shallots and garlic, parsley and a squeeze of lemon is hard to resist. This pie is long and skinny like a ladder, the steps made by slashing the top, the lines sagging apart as the pie bakes. It is moreish on its own hot from the oven but good with tomato salad, particularly one made with chewy, intensely flavoured so-called sun-kissed or sun-blushed tomatoes. Add a few black olives and capers with a crumble of Greek feta cheese to make it even more special.

2 shallots
2 garlic cloves
25g butter plus extra
    for greasing
1 tablespoon olive oil
300g closed-cap mushrooms
20g flat leaf parsley
squeeze of lemon
2 tablespoons fresh white or
    wholemeal breadcrumbs
flour for dusting
250g puff pastry (ready-rolled
    is fine)
1 egg
salt and freshly ground
    black pepper

Peel the shallots, separate the halves and finely chop. Peel the garlic and finely chop. Melt most of the butter in the oil in a frying pan over a medium–low heat and gently soften the shallots and garlic.

Wipe the mushrooms and pulse blitz to a paste with the parsley in a food processor. Stir the mushrooms into the shallots, stirring as the mix darkens and turns moist. Add a squeeze of lemon, salt and pepper and cook for a few more minutes. Stir in the breadcrumbs to take up the juices and spread on a plate to cool.

Preheat the oven to 200°C, Gas Mark 6.

Dust a work surface with flour and roll the pastry out to approximately 13 × 60cm. Pile the cooled mushroom across the middle of one half of the pastry, leaving a 2cm border. Paint the border with the beaten egg. Fold in half, press the edges together and tidy up using a knife and ruler. Make 10 horizontal cuts within the border and paint with egg. Use a palette knife to carefully lift onto a buttered parchment-lined baking sheet. Bake for 10–15 minutes, or until puffed and golden.

MUSHROOM, CHORIZO AND CHICKPEA STEW

SERVES 4 | **PREP** 20 MINUTES | **COOK** 35 MINUTES

This is a variation on one of my favourite quick and easy, almost storecupboard suppers. Piquillo peppers from a jar, canned chickpeas and chopped tomatoes, sliced chorizo on standby in the fridge; only mushrooms and spinach need to be bought freshly. Small boiled new potatoes make the stew go further. Serve it with a spoon and fork and crusty garlic bread for dipping and crunching.

2 small onions
1 tablespoon olive oil
2 garlic cloves
350g medium chestnut
   mushrooms
100g sliced chorizo
400g can chopped tomatoes
¼ teaspoon dried chilli flakes
400g can chickpeas
6 piquillo peppers from a jar
½ chicken stock cube
200g young spinach
salt and freshly ground
   black pepper

Halve, peel and chop the onions. Soften in the oil in a spacious, lidded sauté pan. Give the occasional stir while you peel and thinly slice the garlic into rounds and wipe the mushrooms. Separate the chorizo slices into the pan, giving the odd stir as they wilt and give their juices. Stir in the garlic and mushrooms, tossing constantly as the mush gradually turn juicy and dark. Add the tomatoes, chilli and rinsed, drained chickpeas. Slice the peppers in chunky strips and add to the pan.

Boil the kettle. Dissolve the stock cube in 250ml boiling water and add to the pan. Give a good stir with a generous seasoning of salt and pepper. Simmer, covered, for 15 minutes.

Taste and adjust the seasoning. Fold in what initially seems a lot of spinach. Once wilted, the dish is done.

POLENTA WITH LEMON MUSHROOMS

SERVES 6 | **PREP** 25 MINUTES | **COOK** 20 MINUTES

Cooking on a boat, which I did for a week one summer, concentrates the mind and having a vegetarian skipper concentrated it even more. Quick and easy but satisfying meals were the order of the day. Quick-cook polenta made a great change from pasta, while a bottle of decent olive oil, a slab of Parmesan and plenty of lemons proved worth their weight in gold. Slippery, lemony mushrooms over buttery, cheesy soft polenta was a hit with everyone, and my pot of Greek basil and stash of flat leaf parsley came up trumps for a fresh, vibrant garnish.

500g closed-cup mushrooms
2 garlic cloves
50g flat leaf parsley
2 tablespoons olive oil
1 lemon
½ chicken stock cube
500g quick-cook (1 minute) polenta
50g butter
75g finely grated Parmesan cheese
1 tablespoon Greek or regular chopped basil
salt

Wipe the mushrooms to remove any dirt. Slice thinly. Peel and finely chop the garlic. Pick the leaves off the parsley stalks and chop (discard the stalks).

Heat the olive oil in a spacious pan and stir in the mushrooms. Keep tossing them around until they begin to shrink, darken and turn juicy. Stir in the garlic and continue stir-frying until aromatic. Season with salt, juice from half the lemon and half the parsley.

Boil the kettle and measure out 2 litres boiling water. Pour 1.5 litres into a deep pan, return to the boil and crumble in the stock cube, stirring to dissolve. Add the polenta, stirring constantly with a long wooden spoon as it thickens almost immediately. Add the butter and half the grated Parmesan. Stir, adding extra boiling water if too stiff; you want it sloppy but thick.

Divide the polenta between 6 plates and sprinkle with the last of the Parmesan. Quickly reheat the mushrooms, spoon them over the polenta and garnish with the last of the parsley, offering a final squeeze of lemon.

PORCINI AND CHESTNUT MUSHROOM MAFTOUL RISOTTO

SERVES 4 | **PREP** 20 MINUTES | **COOK** 30 MINUTES

The idea for this style of mushroom risotto can be traced back to a visit I made to *MasterChef* winner Dhruv Baker's pub, *The Jolly Gardeners*, in Earslfield. He used similar Sardinian fregola for a risotto with mushroom and truffle; my version is intensely mushroomy with a background lemon tang.

10g dried porcini
200g giant couscous (maftoul)
1 large celery stick
1 small onion
1 garlic clove
25g butter
1 tablespoon olive oil
300g chestnut mushrooms
1 tablespoon lemon juice
200ml chicken or vegetable
   stock
salt
chunk of Parmesan cheese,
   to serve, optional

Boil the kettle. Place the porcini in a mug and cover with 200ml boiling water from the kettle, then use 1 litre to boil the giant couscous with a generous seasoning of salt. Drain the couscous after 8 minutes and leave the porcini to soak for 20 minutes.

Peel and finely dice the celery. Peel and finely chop the onion and garlic. Soften all 3 in the butter and olive oil in a spacious frying/sauté pan.

Wipe the mushrooms clean, set aside about 75g and briefly pulse the rest in a food processor to chop finely. Scoop the porcini out of the soaking liquid (reserve this) and chop. Coarsely chunk the reserved mushrooms. Stir all into the softened onion mix, adding ½ teaspoon salt, tossing constantly until dark and juicy. Add the lemon juice, couscous, porcini soaking liquid and stock, stirring for a few minutes as the flavours consolidate and the liquid is absorbed. Eat immediately with or without grated Parmesan, or reheat later but add extra liquid.

MUSHROOM OPEN LASAGNE WITH PARSNIP PURÉE

SERVES 2 | **PREP** 20 MINUTES | **COOK** 30 MINUTES

Who'd have thought that parsnip purée and mushrooms would work well? Not me, until I had some purée left over from another recipe and big flat mushrooms in need of eating. The purée took the place of a creamy sauce for this simple yet delicious way of using lasagne to loosely wrap the food.

350g young parsnips
300ml milk
1 teaspoon Dijon mustard
1 lemon
4 large or 6 small sheets
   of dried lasagne
4 portobello or other large
   flat mushrooms
4 slices of ham, optional
1 tablespoon sunflower oil
30g butter
freshly grated Parmesan
   cheese
salt

Peel and chunk the parsnips. Simmer, covered, in the milk until tender. Strain but save the milk. Blitz in a food processor with 2–4 tablespoons of the milk, mustard, a pinch of salt and a squeeze of lemon to make a thick purée. Add extra salt and lemon to taste. Pass through a sieve into a small pan and set aside.

Half-fill a pan, wide enough to hold the lasagne flat, with water. Boil, then add salt and the lasagne. Cook according to the packet instructions until tender, scoop onto a plate and cover, flat, with clingfilm to keep warm.

Meanwhile, wipe the mushrooms and slice each into 4 or 5 thick pieces. Tear the ham, if using, into scraps. Heat the oil in a frying pan and quickly fry the ham, turning as it colours and crisps. Scoop onto kitchen paper.

Add the butter to the pan and stir-fry the mushrooms until juicy. Add a squeeze of lemon; toss again. Quickly reheat the parsnip. Lay the lasagne on warmed plates. Pile half each sheet with parsnip, top with mushrooms, loosely fold over the lasagne, add ham, if using, and grated Parmesan. Eat.

MUSHROOM STROGANOFF, BROWN RICE AND CHIVE CREAM

SERVES 2 | **PREP** 20 MINUTES | **COOK** 45 MINUTES

Inexpensive bog-standard mushrooms get their flavour bolstered with a few dried porcini in this vegetarian take on a meaty classic. Colour and slippery sweetness comes from red peppers, while brown rice lends a pleasing nuttiness, and soured cream and chives add luxury and freshness.

10g dried porcini
150g brown basmati rice
knob of butter
1 medium red onion
1 garlic clove
1 tablespoon olive oil
300g closed-cup mushrooms
1 Romano red pepper,
    about 100g
1 teaspoon paprika
1 lemon
4 tablespoons soured
    cream, crème fraîche
    or thick yoghurt
small bunch of chives
salt

Boil the kettle. Cover the porcini with 150ml boiling water and cover with clingfilm. Leave for 20 minutes.

Rinse the rice in cold running water. Cook in 450ml boiling water for 20 minutes. Drain and return to the pan with the butter and a pinch of salt. Cover and leave for 10 minutes or until required.

Halve, peel and finely chop the onion and garlic and cook in the oil, stirring often, for 5 minutes in a spacious, lidded frying/sauté pan.

Wipe the fresh mushrooms clean and quarter. Trim and quarter the pepper lengthways, slice into strips and dice, then rinse to remove the seeds. Stir the pepper into the onion. Cook, stirring occasionally, for 5 minutes.

Add the fresh mushrooms and stir, continuing until wilted and shiny. Add the scooped-out porcini (reserve the liquid) and paprika. Stir well and add the juice of half the lemon and the strained mushroom water (it will be gritty). Cover and cook for 10 minutes or until tender and juicy.

Adjust the seasoning with salt and lemon juice. Serve over the rice with soured cream, crème fraîche or yoghurt and the finely snipped chives.

ONIONS AND LEEKS

Onion is the bedrock of the kitchen, the starting point of so many dishes that it gets overlooked as a star in its own right. I love it caramelized, cooked into a sloppy, soft goo to turn into soup or stir into pasta. Onion tart, the onions cooked without colour and mixed with a creamy egg custard, is heaven indeed.

Leeks, rightly known as the softy of the onion family, will keep happily in the bottom of the fridge salad drawer for several days. Gently stewed for pie or risotto, leeks love ham and cheese, but remember it, too, for variations on leek vinaigrette.

ONION TART WITH SPINACH AND FETA

SERVES 4–6 | **PREP** 30 MINUTES, PLUS CHILLING | **COOK** 45 MINUTES

The pastry is homemade for this quiche-style tart, but the main ingredients are a cheat. I used chopped fried Spanish onions in a can and frozen spinach, mixing them with eggs, yoghurt, feta and Parmesan, and the result was fantastic. If you are cooking from scratch, you will need 500g each of fresh onions and spinach.

8 nuggets frozen spinach, about 200g

390g can Eazy Fried Onions

150g plain flour plus extra for dusting

50g butter plus extra knob for greasing

25g lard

3 large eggs

250g Greek yoghurt

4 tablespoons freshly grated Parmesan cheese

200g Greek feta cheese

generous grating of nutmeg

salt and freshly ground black pepper

Boil a kettle. Use to fill a bowl. Place the spinach on a plate, then place the plate over the hot water. Tip the onions into a sieve to drain.

Sift the flour with a pinch of salt into a mixing bowl or the bowl of a food processor. Add the diced butter and lard. Rub the fat into the flour by hand or pulse to blend. Quickly mix in 3 tablespoons cold water. Knead into a ball, wrap in clingfilm and chill for 30 minutes.

Whisk the eggs in a bowl. Stir in the yoghurt, half the Parmesan, the crumbled feta, grated nutmeg, onions and squeezed, chopped spinach, a pinch of salt and a generous seasoning of freshly ground black pepper.

Preheat the oven to 200°C, Gas Mark 6. Butter a 23cm loose-based flan tin. Dust with flour and shake out the excess.

Roll out the pastry on a flour-dusted surface to fit the tin, leaving an overhang. Cover loosely with foil, then top with baking beans or raw rice and bake for 10 minutes. Remove the foil and cook for a further 5–10 minutes until pale golden.

Tip in the filling, smooth the top and dust with the remaining Parmesan. Bake for 35–45 minutes until just set. Trim the excess pastry, then stand the tart on a can to remove the collar. Bingo.

BIGOLI WITH CARAMELIZED ONIONS AND ANCHOVIES

SERVES 2 | **PREP** 15 MINUTES | **COOK** 30 MINUTES

When my son went off to college, he left with a box of emergency provisions. Onions, canned tomatoes and anchovies, pasta and a bottle of olive oil were the cornerstones of his personal stash, and this simple pasta dish became a favourite.

Wholewheat pasta isn't normally my first choice, but there are times, and this recipe is one of them, when its dense texture suits the dish. Bigoli is the name of stubby wholewheat pasta with a fine hole running through it (www.linastores.co.uk), but quick-cook wholewheat spaghetti, if you can find it, is a good alternative. The sauce is very easy to make and involves gently softening plenty of sliced onions and mixing them with pounded anchovy and a generous slug of olive oil. The intensely savoury and piquantly salted slippery onions are mixed into the cooked pasta and tossed together so that every strand of pasta is coated. You will be surprised at how delicious this tastes.

200g bigoli or thick
   wholewheat spaghetti or
   another wholewheat pasta
1 large Spanish onion
6 tablespoons olive oil
50g can anchovy fillets in
   olive oil, drained
salt and freshly ground
   black pepper

Boil a kettle. Three-quarters fill a large pan with the kettle water. Salt it sparingly (remember, anchovies are very salty) and cook the pasta according to the packet instructions. Note: A bit of judicious timing is necessary for this simple dish because you want the cooking of the onions – which need at least 20 minutes to get to the right state – to coincide more or less exactly with the pasta. There are few things worse than overcooked wholewheat pasta.

Halve, peel and finely slice the onion. Heat 2 tablespoons of the olive oil in a spacious, lidded frying/sauté pan over a medium heat and stir in the onions. Toss constantly for 2–3 minutes, then reduce the heat and cook, stirring often, for about 10 minutes until beginning to flop and take a little colour. Add 4 tablespoons water and simmer on until disappeared, leaving soft, juicy onions; about 20 minutes.

Chop the anchovy fillets and use a pestle and mortar or the back of a wooden spoon to pound to a paste. Add the anchovy paste to the onions and cook gently for a couple of minutes, stirring the mixture constantly. Add the remaining olive oil to make a homogeneous sauce and season generously with black pepper.

Drain the pasta, reserving 2 tablespoons of the cooking water. Add the pasta and reserved water to the onions. Mix thoroughly so that each strand of pasta is coated.

SAFFRON ONION SOUP WITH COUSCOUS AND TOMATO

SERVES 4 | **PREP** 25 MINUTES | **COOK** 40 MINUTES

Scratching around my bare food cupboards after a few days away resulted in this light, elegant but satisfying soup. It was so good that I immediately made it again, twice. Sloppy saffron-scented onions thickened by couscous with occasional bursts of chilli-hot, creamy green olives get a finale of fresh and vibrant tomato with coriander.

6 medium onions
1 tablespoon olive oil
15g butter
3 garlic cloves
70g pitted green olives
   with chilli
4 vine tomatoes
generous pinch of saffron
   threads
2 thyme sprigs
2 chicken stock cubes
100g couscous
50g coriander
salt

Boil a full kettle. Halve, peel and finely slice the onions. Cook, covered, stirring occasionally, in the oil and butter in a spacious, lidded pan with a generous pinch of salt for 10 minutes.

Peel and finely slice the garlic. Slice the olives into 3 rounds. Pour boiling water over the tomatoes, count to 30, drain, quarter, peel and scrape the seeds into a sieve over a bowl. Dice the flesh and crush the juice out of the seeds with the back of a wooden spoon.

Stir the saffron, garlic and thyme into the onions, cover again and cook for a further 10 minutes.

Dissolve the stock cubes in 1 litre boiling water and add to the pan with the couscous. Simmer, half covered, for 15–20 minutes, then add the tomato juices and flesh. Check the seasoning, stir in the chopped coriander and olives and serve. The tomatoes do not disintegrate. If you find the soup too thick, add extra stock. Discard the thyme sprigs.

HAM, LEEK AND EMMENTAL GRATIN

SERVES 2, GENEROUSLY | **PREP** 15 MINUTES | **COOK** 30 MINUTES

A sudden craving for silky steamed leeks bundled in thick slices of English ham under a Dijon and lemon-flavoured white sauce prompted this take on a bistro classic. The soft shaggy bundles and their piquant sauce are perfectly offset by a crisp thin layer of breadcrumbs and cheese eked out for every mouthful. Pop under the grill until the carapace forms or leave to go cold, then bake for about 20 minutes in a hot oven. Serve alone or with mash and greens.

400g trimmed leeks
120g Wiltshire cured ham
100g grated Emmental cheese
50g butter plus extra knob
40g plain flour
1 tablespoon Dijon mustard
400ml milk
squeeze of lemon
25g fresh white breadcrumbs
salt and freshly ground
   black pepper

Boil a full kettle. Cut the leeks into lengths about 8cm. Agitate in cold water to clean, then drain. Place in a steamer (or drop into boiling salted water) placed over a half-filled pan of boiling water. Cover and cook for 6–8 minutes until tender. Squeeze to rid excess liquid, then loosely wrap in a tear of ham and arrange in a single layer in a 24 × 18 × 4cm gratin dish. Top with a handful of cheese.

Meanwhile, melt the 50g butter in a medium pan and stir in the flour, then the mustard. Off the heat, add the milk, stirring constantly, to make a smooth sauce. Simmer for 5 minutes; whisk if lumpy. Add salt, pepper and lemon to taste.

Pour the sauce over the leeks. Scatter the remaining cheese mixed with the crumbs over the top. Add dots of butter. Place under a hot grill or bake for 20 minutes at 200°C, Gas Mark 6 or until the top is crusty.

LEEK RISOTTO WITH LEMON COD

SERVES 2 | **PREP** 15 MINUTES | **COOK** 35 MINUTES

I often serve a simple vegetable risotto with fish and this combination of leeks, rice and lemon cod works particularly well. The leeks are softened in butter, with a generous splash of white wine, and a light fish or chicken stock gives plenty of flavour to the rice. The fish is quickly roasted in a hot oven as the risotto finishes and the juices aren't wasted. A few thinly sliced runner beans between risotto and fish is a good addition.

300g trimmed leeks
40g butter
200g Arborio rice
150ml dry white wine
1 chicken stock cube
2 thick cod fillets, skin on
1 tablespoon olive oil
½ lemon
250g runner beans
salt

Trim and chop the leeks into 2cm-thick slices. Rinse and drain.

Melt the butter in a spacious, lidded frying/sauté pan, stir in the leeks, season lightly with salt, cover and cook, stirring a few times, for about 10 minutes until slippery soft.

Boil the kettle. Stir in the rice, add the wine and stir until absorbed. Dissolve the stock cube in 600ml boiling water from the kettle and add in 3 batches, stirring occasionally as each batch is absorbed, cooking until the rice is tender with a slightly chalky centre. Allow about 25 minutes in total. Cover and leave for 5 minutes.

Meanwhile, preheat the oven to 200°C, Gas Mark 6. Place the fish, skin-side down, on a lightly oiled small roasting tin. Squeeze over the lemon juice, adding the remaining oil. Roast for 10–15 minutes depending on the thickness of the fillets.

Slice the beans and boil for 5 minutes. Drain.

Serve the risotto topped with the beans, then quickly invert a fish fillet, remove the skin and pour over the cooking juices.

GREEN CHICKEN COUSCOUS WITH LEEKS

SERVES 4 | **PREP** 25 MINUTES | **COOK** 20 MINUTES

For an almost instant supper I often combine leeks with couscous, usually with hard-boiled eggs. This time I've zizzed up the flavours with watercress, lemon zest and garlic, and mixed this vivacious green backdrop with quickly fried chicken nuggets and golden Marcona almonds. This lovely combination can be served hot or cold, and leftovers are perfect for fridge cruising or the lunch box.

400g trimmed leeks
350g skinned chicken
    thigh fillets
1 small lemon
4½ tablespoons olive oil
    plus extra for drizzling
½ chicken stock cube
175g couscous
100g watercress
1 garlic clove
30 blanched almonds,
    preferably Marcona

Cut the leeks into 6cm lengths. Agitate in cold water, drain and boil or steam for about 4 minutes until tender to the point of a sharp knife. Drain and keep warm.

Meanwhile, slice the chicken into 5cm-long, thin strips. Pile them into a mixing bowl.

Boil the kettle. Remove the zest from the lemon. Squeeze half the lemon juice over the chicken, add 1 tablespoon olive oil and toss thoroughly.

Dissolve the stock cube in 300ml boiling water and pour the stock into a large serving bowl. Add 1 tablespoon lemon juice and 1 tablespoon olive oil and stir in the couscous. Leave for about 10 minutes until all the liquid has been absorbed and the couscous is tender. Scrape across the surface with a fork to separate the grains.

Place the watercress, lemon zest and peeled garlic in the bowl of a food processor. Blitz until finely chopped.

Heat a heavy frying pan over a medium heat with ½ tablespoon olive oil and stir-fry the almonds until golden. Tip onto a plate. Add the remaining 2 tablespoons olive oil to the empty pan and brown the chicken in 2 batches, cooking for about 45 seconds on each side, or until golden and cooked through.

Stir the watercress mixture into the couscous and add the almonds, chicken and leeks. Toss and serve now or later with a drizzle of olive oil and a squeeze of lemon juice.

FLAMICHE

SERVES 4–6 | **PREP** 30 MINUTES | **COOK** 45 MINUTES

Flamiche is the name of a Belgian leek pie that is very simple to make and extremely delicious. I've tinkered with the recipe many times, adding white wine to the cooked leeks before the cream and tried adding bacon or ham, but have come to the conclusion that the original is best. Serve on its own or with roast tomatoes, but remember that it is also a spectacular accompaniment to poached gammon or gammon steaks.

800g trimmed leeks
75g butter
5–6 tablespoons double
   cream
500g puff pastry
flour for dusting
1 egg yolk
splash of milk
salt and freshly ground
   black pepper

Slice the leeks into thick rounds, agitate them in cold water to clean and drain thoroughly.

Use a little of the butter to smear a parchment-lined baking sheet. Melt the rest in a large, lidded frying pan and cook the leeks gently, stirring occasionally, for about 20 minutes until soft. Remove the lid and bubble away any liquid. Season with salt and pepper, add the cream and cook, stirring, until thick and creamy. Leave to cool.

Preheat the oven to 220°C, Gas Mark 7. Halve the pastry, dust a work surface with the flour and roll into 2 circles, approximately 22cm, one slightly larger than the other.

Place the smaller pastry circle on the buttered sheet and spoon the cooled leeks over, spreading within a 2.5cm border. Paint the border with the egg yolk beaten with a splash of milk. Make a lid with the larger circle and gently press the edges together. Now brush the whole surface with egg wash and go round the border again, this time with the tines of a fork, pressing firmly. Make a central steam hole and decorate, if you fancy, by etching with the backside of a knife. Bake for 25 minutes or until puffed, golden and spectacular. Cool for a few minutes before serving in wedges.

POTATOES AND SWEET POTATOES

You are never far from a decent supper if you've got some potatoes tucked away. Think of it now: potato soup, potato salad, crusty jacket potatoes with cold grated cheese, roast potatoes, the first early new potatoes, Spanish omelette, curried potato, fluffy mashed potato, crusty-topped potato gratins, potato pies and potato gnocchi. Potatoes just keep on giving. Sweet potatoes are almost as versatile, their golden flesh quickly baked into fluffy mash, roasted into chips and boiled in half the time of regular potatoes.

BONFIRE NIGHT POTATO TAGINE

SERVES 4–6 | **PREP** 30 MINUTES | **COOK** 50 MINUTES

If you are scratching around for something to complement the inevitable Bonfire Night sausages, here's a bracing storecupboard alternative to baked potatoes. The basics are potatoes and onions, garlic and a pinch of saffron, but it is ras el hanout Moroccan spice mix, green olives, salt-preserved lemons or scraps of lemon zest and a big bunch of coriander that give this curry its excitement. A can of rinsed, drained chickpeas and a handful of blanched, halved green beans, thrown in just before serving, will extend the dish.

2 Spanish onions
2 tablespoons olive oil
10g butter
4 large garlic cloves
generous pinch of saffron
    threads
4 teaspoons ras el hanout
    Moroccan spice mix
700–900g potatoes
½ chicken stock cube
6 salt-preserved lemons
    or 1 lemon
70g pitted, sliced green olives
80g bunch of coriander
1 lemon
salt and freshly ground
    black pepper

Peel, halve and chop the onions. Add the oil to a spacious, heavy-based lidded pan (or tagine). Melt the butter in the oil and stir in the chopped onions. Stir occasionally for about 10 minutes until juicy and glassy.

Peel, chop and crush the garlic to a paste with a pinch of salt. Sprinkle the saffron over the onions, stirring as it bleeds colour into the hot juices. Stir in the garlic, followed by the ras el hanout, stir-frying for a couple of minutes.

Boil the kettle. Peel the potatoes, cut into big bite-sized pieces and rinse. Stir into the onions until all the pieces change colour. Dissolve the half stock cube in 400ml boiling water and add to the pan.

Quarter the preserved lemons, scrape away the pulp and slice the peel. Stir the sliced peel or shirt-button-sized scraps of lemon zest and the olives into the stew. Chop the coriander, slicing the stalks finely. Add the stalk half of the bunch to the pot. Establish a gentle simmer, cover and cook for 20–30 minutes until the potatoes are tender and most of the liquid absorbed.

Adjust the seasoning with salt, pepper and lemon juice. Stir in the coriander leaves just before serving.

TARTIFLETTE

SERVES 4 | **PREP** 20 MINUTES | **COOK** 35 MINUTES

There were murmurs of approval when I cooked this for my son, a tartiflette aficionado since his skiing season in the Alps. There it's made with Reblochon or Beaufort cheese, but Taleggio is a good alternative. Serve it with gherkins and green salad leaves with walnut oil vinaigrette.

1 large or 2 medium onions
2 tablespoons olive oil
1 teaspoon thyme leaves
200g pancetta or other smoked, streaky bacon lardons
1kg medium Charlotte or similar waxy potatoes
600ml milk or 300ml milk and 300ml crème fraîche
400g Reblochon, Beaufort or fridge-cold Taleggio cheese
salt and freshly ground black pepper

Preheat the oven to 200°C, Gas Mark 6.

Halve, peel and finely chop the onion. Heat the oil in a spacious frying pan and stir in the onion and thyme, followed by the lardons. Cook for about 15 minutes until the onion is slippery soft and the lardons crisp. Tip into a sieve to drain.

Meanwhile, scrub and chop the potatoes into 5mm-thick slices, then rinse and shake dry. Simmer in the milk or milk mixture with a generous seasoning of salt and pepper for about 12 minutes until tender, not worrying if the milk fluffs. Drain the potatoes and reserve the milk.

Slice the cheese thinly, trimming away the rind. Layer up the potatoes, onion and lardons, slices of cheese, a dribble of the reserved milk and a seasoning of salt and pepper in a 30 × 20 × 5cm gratin dish, saving a layer of cheese for the top. Add the last of the milk and bake for 15–20 minutes until the cheese is bubbling and browning.

PAN HAGGERTY

SERVES 2–4 | **PREP** 20 MINUTES | **COOK** 1 HOUR

Pan Haggerty is a Northumberland dish of thinly sliced potatoes layered with onion and cheese. Traditionally it's cooked in beef dripping, but this version uses butter and a smidgen of oil. Good on its own, it goes well with steak, roast chicken, crisp streaky bacon or poached eggs.

2 medium onions
50g butter
1 dessertspoon sunflower oil
4 large potatoes, about 600g
100g mature Cheddar cheese
salt and freshly ground black pepper

Halve, peel and finely slice the onions. Melt the butter in the oil in an ovenproof, heavy-based frying pan and soften the onions, adding a generous pinch of salt, tossing regularly until very sloppy; about 15 minutes.

Peel, rinse and thinly slice the potatoes using a mandolin, food processor attachment or slicer on the side of a box cheese grater, as if making crisps.

Preheat the oven to 190°C, Gas Mark 5. Grate the cheese.

Scoop the onions into a sieve over the pan so that the buttery juices drain back. Pour half into a cup. Arrange overlapping slices of potato, as if making a French apple tart but going up the sides of the oiled pan, too. Layer with the onion and the grated cheese, plenty of freshly ground black pepper and salt, finishing with potato. Smear the top with the reserved butter.

Bake for 30 minutes. Increase the heat to 220°C, Gas Mark 7 and cook for a further 10–15 minutes until the top is crusty and golden. Loosen with a palette knife and quickly, but carefully, invert onto a warm plate.

POTATO SALAD WITH CRUSHED PEAS, ASPARAGUS AND MINT

SERVES 2–4 | **PREP** 20 MINUTES | **COOK** 20 MINUTES

I used tiny new potatoes from Italy for this pretty potato salad but will be making it again with Cornish earlies and Jersey Royals when they are in season. I always bother to skin potatoes for potato salad and dress them warm so that the dressing gets a chance to soak in. This lovely salad goes with anything from a slab of mature Cheddar or a hard-boiled egg to lamb kebabs or simply cooked fish. I teamed it with chicken drumsticks roasted over rosemary.

400g miniature new potatoes
100g British asparagus tips
200g frozen petits pois
20 mint leaves
salt and freshly ground
   black pepper

For the vinaigrette
1 tablespoon white wine
   vinegar
generous pinch of sugar
1 small shallot
1 teaspoon Dijon mustard
3–4 tablespoons olive oil

Boil the potatoes in salted water until tender. Scoop into a colander (reserve the cooking water) and leave to cool slightly.

Next make the dressing. Place the vinegar in a salad bowl. Stir in the sugar until dissolved and season lavishly with black pepper. Halve, peel and finely chop the shallot. Stir into the vinegar, followed by the mustard. Beat in sufficient olive oil to make a thick, creamy vinaigrette.

By now the potatoes will be cool enough to handle. Quickly remove their skins. Stir the potatoes into the vinaigrette.

Re-boil the potato water. Cut the asparagus into 3cm lengths. Boil for 2 minutes. Scoop into a colander. Re-boil the water and add the peas. Boil until tender. Drain and use a potato masher to crush coarsely.

Chop the mint and stir through the peas. Mix the peas through the potato salad, then add the asparagus. Mix and serve now or later.

SWEET POTATO, GINGER AND COCONUT SOUP WITH CHORIZO

SERVES 4 | **PREP** 20 MINUTES | **COOK** 35 MINUTES

This soup is a true winter warmer, good to look at, rich and creamy with hot back notes. It's thick, smooth and glossy, a deep, golden terracotta colour with a splash of green from chopped coriander and has a crisp chorizo garnish. It's filling, too, particularly when served with garlic-rubbed toasted sourdough splashed with your finest olive oil. After a couple of bowlfuls of this, there won't be room for much else.

1 medium onion
1½ tablespoons groundnut oil
2 garlic cloves
25g fresh root ginger
1 red bird's eye chilli
550–650g sweet potatoes
1½ chicken stock cubes
160ml can coconut cream
1 lime
100g whole chorizo sausage
25g coriander
salt
bruschetta, to serve

Halve, peel and chop the onion. Heat 1 tablespoon of the oil in a pan that can accommodate the soup, stir in the onion and cook, stirring occasionally, over a medium heat for about 10 minutes while you prepare the other veg.

Crack the garlic and flake away the skin. Slice lengthways and chop. Peel and finely slice the ginger. Split the chilli, scrape out the seeds and chop. Stir everything into the onion with a generous pinch of salt. Reduce the heat slightly and leave to soften.

Boil the kettle. Peel the sweet potatoes and cut into kebab-sized chunks. Stir the potatoes into the onion. Crumble the stock cubes over the top and add 1 litre boiling water. Stir to dissolve the cubes, establish a steady simmer, partially cover the pan and cook for 15–20 minutes until soft.

Add the coconut cream and blitz in batches. Return to the pan and taste and adjust the seasoning with salt and lime juice. Peel the chorizo, split lengthways and slice thinly. Quickly fry in the remaining oil until crisp. Drain on kitchen paper.

Serve the soup topped with the chopped coriander and crisp-fried chorizo plus bruschetta for dunking.

TOMATOES

Tomatoes are the perfect starting point for super-quick, super-easy and super-delicious tarts that can be served as a starter or light supper with salad. Tomato salads are another sure-fire winner, dressed with a swirl of balsamic and another of olive oil with a few basil leaves, building up flavour with crumbled feta cheese, capers and black olives.

My favourite tomato standby, perfect for transforming lack-lustre tomatoes or to be remembered when there is a glut, is roast tomato halves. I make a tray at a time and store them in the fridge in a plastic box. They can be quickly warmed for breakfast-supper with bacon or scrambled eggs, turned into soup, stirred into pasta or piled onto garlic-rubbed toast for instant starters or snack suppers. They also make great risotto.

Cherry tomatoes can be popped in the mouth like sweets, but cheer up unseasonal tomato sauces and salads, although I tend to open a can in the winter months.

PANZANELLA

SERVES 4 | **PREP** 30 MINUTES | **COOK** 20 MINUTES

I had a very pretty version of this Tuscan bread and tomato salad at The Walnut Tree, Abergavenny. Shaun Hill makes it with small heritage tomatoes, while my version is more rustic, a delicious mess of juicy ripe tomato, slippery sweet roast red pepper and garlicky, soggy and crusty croutons, all livened by capers, basil and cucumber. It's a great starter or light meal, but controversially good with olive oil and lemon-splashed roast cod, and peas.

1 large red pepper
½ cucumber
3 thick slices of sourdough
  bread or similar
1 garlic clove
7 tablespoons olive oil
750g very ripe tomatoes
1 tablespoon red wine
  vinegar
1 tablespoon capers in
  brine, drained
handful of basil leaves
salt and freshly ground
  black pepper

Preheat the oven to 220°C, Gas Mark 7.

Halve the pepper through the stalk and arrange, cut-side down, on a foil-lined small roasting tin. Bake for 20 minutes or until the skin is black and puffy. Lift the foil and pepper onto a plate, cover with clingfilm and leave for 15 minutes before skinning and chopping.

Peel, deseed and chop the cucumber, place in a colander and sprinkle with 1 teaspoon salt. Leave for 15 minutes, rinse and pat dry.

Tear the bread into chunky croutons. Smash and peel the garlic, then stir-fry in 3 tablespoons of the oil in a spacious frying/sauté pan until golden and aromatic. Discard the garlic, add the bread, increase the heat and stir-fry until crisp and golden. Rest on a fold of kitchen paper to drain.

Boil the kettle. Pour boiling water over the tomatoes. Count to 30, drain, quarter, peel and scrape the seeds into a sieve over a bowl. Chop the tomato flesh. Crush the seeds to extract juice. Whisk the vinegar and remaining olive oil into the juice. Place all the ingredients in a bowl, add salt and pepper, toss, leave for 15 minutes, toss again and serve.

ROAST TOMATO TARTE TATIN

SERVES 2–4 | **PREP** 25 MINUTES, PLUS CHILLING | **COOK** 35 MINUTES PLUS 1½ HOURS
FOR ROASTING THE TOMATOES

When it's good, the tomatoes soft and intensely flavoured and the pastry a tad gooey with luscious juices, there are few tomato tarts better than upside-down tomato tarte Tatin. It can, though, be disastrous and a reader's failure to succeed with the recipe in my book *The Big Red Book of Tomatoes* prompted this sure winner. Instead of the usual puff pastry, I made buttery shortcrust in minutes in my food processor, and used tomatoes already roasted on standby, as it were, in the fridge. Balsamic vinegar and Parmesan were my secret add-ons and the result, eaten warm with a scattering of basil leaves, was so good that I made it again the very next day.

6 ripe vine tomatoes,
  about 500g
1–2 tablespoons olive oil
100g plain flour plus extra
  for dusting
50g butter
1 tablespoon thick balsamic
  vinegar, such as Belazu
2 tablespoons freshly grated
  Parmesan cheese
handful of basil leaves
salt

Heat the oven to 170°C, Gas Mark 3. Halve the tomatoes through their middles. Lay out, cut-side up, on a shallow roasting tin. Smear the cut surfaces with olive oil and season with salt. Place near the top of the oven and cook for 1–1½ hours until the tomatoes are soft and squidgy, juicy rather than very wet. This could be done up to 48 hours in advance, the tomatoes kept, covered, in the fridge.

To make the pastry, sift 100g of the flour into the bowl of a food processor. Add the diced butter and a pinch of salt. Blitz briefly, just until flour and butter resemble breadcrumbs. Add 2 tablespoons cold water. Pulse, adding extra water if necessary, to make a cohesive dough. If very wet, sift a little extra flour over the top. Form into a ball, place in a plastic bag and chill for at least 30 minutes.

Nudge the tomatoes, cut-side up, together in an 18cm ovenproof frying pan or heavy-duty flan tin. Paint them with the balsamic and dredge with the Parmesan. Dust a work surface with flour and roll out the pastry into a circle slightly larger than the pan or tin. Place it over the tomatoes, tucking the edges inside the pan. Increase the oven temperature to 200°C, Gas Mark 6 and bake for 25–35 minutes until the pastry is cooked through. Run a knife round the inside edge, place a plate over the top and deftly invert. Scatter the basil leaves over.

ROAST AND FRESH TOMATO SOUP

SERVES 4 | **PREP** 30 MINUTES | **COOK** 1 HOUR

I've been extra conscious lately of only buying British tomatoes, particularly intensely flavoured Isle of Wight fruit, and that's what I used for this sublimely simple recipe. When tomatoes really drop in price I make versions of this intense tomato nectar-cum-soup all the time. The flavour can be fine-tuned with different herbs while the tomatoes roast, but another delicious idea is adding a little honey and saffron, as I did in this version. The lion's share of the soup is blitzed and sieved roast tomatoes, but flavour and colour is sharpened with fresh cherry tomatoes. It's lightened with chicken stock and is an occasion to use freshly made so that there are no artificial flavours interfering with the clean, tomato taste. It can be served hot or cold. Try a dollop of crème fraîche and a generous garnish of chopped chives for the former and a nip of vodka for the latter, but both ideas are really gilding the lily.

10 vine tomatoes, about 1kg
1 tablespoon olive oil
several thyme sprigs
100g piccolini cherry
    tomatoes
pinch of saffron threads
2 teaspoons clear honey
500ml light chicken stock
1 lemon
salt

Line a shallow roasting tin with foil. Preheat the oven to 150°C, Gas Mark 2.

Halve the vine tomatoes through their middles and arrange, cut-side up, on the foil. Smear with olive oil and season lightly with salt. Spread the thyme over the tomatoes, arranging so that it touches all the cut surfaces. Place the tin on a middle shelf and cook for 1 hour or until very aromatic and the tomatoes are soft to the prod. Remove the thyme – the dried leaves could be used for something else – and leave to cool slightly.

Dissolve the saffron in 1 tablespoon boiling water from the kettle. Turn the tomatoes over and pinch off the skins. Tip the tomatoes and juices into the bowl of a food processor. Add the cherry tomatoes. Blitz for several minutes until smooth. Pass through a sieve into a saucepan, pressing hard to get everything except pips and core into the pan. Scrape underneath so that nothing is wasted.

Add the saffron, half the honey and the stock to the pan. Simmer gently for 5 minutes, taste and adjust the seasoning with salt, honey and a squeeze of lemon. For a super-smooth finish, sieve again. Serve very hot or chilled.

PASTA WITH FRESH TOMATO SAUCE

SERVES 4 | **PREP** 15 MINUTES | **COOK** 30 MINUTES

There are so many ways to make tomato sauce for pasta, but this is a new favourite. It's extremely simple, but because there are no support ingredients like onion and garlic, it's vital to use tomatoes with flavour. They are blitzed to a purée, passed through a sieve to catch pips and pith, then simmered very gently with a splash of olive oil until thick and creamy. Whisking in a spoonful of butter at the end adds richness beyond expectation. You can make the sauce as thick as you like by continued simmering and it can be flavoured with orange or lemon juice, saffron or herbs. Add anything from crumbled feta to meatballs.

600g cherry or vine tomatoes
1 tablespoon olive oil
sugar, to taste, optional
40g butter
400g short pasta
freshly grated Parmesan
   cheese
salt

Place the cherry tomatoes or chopped vine tomatoes in the bowl of a food processor and blitz for several minutes until liquidized. Pass through a sieve into a medium saucepan with the oil. Simmer gently, stirring regularly, for about 15 minutes until thickened and sauce-like. Taste and adjust the seasoning with salt and possibly sugar.

Beat in half the butter. Use immediately or keep covered in the fridge for up to 48 hours. Reheat gently when you are ready to serve.

Cook the pasta according to the packet instructions, then drain and return to the pan with the remaining butter. Toss and serve with grated Parmesan and a generous dollop of the hot tomato sauce.

TOMATO, ONION AND ANCHOVY TART

SERVES 4–6 | **PREP** 25 MINUTES | **COOK** 45 MINUTES

This large tart looks as stunning as a tastes, a mass of lightly cooked slices of large, ripe tomatoes arranged concentrically like a French apple tart. They lie on a bed of gently stewed, piquantly seasoned onion in a pastry case made with crushed walnuts, rapeseed oil and spelt or plain flour. The dough ends up a bit like Play-Doh, so broken into chunks and pressed into the tart tin rather than rolled in the usual way. Serve it hot or warm.

50g walnut pieces

200g spelt or plain flour
plus extra for dusting

8 tablespoons cold-pressed
rapeseed oil

knob of butter for greasing

3 Spanish onions

4 tablespoons olive oil

2 thyme sprigs

4 anchovy fillets in olive oil,
drained

3 vine tomatoes, about
225g each

salt and freshly ground
black pepper

Preheat the oven to 200°C, Gas Mark 6.

Briefly blitz the walnuts or place in a plastic bag and bash with a rolling pin. In a mixing bowl, use a fork to mix the flour and walnuts, ½ teaspoon salt, the rapeseed oil and 2 tablespoons water.

Smear a loose-based 26cm tart or flan tin with butter, dust with flour and shake out the excess. Quarter the pastry, then cut off pieces, pressing them to cover the base and sides of the tin. Bake, uncovered, for 10 minutes.

Trim, halve, peel and finely slice the onions. Heat 2 tablespoons olive oil in a spacious, lidded frying/sauté pan and stir in the onions. Toss over a high heat for 2–3 minutes, sprinkle over 1 teaspoon salt, add the thyme, cover and cook for 15–20 minutes, giving the odd stir, until soft and juicy. Chop the anchovies and stir into the onion. Cook for another 5–10 minutes until completely tender and the anchovies have completely broken down.

While the onion cooks, cut the cores out of the tomatoes in a pointed plug shape. Halve through the depth of the fruit and cut into 5mm-thick slices. Discard the thyme stalks and spread the onion over the tart base. Arrange overlapping tomato slices on the onion. Season with salt and black pepper and drizzle over the remaining oil. Bake for 10–15 minutes until the tomatoes are lightly cooked rather than merely hot. Rest for 5 minutes, then stand on a can to remove the collar. This reheats well.

CHICKEN ALLA PUTTANESCA

SERVES 2 | **PREP** 20 MINUTES | **COOK** 20 MINUTES

Puttanesca is hot and spicy, a tomato sauce with attitude. As I cooked this version, intending to serve it with chicken, I decided to add it to the pot. The combination worked so well, I'm passing the recipe on. Serve over green beans or spiralized courgettes instead of the usual penne.

1 small red chilli
2 tablespoons olive oil
1 medium red onion
1 garlic clove
10 pitted black olives
4 vine tomatoes, about 400g
4 skinned chicken thigh fillets
knob of butter
squeeze of lemon
salt and freshly ground
    black pepper
few flat leaf parsley sprigs,
    to garnish

Trim, halve, deseed and slice the chilli into skinny strips, then into tiny dice. Immerse in 1 tablespoon olive oil.

Halve, peel and finely chop the onion. Soften in the remaining 1 tablespoon olive oil in a spacious frying/sauté pan while you peel and finely chop the garlic, halve the olives round their middles and boil the kettle. Pour boiling water over the tomatoes, count to 30, drain, cut out the core, quarter lengthways, peel and chop. Slice the chicken into bite-sized strips.

Stir the garlic and half the chilli and oil – save the rest for another occasion; it will keep for several days – into the onion. Stir-fry briefly, increase the heat and add the chicken. Stir-fry to brown, then add the tomatoes and keep stirring, reducing the heat slightly, until sloppy and sauce-like, and the chicken is cooked through. Stir in the olives and butter, and season to taste with salt, pepper and lemon. Eat now or later garnished with the chopped parsley.

TOMATO TARTS WITH GOATS' CHEESE AND BASIL

SERVES 4 | **PREP** 20 MINUTES | **COOK** 30 MINUTES

Intensely flavoured gooey roast tomatoes, crisp flaky pastry, creamy soft goats' cheese and pungent pounded basil are a combination made in heaven. Easy to make, these simple tarts are a gorgeous mix of textures and flavours.

flour for dusting
320g ready-rolled puff pastry
5 tablespoons olive oil
12 medium tomatoes,
    about 700g
2 tablespoons fresh white
    breadcrumbs
2 heaped tablespoons freshly
    grated Parmesan cheese
generous handful of basil leaves
2 tablespoons pine nuts
150g soft French goats' cheese
salt

Preheat the oven to 220°C, Gas Mark 7. Dust a work surface with flour. Divide the puff pastry into 4 equal pieces and roll each out to 15 × 18cm. Lightly oil a baking sheet with some of the olive oil and transfer the pastries. Leaving a 1cm border, prick all over with a fork. Paint the border with olive oil.

It's not essential to peel the tomatoes, but I think it's worth it. Boil the kettle. Cover the tomatoes with boiling water, count to 30, drain, cut out the core in a pointed plug shape and peel off the skin. Cut into medium-thin slices. Arrange the slices nudged close up to the border. Dribble with a little olive oil and sprinkle with the breadcrumbs and Parmesan.

Bake on a top shelf for 25–30 minutes until the border is puffy and golden, the tomatoes soft and juicy and the pastry underneath cooked.

Blitz the basil, pine nuts and a pinch of salt to a rough paste in a food processor or pound with a pestle and mortar, then stir in the remaining oil.

Top the tarts with intermittent teaspoons of the goats' cheese. Add a swirl of basil dressing and serve.

Seafood

Many people, and I was brought up by one of them, don't like fish. Well, that's what they say (my mother loved smoked salmon and Dover sole), but anxiety about bones and cooking the different types of fish is often the real reason. Fish, though, is perfect fast food, fat free, healthy and versatile.

To check the sustainability of specific fish from particular waters, check out www.goodfishguide.org. The site, which was set up by the Marine Conservation Society (MCS), is crystal clear and easy to use.

COD, HADDOCK, HAKE, POLLACK AND SEA BASS

I could happily live on fish, particularly the cod family, and often do, two or three times a week. It's such a quick and easy way of eating healthily and is usually best when cooked simply, fried with a dusting of flour, or grilled or roasted with olive oil and lemon juice. I love it with rich, luscious salsa verde that can be whipped up in moments. Presentation helps with fish. I often serve it draped over boiled and then crushed peas and/or a spray of squashy grilled or roasted cherry tomatoes with a lavish swirl of my best olive oil, adding a big wedge of lemon to squeeze over the top.

Packs of frozen cod from the supermarket are perfect for fish fingers, fish pie or roasting with lemon and olive oil. The flavour and texture is improved by lightly dusting the defrosted fish with salt, leaving it for at least 10 minutes, preferably 30, then rinsing and mopping dry with kitchen paper before cooking. My mother-in-law, who lived in a Cornish fishing village, used to make fish pie with ling. Like coley, also known as pollock, and increasingly fashionable pollack, it's part of the cod family. All these fish have always been regarded as inferior to cod. While none have such big, firm flakes as cod, and ling is bonier, they are beginning to be recognized as good fish.

I can never resist smoked haddock, but it has to be decent stuff, naturally smoked, not dyed, with a pale saffron colour and pearly luminescence. Its dense texture and intense flavour go particularly well with eggs, creamy sauces, potatoes and rice. This combination works in all manner of guises and there are many variations on similar themes. Proper smoked haddock can stand up to quite powerful flavours. Even curry spices can't dominate; in fact, they are the perfect foil for the assertive smokiness of the fish. Which brings me neatly to kedgeree, the Anglo-Indian dish that was once a feature of the country-house breakfast sideboard but perfect for mid-week suppers.

The fish we eat most often is white. There are two basic types: flat fish, such as the sole family and plaice (see page 86), and round fish, like cod and its extended family of hake, haddock, pollack, whiting and ling. If you buy fish in the supermarket, it is rare to see either type whole, so it's difficult to know which is which. Broadly speaking, round fish vary in thickness, density and their ability to flake as they cook. The reason we love cod so much is because it flakes in tempting big pearly white pieces and has big bones that are easy to see and remove. Haddock, hake, pollack and pollock are all interchangeable with cod, but their flakes are less pronounced, the texture softer and the bones smaller. Wild sea bass from Cornwall is a very fine fish. This fish is also extensively farmed in Greece and is available in small one or two size portions. Its texture and pink-tinged flesh is closer to mackerel than cod but has a delicate flavour. All white fish recipes are interchangeable, but timing will vary bearing in mind thickness of fillet and density of texture.

COD PARCELS WITH GINGER, SOY AND LIME

SERVES 2 | **PREP** 15 MINUTES | **COOK** 25 MINUTES

This is a favourite fast fish supper. Any firm white fish is suitable and I suspect the clean, tangy, vaguely Chinesey flavours would be good with salmon or mackerel, too. One of the great things about parcelling fish up in foil, which is what you will be doing, is that it saves on washing-up and contains the fishy smells that some people find off-putting, particularly when it comes to salmon and other oily fish like mackerel.

Although the quantities given here are for two servings, it is easy to scale up and would be a good dish to make if you're having friends over and want something that can be prepared ahead and stashed in the fridge until needed. In that case, add a few extra minutes to the cooking time. If you are unsure about including chilli, just leave it out or add a tablespoon of Thai sweet chilli sauce, which gives a gentler snap to the flavours. Baby pak choi leaves end up soft and wilted and the stalks will be juicy and tender.

150g basmati rice
2 cod, pollack or other firm
　white fish fillets
10g piece of fresh root ginger
1 large garlic clove
1 red bird's eye chilli
2 limes
1 tablespoon soy sauce
1 tablespoon mirin or
　sweet sherry
10g bunch of coriander
90g baby pak choi
salt
Thai sweet chilli sauce,
　to serve

Preheat the oven to 200°C, Gas Mark 6. Rinse the rice until the water runs clear. Place in a pan with 225ml cold water and bring to the boil. Immediately turn the heat very low, as low as possible, cover and cook for 10 minutes. Turn off the heat and leave, covered, for 10 minutes to finish cooking in the steam.

Tear off 4 sheets of foil, approximately 20cm square. Lay the fish in the middle of 2 sheets and turn up the edges to make a quasi boat. Peel and finely chop or grate the ginger. Crack the garlic with your fist, flake away the skin, coarsely chop and then crush to a paste with a pinch of salt. Trim and split the chilli lengthways. Scrape away the seeds, slice thinly and chop. Place all 3 in a bowl and stir in 1 tablespoon lime juice, the soy, mirin or sherry and most of the coriander, chopped finely, setting aside a few of the best sprigs. Quarter the pak choi lengthways.

Spoon the ginger mix over the fish and lay the pak choi on top. Quickly place a sheet of reserved foil over the top and crimp the edges, firmly and securely but not too tightly. Lift onto a baking sheet. Bake for 15 minutes.

Tip the contents of the parcel over a mound of rice. Serve with a lime wedge, the remaining coriander sprigs and Thai sweet chilli sauce.

COD TAPENADE

SERVES 2 | **PREP** 15 MINUTES | **COOK** 15 MINUTES

Shiny black olive tapenade made by pounding olives, anchovy and capers (but sold in jars) is second to hummus as my favourite standby. It is particularly good with tomatoes, but have you thought of matching it with quickly fried fillets of cod? Here the blackened fish is arranged over lightly cooked green beans, then finished with a tumble of diced cherry tomatoes and a swirl of olive oil.

It is child's play to make for more people, and if it is easier, the fish could be roasted with a smear of olive oil to prevent sticking. In that case, allow 10–15 minutes in a hot oven (200°C, Gas Mark 6), depending on thickness of fillet and number of portions; you want the fish firm yet just cooked through and showing its handsome flakes.

250g green beans, runner or French
8 cherry tomatoes
2 thick cod fillets, skin on
1 tablespoon olive oil
4 teaspoons black olive tapenade
best olive oil
2 lemon wedges
salt

Boil the kettle. If using runner beans, top and tail and slice long and thin on the diagonal to make pieces about 5cm long. Top and tail French beans and snap or cut in half. Quarter the tomatoes and halve the quarters.

Smear the fish with olive oil and heat what remains in a frying pan. Cook, skin-side down, for 2–3 minutes over a high heat, turn and ease the skin loose with a spatula while cooking the other side for a further 2–3 minutes until pearly and just cooked through. Smear the freshly exposed surface with the tapenade.

As the fish cooks, drop the beans into a pan of boiling salted water from the kettle. Boil for 2–3 minutes until al dente. Drain the beans and pile in the middle of 2 warmed dinner plates. Top with the cod, carefully lifted with a spatula, scatter with the chopped tomato and serve with a swirl of best olive oil and a lemon wedge.

MISO COD WITH CRUNCHY VEGETABLE SALAD

SERVES 6 | **PREP** 20 MINUTES | **COOK** 15 MINUTES

I have an on-off love affair with miso but am rarely without miso soup paste, useful for quick, healthy hunger stop-gaps while supper is on the go. It's useful, too, for this neat way of seasoning grilled fish. Miso has umami (the fifth flavour) qualities and forms an intriguing soft layer under crisp-grilled Parmesan, this disparate combination making a beguiling topping for fish. I've specified white fish fillets, though salmon would also be good. It suits being served with batons of crisp green vegetables, but here I've added carrot, too; it's an idea to play around with.

1 tablespoon groundnut oil

6 cod, haddock, pollack or pin-boned whiting fillets, skin off

3 × 15g miso soup paste sachets or 2 tablespoons white miso paste

2 tablespoons finely grated Parmesan cheese

150g mangetout

200g courgette

200g carrot

1 celery heart

1 tablespoon soy sauce

½ tablespoon toasted sesame oil

Line a grill pan with foil. Rub the groundnut oil over the fish fillets and arrange on the grill pan. Spread the surface with the miso soup paste or white miso paste, making an even but not overly thick covering. Carefully dust the paste with Parmesan to entirely cover. Turn the grill to its highest setting, and when up to temperature, position the grill pan about 4cm from the heat. Cook the fish for 4–8 minutes, depending on the thickness of the fillets, until just cooked through, with a crusty topping.

Meanwhile, boil a kettle and half-fill a saucepan. Slice each mangetout into 2 or 3 strips and use a potato peeler to slice the other veg in thin, wide batons, then into long strips. Drop all the veg, one after the other, into the boiling water for 30 seconds. Scoop out and toss with the soy and toasted sesame oil. Serve the fish over the veg.

HADDOCK WITH CRUSHED PEAS

SERVES 2 | **PREP** 10 MINUTES | **COOK** 10 MINUTES

This is such a simple idea that it hardly needs a recipe. It's one of my regular standbys when I can't think what to cook. It is basically fish and peas; however, it's the way they are cooked and presented that lifts them into a different league. Serve with new potatoes if you are big eaters.

200g frozen petits pois
  or fresh peas
2 haddock, cod, hake or
  other firm white fish fillets,
  skin off
2 tablespoons olive oil
2 × sprays 8-strong cherry
  tomatoes on the vine
1 lemon
best olive oil, to serve

Put the kettle on to boil. Use some of the water to cook the peas and put the rest in the steamer pan. If, incidentally, you don't have a steamer, you could cook the fish in a hot oven for 10 minutes, seasoned with a squeeze of lemon. Failing that, if it's easier, fry it, dusted with flour, in hot oil. If steaming, smear the fillets with half the olive oil, place in the steamer tray, cover and cook for 8 minutes.

Meanwhile, place the tomato sprays in a frying pan or roasting tin (spike them with a small, pointed knife to avoid bursting) and cook under a hot grill for about 5 minutes until they begin to pop but before they disintegrate.

When the peas are ready, drain and return to the pan with the remaining olive oil and a generous squeeze of lemon. Crush a few times with a potato masher, tip onto warmed plates and top with the fish. Drape a spray of tomatoes over the top and serve with a swirl of olive oil and a lemon wedge.

SMOKED HADDOCK AND PARMESAN RISOTTO

SERVES 3–4 | **PREP** 15 MINUTES | **COOK** 35 MINUTES

Smoky haddock flaked into creamy risotto rice with hints of lemony crème fraîche and gentle Dijon mustard, a background tang of bay with lashings of freshly grated Parmesan, is perfect week-night food. Easy to cook and comfort factor extremely high.

300g naturally smoked
  haddock, skin on
150ml milk
1 bay leaf
2 shallots
25g butter
250g Arborio rice
1 dessertspoon Dijon mustard
50g Parmesan cheese
2 tablespoons chopped flat
  leaf parsley
1 tablespoon crème fraîche
salt and freshly ground
  black pepper

Place the fish, milk, bay and 250ml water in a pan that can submerge the fish in a single layer. Simmer for a few minutes until just tender. Boil the kettle. Lift the fish onto a plate and tip the liquid into a measuring jug. Make up to 1 litre with boiling water from the kettle.

Meanwhile, peel and finely chop the shallots, then gently soften in the butter in a spacious, lidded frying/sauté pan. Stir in the unwashed rice, stirring until it glistens, then add the mustard and one third of the fish liquid. Simmer briskly, stirring constantly, until thick and creamy. Add another third of the liquid and simmer steadily, giving the occasional stir while you flake the fish off its skin, discarding any bones. Season it lightly with salt, generously with pepper, and grate half the cheese over the top. Add the parsley. Add the last of the hot liquid and cook as before. When thick and creamy, stir in the fish mix and crème fraîche. Cover and leave for 5 minutes before serving with the remaining grated Parmesan.

SMOKED HADDOCK WITH POACHED EGG AND DIJON MUSTARD SAUCE

SERVES 4 | **PREP** 20 MINUTES | **COOK** 30 MINUTES

Variations on this combination of thick flakes of smoky, salty fish with fluffy, buttery mashed potato and lashings of creamy tangy sauce is one of my favourite plates of food. Add a soft-poached egg and flourish of chives and it's Proper Job, as they say in Cornwall.

4 large potatoes, about 800g

80g butter

500ml milk

4 thick naturally smoked haddock fillets, skin on

40g plain flour

1 tablespoon Dijon mustard

squeeze of lemon

4 eggs

splash of red wine vinegar

1 tablespoon chopped chives or flat leaf parsley

salt and freshly ground black pepper

Peel, chunk, rinse and boil the potatoes in salted water. Drain. Melt 30g of the butter in 100ml of the milk in the potato pan, return the potatoes, mash smooth, then beat thoroughly. Cover to keep warm.

Meanwhile, place the fish fillets, skin-side down, in a pan that can hold the pieces in a single layer. Add the remaining milk and sufficient water to just cover. Simmer for 5 minutes, then carefully turn the fish and cook for a further 5 minutes or until the fish is just cooked through.

Melt the remaining butter in a medium pan and stir in the flour, then the mustard. Off the heat, carefully strain the fish liquid into the pan, stirring constantly to make a smooth sauce. Return to the heat and simmer for 5 minutes. Add salt, lemon juice and pepper to taste.

Boil the kettle. Crack one egg at a time into a cup and slip into a pan of vinegar-seasoned simmering water from the kettle. Simmer for 1–2 minutes until the white is set yet the yolk is still soft.

Serve a mound of mash in the middle of hot plates, then top with the fish, remove the skin and add an egg (lifted with a perforated spoon and rested on a fold of kitchen paper to drain), hot sauce and the chives or parsley. Phew.

SIMPLE KEDGEREE

SERVES 2–3 | **PREP** 15 MINUTES | **COOK** 30 MINUTES

Pale, soft naturally smoked haddock rather than bright yellow, hard-textured fillets that get passed off as the real thing is what you need for this family favourite. Turmeric colours the rice a complementary hue so that the dish is a pretty mixture of pale yellow and white. Smoky fish, curry-scented rice with creamy soft-boiled eggs and the grassy finish of parsley is so good, I could eat it once a week. One thick fillet of smoked haddock will suffice for two people, or use two and up the quantity of rice slightly to extend the dish for four. Mango chutney is a must.

1 bay leaf

1 large naturally smoked haddock fillet, skin on

1 small onion

20g butter

1 teaspoon groundnut oil

2 teaspoons mild curry powder

½ teaspoon turmeric

150g basmati rice

few flat leaf parsley sprigs

2 hard-boiled eggs, peeled and halved

freshly ground black pepper

mango chutney, to serve

Place the bay leaf in a pan that can hold the fish fillet, skin-side down, snugly. Add the fillet and just enough water to cover it, and simmer for 5 minutes. Turn the fish and leave.

Meanwhile, peel and finely chop the onion. Melt the butter in the oil in a medium pan with a well-fitting lid and soften the onion, stirring often. Stir in the curry powder and turmeric, stir-frying to evenly coat. Add the washed rice, stirring to coat that, too. Drain the juices from the fish into a measuring jug and top up to 250ml with water. Add the liquid to the rice, bring slowly to a simmer, clamp on the lid, turn the heat as low as possible and cook for 10 minutes. Turn off the heat and leave, lid untouched, for a further 10 minutes.

Fork up the rice into a warmed serving bowl. Flake the skinned fish over the top and fold together. Season with black pepper, add the chopped parsley, fold again, then add the halved eggs. Eat hot or cold, with mango chutney.

HAKE IN COCONUT MILK WITH RICE NOODLES

SERVES 2 | **PREP** 15 MINUTES | **COOK** 35 MINUTES

Coconut milk has a gentle effect on fish, rendering it creamy and luscious. That is certainly the case with this dish, where the coconut milk is flavoured with ginger, lemon grass, chilli and Thai fish sauce. The seasoned brew could be made in advance and the noodles soaked, both ready on standby for a quickly finished dish. The sauce ends up salty, sour, creamy and with snaps of chilli heat, all rounded off by coriander. So good and so easy.

1 small onion
1 tablespoon groundnut
　or sunflower oil
½ large red chilli
1 plump lemon grass stalk
15g fresh root ginger
200ml can coconut milk
1 lime
2 teaspoons Thai fish sauce
　(nam pla)
100g rice noodles
2 hake or similar firm white
　fish fillets, skin off
few coriander sprigs

Halve, peel and finely chop the onion. Soften gently in a medium pan in the oil while you deseed and slice the chilli into thin rounds. Unfurl the outer layers of the lemon grass to reveal the tender inner stem. Slice the stem finely. Peel the ginger and slice into small slivers. Stir the chilli, lemon grass and ginger into the softening onion, cooking gently, stirring often to wilt rather than fry.

Add the coconut milk, stirring to mix, then add the juice of half the lime and the fish sauce. Simmer gently, tasting after 5 minutes and adjusting the seasoning with nam pla and lime juice.

Meanwhile, pour boiling water over the noodles and leave to soften. Drain and reheat with fresh boiling water just before serving.

Slip the fish into the gently simmering coconut milk mixture and cook for 8–12 minutes, depending on thickness, until just cooked through.

Drain the noodles and place in bowls. Top with the fish and spoon over the broth with a final flourish of torn coriander.

ROAST HAKE WITH BLACK BEANS AND TOMATOES

SERVES 2 | **PREP** 20 MINUTES | **COOK** 20 MINUTES

There are two parts to this dish: roasted fish cooked with lemon juice and olive oil alongside sprays of cherry tomatoes, and jazzed up turtle beans. Both are quick and undemanding to prepare, and the result is stunning. Instead of hake or a similar firm white fish, it could be made with salmon.

1 large shallot or small onion
2 tablespoons olive oil
generous pinch of dried
    chilli flakes
1 rosemary sprig
400g can black turtle beans
150ml fish or light chicken
    stock
200g boiled beetroot
1 lemon
2 hake fillets, skin off
2 × sprays 8-strong cherry
    tomatoes on the vine
best olive oil
salt and freshly ground
    black pepper

Preheat the oven to 200°C, Gas Mark 6. Peel and finely chop the shallot or onion and soften gently in a spacious, lidded frying/sauté pan in 1 tablespoon of the olive oil. Add the chilli, rosemary, drained, rinsed beans and stock. Simmer gently, stirring regularly as it thickens, while you peel and chunk the beetroot. Toss the beets with juice from half the lemon and a generous pinch of salt. Stir the beets into the beans, cook for a few minutes to heat through, then cover the pan and leave off the heat.

Smear the fish with the remaining oil and arrange on one side of a small roasting tin. Pierce the tomatoes with the point of a sharp knife to avoid bursting and lay out next to the fish. Add a squeeze of lemon to the fish, season with salt and pepper and roast for 10–15 minutes until just cooked through. Carefully drain the juices into the sauce-like – rather than wet – beans; if necessary, quickly simmer to thicken. Serve beans topped with fish topped with tomatoes. Add a swirl of best olive oil.

HAKE AND CHORIZO BEAN STEW

SERVES 2 | **PREP** 15 MINUTES | **COOK** 25 MINUTES

Hake and chorizo is a good combination, but other cod-like fish fillets would work in this dish. It's one of those forgiving recipes that could be reduced or expanded to suit the number of mouths around the table. Flavours are surprisingly robust considering how quickly the dish is ready to eat.

1 medium onion
1 tablespoon olive oil
2 hake fillets, skin off
½ teaspoon thyme leaves or
    good pinch of dried thyme
90g sliced chorizo
400g can haricot beans
150ml chicken or fish stock
100g young spinach
salt
crusty bread and/or green
    beans, to serve

Halve, peel and finely chop the onion. Cook, tossing regularly, for 5 minutes in the hot oil in a spacious, lidded frying pan. Reduce the heat, add a generous pinch of salt, cover and cook for 10 minutes while you slice the fish into bite-sized chunks.

Stir the thyme into the softened onion and add the chorizo slices, tossing as they shrivel and weep their oil. Add the drained, rinsed beans and stock. Simmer until juicy rather than wet.

Fold through the spinach, and when semi-wilted, add the fish. Cover and cook for 5 minutes, or so, until the fish is firm. Serve from the pan with crusty bread and/or green beans.

LAZY FISH PIE WITH SPINACH

SERVES 2 | **PREP** 15 MINUTES | **COOK** 35 MINUTES

This is very lazy fish pie. No sauce, just grated Emmental, a fillet of fish per person, spinach and mashed potato. The mash is enriched with beaten egg, so it holds its shape and crisps as it bakes.

2 thick cod, haddock or
  salmon fillets, skin off
25g butter
350g potatoes
1 egg yolk
75g young spinach
50g Emmental cheese
salt

Dust the skinned fish with ½ teaspoon salt. Set aside to firm and weep.

Smear a 12 × 16 × 4cm gratin dish or 2 small ovenproof dishes with a little of the butter. Peel, chunk and boil the potatoes in salted water until tender. Drain and pass through a mouli-legume or ricer, or mash smooth. Beat in the remaining butter, then the egg yolk.

Meanwhile, boil the kettle. Place the spinach in a mixing bowl and cover with water from the kettle. Leave briefly to wilt. Drain, squeeze dry and slice through the ball a few times.

Preheat the oven to 200°C, Gas Mark 6. Spoon the mash into a piping bag or stiff plastic bag with the corner cut off. Rinse the fish and pat dry. Line up in the prepared dish/es and cover with a layer of spinach and most of the grated cheese, then pipe or fork the mash in swirls, furrows or spikes over the top. Add a little more cheese. Bake for 20–25 minutes until crusty and golden.

SEAFOOD LASAGNE

SERVES 4 | **PREP** 25 MINUTES | **COOK** 45 MINUTES

This seafood version of lasagne uses virtually the same ingredients as fish pie, but they are layered up with lasagne in a thick, creamy sauce, the top finished with a layer of grated Parmesan.

2 eggs
300g white fish fillet such as
  pollack, hake or cod, skin off
300g smoked haddock fillet
750ml milk
2 thyme sprigs
1 bay leaf
40g butter
40g plain flour
150ml double cream
150g young spinach
25g bunch of flat leaf parsley
340g lasagne sheets
160g cooked peeled prawns
3 tablespoons grated Parmesan
salt and freshly ground
  black pepper

Preheat the oven to 180°C, Gas Mark 4.

Boil the eggs in a small pan for 9 minutes. Drain; return to cold water.

Put the fish and milk in a medium pan and add the thyme and bay leaf. Simmer for 6–8 minutes. Lift the fish onto a plate and strain the milk.

Melt the butter in a medium pan, stir in the flour until smooth, add the strained fish milk and stir briskly, with a whisk if necessary, to make a smooth sauce. Simmer for 5 minutes. Season and add the cream.

Rinse and shake the spinach dry. Place in a covered pan and cook for 2 minutes until wilted. Squeeze dry and chop. Peel and chop the eggs. Chop the parsley leaves.

Smear a 24 × 18 × 4cm gratin dish with 2 tablespoons of the sauce and cover with lasagne. Top with half the fish, broken into chunks. Scatter with half the prawns, egg, spinach and parsley. Cover with one third of the sauce, more lasagne, the rest of the other ingredients, more sauce, more lasagne and the last of the sauce. Dredge with Parmesan. Cook in the oven for 25–35 minutes until crusty, golden and bubbling round the edges.

BALSAMIC SEA BASS WITH GREEK BEETROOT

SERVES 4 | **PREP** BEETROOT: 10 MINUTES; FISH: 5 MINUTES
COOK BEETROOT: 30 MINUTES; FISH: 15 MINUTES

Cooking fish with balsamic vinegar is an idea I picked up in Verona and makes an interesting change from the usual lemon and olive oil. Thick syrupy balsamic vinegar is what you need – Belazu is a good one – which clings to the fish, giving it a sweet, rich and beguiling succulence.

2 bunches of small beetroot, with stalks and leaves
1 tablespoon lemon juice or white or red wine vinegar
4 tablespoons Greek olive oil
4 sea bass fillets, skin on
2 tablespoons olive oil
4 tablespoons thick balsamic vinegar, such as Belazu
salt and freshly ground black pepper

Cut the stalks and leaves from the beetroot. Discard any withered or yellowing leaves, wash and shake dry. Wash the beetroot without breaking the skin, leaving the roots intact. Boil the beets in plenty of salted water for about 30 minutes until tender to the point of the knife. Don Marigolds and rub away the skin and trim the ends. Boil the stalks and leaves in a separate pan of salted water for about 5 minutes until tender. Drain. Coil the drained stalks and leaves into a serving bowl and cover with big chunks of beetroot, leaving the smaller beets whole. Whisk the lemon juice or vinegar and Greek olive oil briefly and pour over the top.

Preheat the oven to 200°C, Gas Mark 6. Place a sheet of foil in a small, shallow roasting tin. Smear the skin side of the fish with olive oil and lay the fillets, skin-side down, in the pan. Dribble the flesh with the balsamic and a splash of olive oil. Season with salt and pepper. Roast for 10–15 minutes until just cooked through to the point of a knife. Transfer to warmed plates and dribble any juices left in the foil over the top. Serve with the beetroot.

PROVENÇAL FISH WITH BOULANGÈRE POTATOES

SERVES 2 | **PREP** 20 MINUTES | **COOK** 55 MINUTES

This is a useful dish to know about because it adapts easily for any number of people and virtually cooks itself. Although I've specified sea bass, you can use any flat fish fillets you like. I often make it for a home-alone supper or for two or three, but it is easy to scale up for more, adding all the ingredients in proportion. The only point to remember is that the potatoes should be tender before the fish is added.

Black olives and capers with a splash of olive oil, a few basil leaves and soft, squashy roast cherry tomatoes give fish and potatoes a taste of the south of the South of France, but use this recipe as a template, introducing other flavours like chopped anchovies with garlic and rosemary, or saffron with tomatoes and green olives for a taste of the Maghreb.

1 banana shallot
400g potatoes
300ml light chicken or
  fish stock
3 tablespoons olive oil
10 pitted black olives
100g cherry tomatoes
½ tablespoon capers in
  brine, drained
2 sea bass fillets, skin off
few basil leaves
salt and freshly ground
  black pepper

Preheat the oven to 220°C, Gas Mark 7. Peel, halve and finely chop the shallot. Place in a mixing bowl. Peel and thinly slice the potatoes. Rinse and add to the shallot. Season with salt and pepper and mix thoroughly.

Pour the stock into a pan and bring to the boil. Tip the potato mixture into a 24 × 18 × 4cm gratin dish, smooth the top and pour on the boiling stock. Splash 1 tablespoon of the olive oil over the top and bake for 10 minutes. Reduce the heat to 200°C, Gas Mark 6 and cook for a further 30 minutes until the potatoes are tender and some of the liquid absorbed.

Halve the olives and pierce the tomatoes with a sharp knife. Trickle the capers and olives into the potatoes, add the tomatoes and lay the fish over the top. Season with salt and pepper and add 1 tablespoon of the olive oil. Bake for 10–15 more minutes, depending on the thickness of the fish fillets. Serve with a flourish of basil leaves and drizzle over the remaining olive oil.

PLAICE, SOLE AND SKATE

What all these fish have in common is that they are flat fish; they have thin fillets, soft flesh and are often sold in pairs or sets of four fillets, so one or two whole fish. The flesh is mildly flavoured and cooks quickly. Apart from its main carcass, most flat fish are fringed with tiny bones that form a skirt around the fish. Dover sole has dense, chewy but mildly flavoured flesh and is regarded as the king of flat fish, but turbot and then brill, bream and halibut are close seconds. There are various soles – lemon and megrim, now often called Cornish sole, and plaice are the most popular. Their flesh is softer, the texture looser and the flavour slightly more pronounced than Dover. The exception is skate, an altogether different flat fish (see below).

Look out for Cornish sole (formally known as megrim), unique to the western coast of the UK, flourishing off the Cornish coast to Ireland and occasionally found in Scottish waters. Megrim is abundant 12 months of the year, less so during March and April when it's breeding, and ranges from 180g to a kilo in weight. It is a loose-textured sole with a sweet, clean flavour and is far superior, in my view, to witch or Torbay sole, which are also prolific in south-westerly waters. The jury is out on whether it really measures up against lemon sole, to which it is often compared, but it is a lovely fish in its own right. It's popular in France, where it's called *cardine*, but most of it goes to Spain, where it's called *gallos*, pronounced galios. It's usually cheaper than lemon sole, half the price of Dover and is so plentiful that we are unlikely to outfish its European quota restrictions. I eat it all the time in the West country and love it grilled or roasted whole with plenty of butter, olive oil and lemon, but fillets are endlessly versatile. Ask for it.

There are many different types of skate, or ray, in our waters, but according to the Marine Conservation Society (MCS), an independent, global, non-profit organization established to find a solution to the problem of over-fishing, only the smaller species – spotted, cuckoo and starry ray – are sustainable. It's rare to see anything other than skate wings on sale, although skate knobs, the fleshy lump at the base of the tail, are increasingly available. Wings are always sold skinned at British fishmongers and the mild-flavoured, meaty flesh is supported by cartilaginous long, knobbly finger 'bones'; it looks like snowy-white jumbo cord when poached. It's satisfying to 'stroke' the fish off the cartilage and not to have to worry about bones.

HOMEMADE FISH FINGERS WITH CHEAT'S TARTARE SAUCE

SERVES 4 | **PREP** 20 MINUTES | **COOK** 20 MINUTES

Recently, when inspiration faltered in front of the ketchup bottle as I wondered what to serve with homemade fish fingers, I remembered tartare sauce. Creamy, yet tangy, crunchy and lemony, with a hint of parsley, it gives this simple supper an instant upgrade.

Skinny chips is what you really want on the side, but I settled on watercress, and ate the whole lot with my fingers watching the completely brilliant Giorgio Locatelli frying freshly caught little whitebait lookalikes on *Italy Unpacked*, his BBC 2 series with Andrew Graham-Dixon. The shape and size of these fish fingers is immaterial; in fact, wonky and irregular is good. Sole, plaice, cod, pollack and other lesser members of the cod family are ideal – just ensure there are no bones.

8 plaice or sole fillets
3 tablespoons plain flour
2 eggs
3 slices of white or
   wholemeal bread without
   crusts, about 75g
2 tablespoons sunflower
   or other flavourless oil,
   for frying

For the tartare sauce
6 cornichons
4 tablespoons Hellmann's
   or other decent mayo
2 lemons
2 teaspoons Dijon mustard
1 tablespoon capers in
   brine, drained
2 flat leaf parsley sprigs
salt and freshly ground
   black pepper

Halve the skinned fillets lengthways and across their middles. Pat dry and dust with the flour, shaking away the excess. Whisk the eggs in a shallow cereal bowl. Tear the bread into the bowl of a food processor and blitz to fine crumbs. Swipe the fish pieces through the beaten egg, then press into the crumbs to completely cover.

Next make the tartare sauce. Quarter the cornichons lengthways, then slice across to make tiny dice. Spoon the mayo into a bowl and add 1 tablespoon lemon juice, the mustard, lightly squeezed capers (to eliminate vinegar) and finely chopped parsley leaves. Mix, taste and add extra lemon juice, salt and pepper to taste and a little water if too thick.

Preheat the oven to 150°C, Gas Mark 2. Heat the oil in a non-stick frying pan and fry the fish in uncrowded batches for 2–3 minutes a side, depending on thickness, adjusting the heat so that the crumbs turn evenly golden and the fish cooks through. Continue thus, keeping the cooked fillets warm in the oven. Serve with the sauce and lemon wedges.

KOREAN PLAICE WITH SOY AND GINGER

SERVES 2 | **PREP** 15 MINUTES | **COOK** 10 MINUTES

Yongja Kim is a Korean Delia, skilled at simplifying her thrilling food as exemplified in *Korean Cuisine*, a book of mainly quick, elegant recipes. When she cooked dinner for eight of us, she kicked off with a stylishly simple tofu appetizer that adapts perfectly for thin fillets of fish, served here with quickly wilted pak choi. Rice goes well with this. Ms Kim is a stickler for brown glutinous rice (a Korean speciality), adding a small amount of white rice at the end to freshen the flavour.

20g fresh root ginger
1 tablespoon soy sauce
2 tablespoons toasted
  sesame oil
2 tablespoons finely
  snipped chives
2 pak choi, about 250g
2 plaice fillets, skin off
2 tablespoons cornflour
3 tablespoons light olive oil

Peel and finely grate the ginger into a small bowl, pressing to extract the maximum juice into a second bowl. Add the soy to the juice, taste and add up to 1 tablespoon water if very salty. Stir in half the sesame oil.

Boil the kettle. Separate the pak choi leaves, halving large leaves lengthways. Rinse and shake dry. Steam or cook the pak choi in boiling water from the kettle for 1 minute. Drain.

Slice the skinned fish fillets in two, following the central dip. Dust the fish with cornflour. Heat the oil in a non-stick frying pan until very hot and quickly fry the fish until golden on both sides.

Pour the ginger sauce onto 2 plates and sprinkle lavishly with most of the chives. Add the fish, turning quickly through the sauce. Add the pak choi on the side, sprinkled with the remaining sesame oil and chives.

GINGER NOODLES WITH BLACK SESAME WHITE FISH

SERVES 2 | **PREP** 15 MINUTES | **COOK** 10 MINUTES

Coating fillets of fish in black sesame seeds gives drama to this stylish oriental fish supper, but ordinary sesame seeds give a similar nutty flavour. The fish is served over egg noodles tossed with scraps of sushi ginger, lime, fresh coriander and a hint of toasted sesame oil, making a moreish base for the quickly fried fish. Serve with chopsticks or fork and spoon.

300g cooked egg noodles
10g bunch of coriander
2 tablespoons black or regular
  sesame seeds
2 plaice or lemon sole fillets,
  skin off
2 tablespoons lime juice
1 tablespoon toasted
  sesame oil
1 tablespoon pickled
  sushi ginger
1 tablespoon vegetable oil
soy sauce, to serve

Place the noodles in a bowl and cover with boiling water. Cover with clingfilm and leave to heat through. Chop the coriander.

Spread the sesame seeds on a plate and press the skinned fillets into the seeds, coating thoroughly all over. Combine the lime juice, sesame oil, torn pickled ginger and coriander ready to stir into the drained noodles.

Heat the vegetable oil in a non-stick frying pan over a medium heat and quickly fry the fish fillets for 1–2 minutes on each side until just cooked through. Rest on kitchen paper to drain.

Strain the noodles, toss them with the lime juice mixture and divide between warmed bowls. Top with the fish and serve with soy sauce to shake over the top.

SKATE WITH BLACK BUTTER AND CAPERS

SERVES 2 | **PREP** 10 MINUTES | **COOK** 30 MINUTES

Smaller wings are perfect for this classic dish, appearing on French menus as *raie au beurre noir*. The fish is poached in acidulated water, carefully drained and served with nut-brown butter seasoned with wine vinegar, capers and chopped parsley. Good with *pommes vapeur*.

1 small onion

1 carrot

1 bay leaf

3 tablespoons white wine vinegar

2 skate wings, skin off

75g unsalted butter

10g bunch of flat leaf parsley

2 tablespoons capers in brine, drained

Peel and chop the onion. Scrape and chop the carrot. Place in sauté pan with the bay leaf, 1 tablespoon of the vinegar and 750ml cold water. Bring to the boil and simmer for 10 minutes. Slip the skate into the simmering court-bouillon, return to the boil and simmer for 15 minutes or until cooked through at the thickest part of the wing. Drain the fish on kitchen paper, place on warmed plates and cover to keep hot. Finely chop the parsley leaves.

Melt the butter in a frying pan, swirling the pan as the butter foams and turns a deep brown and smells nutty. Add the remaining vinegar, swirling the pan again, letting it boil together for a few seconds, then add the parsley and lightly squeezed capers (to eliminate vinegar). Cook for a few more seconds, then pour and spoon the sauce over the fish. Eat by stroking the fish off the cartilaginous bones into the sauce.

SALMON AND TROUT

I often buy packs of salmon fillets for the freezer. Frozen separately, they are useful for simple suppers and endlessly versatile. The firm, dense meat can be steamed, grilled, roasted and fried without oil. I like it lightly cooked so that the centre stays moist and hardly changes colour. Poached fillets are useful for quick trolley-dash suppers.

I'm a bit of a tart when it comes to smoked salmon. I love it but am always on the lookout for a bargain. Hence I buy trimmings one day, London cure another day and the finest wild salmon to carve myself on high days and holidays. It is, though, interchangeable with mildly cheaper smoked trout. A small amount will transform creamy potato gratins and it is perfect for quick pasta dishes. I love it sliced with scrambled egg and with potatoes, but often buy hot smoked salmon in chunky pieces for tarts and pasta dishes.

Oily fish, by which I mean salmon and trout, and mackerel, herring and sardines (see page 98), is rich in omega-3 oil and we should be eating far more of it. The downside, though, particularly with mackerel and its family, is that it stinks the place out when it's cooked, so an efficient extractor fan or handy open window is useful.

POACHED SALMON AND SPINACH GRATIN
SERVES 2–3 | **PREP** 15 MINUTES | **COOK** 35 MINUTES

Poached salmon pieces from the supermarket make a fabulous gratin with spinach and diced tomato, all hidden under a thick, creamy white sauce. It's an occasion to peel and deseed the tomatoes so that the pieces are soft and slippery and don't interfere with the general smoothness of the dish. It's a useful make-ahead supper and doubles up perfectly by increasing all the ingredients in proportion. I have two identical gratin dishes and often make two small rather than one large version and serve it with new potatoes tossed with halved green beans and peas.

100g young spinach
2 vine tomatoes
170g poached salmon flakes
50g fresh white breadcrumbs
2 tablespoons finely grated
  Parmesan cheese
25g butter plus extra knob
25g plain flour
300ml milk
salt and freshly ground
  black pepper

Preheat the oven to 220°C, Gas Mark 7. Boil the kettle. Place the spinach in a bowl or pan and pour over most of the boiling water, stirring a few times as it wilts, then drain and leave to cool in a colander.

Pour the remaining boiling water over the tomatoes, count to 30, drain, peel, halve, scrape out the seeds and dice the flesh. Squeeze the cooled spinach in your hands and chop the ball a few times.

Choose a 1-litre gratin dish and make a layer of half the diced tomato, spinach and fish, seasoning lightly with salt and pepper. Repeat to make a second layer. Mix together the crumbs and Parmesan.

Make a thick white sauce by melting the 25g butter in a small pan, stirring in the flour and adding the milk, stirring briskly with a wooden spoon as you do so. Simmer gently, stirring constantly, for a couple of minutes to cook the flour. Use a whisk if it turns lumpy. Season to taste with salt. Pour the sauce over the filling. Dredge with the cheese crumbs and dot with remaining butter. Bake for 20–25 minutes until the top is golden and the sauce bubbling enticingly round the edges.

SALMON AND DILL GOUJONS WITH PEA PURÉE

SERVES 2 | **PREP** 20 MINUTES | **COOK** 15 MINUTES

Dill and salmon is one of those culinary marriages made in heaven and this is a novel way of pairing them. Salmon fillets, nice big thick ones from the middle of the fish, are sliced through their depth, then halved to make neat, long strips. They are given the escalope treatment of dipping first in flour and then beaten egg and the finale is bright pale green crumbs. These are made by blitzing fresh breadcrumbs with leaves from a whole packet of dill, continuing until there is no trace of the spiky leaves.

It's a pity to tell you that by the time the goujons have been fried only a hint of the green peeks through the crusty, golden finish. The flavour, though, is what it's all about and it sings out as you crunch through the crisp shell onto moist, just-cooked salmon. I like these with creamy pea purée and a mound of green beans, turning the meal into a symphony of green. If you are big eaters, add buttered new potatoes tossed with parsley, or couscous with a hint of saffron and a last-minute addition of chopped mint.

2 salmon fillets, skin on
2 tablespoons plain flour
1 egg
2 slices of white bread
  without crusts
15g pack dill
2 tablespoons groundnut oil
1 lemon

For the pea purée
200g frozen petits pois
1 teaspoon English mint
  sauce
1 tablespoon crème fraîche
salt

Place the fish, skin-side down, on a work surface. To remove the skin, slide a sharp knife along the fillet, pressing the blade close to the skin to remove. Slice away any excess dark grey fat. Slice through the depth of the fillets, to make 2 equal pieces. Halve lengthways to make 4 chunky strips per fillet of fish.

Place the flour in a shallow cereal bowl and beat the egg in a second bowl. Tear the bread into the bowl of a food processor. Strip the dill off the tougher stalk ends and add to the bowl. Blitz for several minutes until the crumbs turn apple green. If the crumbs seem very damp, lay out on a plate for a few minutes to dry out.

Swipe the fish through the flour, shaking off the excess, then through the egg to cover and finally press into the crumbs. Transfer to a plate as you go. Cover with clingfilm and chill until required.

To make the pea purée, cook the peas as usual in boiling salted water. Drain, transfer to the bowl of the food processor, add the mint sauce and crème fraîche and blitz until smooth.

Fry the goujons in the hot oil for about 45 seconds a side, adjusting the heat so that the crumbs turn golden and the fish cooks through.

Serve the purée alongside the goujons with the lemon, cut into wedges.

THAI RED CURRY WITH SALMON AND PRAWNS

SERVES 6 | **PREP** 40 MINUTES | **COOK** 40 MINUTES

Big pieces of salmon, sweet prawns and crunchy bamboo shoots vie for your attention in the chilli-hot, sour and creamy sauce. I like to serve it over tagliatelle-style rice noodles topped with juicy pak choi, quickly fried in finely chopped garlic with Thai basil.

2 medium red onions

2 tablespoons groundnut oil

4 garlic cloves

25g fresh root ginger

2 long red chillies

3 tablespoons red curry paste

2 × 400g cans coconut milk

4–5 tablespoons Thai fish
   sauce (nam pla)

2 lemons

2 limes

1 chicken stock cube

sugar, to taste

2 × 225g cans bamboo shoots

600g salmon fillet, skin off

50g bunch of coriander

400g raw peeled tiger prawns

salt

Peel and finely chop the onions. Soften in the groundnut oil in a large pan while you peel and chop the garlic, peel the ginger and slice into thin scraps and finely dice the deseeded chillies. Stir all 3 into the wilted onion. Stir-fry briefly, then add the curry paste with 2 tablespoons coconut milk, stirring for 2 minutes. Boil the kettle. Add the remaining coconut milk, 4 tablespoons nam pla, the juice of 1 lemon and the 2 limes, the stock cube dissolved in 500ml of the kettle water and a generous pinch of salt. Simmer, stirring often, for 20 minutes, then taste and fine-tune with nam pla, salt, lemon juice and sugar.

Drain and rinse the bamboo shoots, then add to the pan. Following the lines of the fish, cut it into large bite-sized pieces. Chop the coriander, working up the bunch from the stalks. Add the stalk half of the bunch to the pan with the salmon and prawns. Simmer for 10–15 minutes until evenly cooked. Serve stirred with the remaining coriander.

SALMON, PEA AND CUCUMBER TART

SERVES 4–6 | **PREP** 20 MINUTES | **COOK** 40 MINUTES

This is such a pretty tart, so summery and elegant. The cucumber and peas look like disjointed question marks swirling around with chunks of pink salmon nudging them together in a sea of yellow custard. The tart is quiche-style, made with single cream and a couple of eggs in a puff pastry shell. After 30 minutes in a hot oven the custard billows and sets, and it's important not to over-cook it, as it will continue to firm when it's out of the oven.

The tart is prepared with a sizeable pastry overhang because it shrinks and tries to puff as the tart cooks. There is very little to trim away when it's done. Delicious hot, warm or cold.

150g cucumber
150g frozen petits pois
knob of butter
flour for dusting
300ml single cream
2 eggs
200g puff pastry
300g cooked salmon
salt and freshly ground
    black pepper

Boil the kettle. Use a potato peeler to peel the cucumber, then halve lengthways and use a teaspoon to scrape out the seeds. Slice into 5mm-thick half-moons. Using water from the kettle, boil the peas in salted water, adding the cucumber after a couple of minutes. Drain and set aside.

Preheat the oven 220°C, Gas Mark 7 and place a baking sheet on a middle shelf. Lavishly butter a 23cm loose-based flan tin. Dust with flour, turning the tin in your hands and tipping out the excess. Dust a work surface with flour and roll out the pastry to fit the tin with a minimum 2cm overhang. Don't worry about neatness here; it will shrink back and swell to avoid spillage.

Pour the cream into a mixing bowl. Add the eggs and season with salt and pepper. Whisk until smooth. Break the fish into bite-sized chunks over the pastry base. Stir the peas and cucumber into the cream and pour/spoon it over the fish, ensuring everything is immersed. Carefully lift onto the baking sheet and cook for 15 minutes. Reduce the heat to 180°C, Gas Mark 4 and cook for a further 10–15 minutes until the pastry is puffy and the custard just set to the flat of a hand – under- is better than over-cooking. Stand on a can, carefully shave off the pastry overhang, ease out of the collar and serve now or later.

SALMON WITH MOORISH TOMATOES
AND SPINACH LENTILS

SERVES 2 | **PREP** 15 MINUTES | **COOK** 15 MINUTES

Salmon and tomatoes aren't an obvious combination, but the oiliness of the fish is cut by the acidity of the tomatoes. When the tomatoes are cooked with a pinch of saffron and a spoonful of honey, they get a Moorish flavour and this sauce is excellent with pan-fried salmon. This combination goes deliciously well with the earthy flavour of Puy lentils, and for this super-quick dish, I relied on ready-to-eat Puy lentils, adding tomato juice and spinach. A layered presentation makes the dish look like something you might be served in a smart restaurant.

4 vine tomatoes
pinch of saffron threads
1 tablespoon olive oil
½ teaspoon clear honey
about 100ml vegetable or
    chicken stock
250g sachet ready-to-eat
    Puy lentils
150g young spinach
2 salmon tail fillets, skin off
    or skin on
salt and freshly ground
    black pepper

Boil the kettle. Cover the tomatoes with boiling water, count to 30, pierce with a sharp knife and if the skin peels back they are ready to skin; if not, leave for a few more seconds. Cut out the core in a pointed plug shape and remove the skin. Halve the tomatoes, scrape the seeds into a sieve over a bowl and press the juice through, then transfer to a measuring jug. Chop the tomatoes.

Soften the saffron threads in 1 tablespoon boiling water. Place the chopped tomatoes, olive oil, saffron and water, honey and salt and pepper in a small pan. Cook, stirring occasionally, for about 10 minutes until thick and sauce-like.

Make the tomato juice up to 150ml with stock and add to a medium pan with the lentils. Warm through, stirring. Stir the spinach through the lentils; when it's wilted, this part of the dish is ready.

Heat a heavy-based, non-stick frying pan, and when very hot, cook the salmon fillets for 2 minutes on each side until crusty on the outside but moist, rather than dry, inside. (If using skin-on salmon, begin cooking skin-side down, then turn and remove the skin just before serving.) Serve a pile of lentils topped with a fillet of salmon and a goodly dollop of the hot tomato sauce.

SOY SALMON TAILS WITH GINGER RICE

SERVES 2 | **PREP** 20 MINUTES | **COOK** 25 MINUTES

I'm always looking out for quick and interesting ways of cooking salmon, and Japanese seasoning provides a variation on a favourite theme. Apart from soy sauce and pickled sushi ginger, which are likely to be in the storecupboard, you will also need mirin. This is a sweet and salty version of sake with umami powers, lifting and brightening the flavour of meat as well as fish dishes. Toasted sesame oil, which is even more essential to the dish, is thick and powerful, so you only need a few drops to achieve a deep, nutty flavour. Together they enrich a soy-seasoned rice stir-fry with leeks and carrots, while scraps of sushi ginger give each mouthful a sharp tang. The aromatic freshness of lemon thyme is the odd man out, but it provides a surprise wake-up call to the taste buds.

200g basmati rice

1 garlic clove

8 small Chantenay carrots

1 trimmed leek

1 tablespoon groundnut oil

2 teaspoons toasted sesame oil

2 splashes of mirin

3 tablespoons soy sauce

2 salmon tail fillets, skin off

1 dessertspoon pickled sushi ginger

1 teaspoon finely chopped lemon thyme

salt

Rinse the rice until the water runs clean. Peel, chop and crush the garlic with a pinch of salt. Trim, scrape and halve the carrots lengthways. Chop the leek into 1cm-thick slices, rinse and shake dry.

Heat ½ tablespoon of the groundnut oil with ½ teaspoon of the sesame oil over a low heat in a lidded pan suitable for cooking the rice. Stir-fry the garlic for a few seconds until aromatic, then add the carrots and leek, a splash of mirin and 1 tablespoon of the soy, and stir-fry for 2–3 minutes. Now add the rice, stirring to mix. Add 350ml cold water and bring slowly to the boil. Reduce the heat as low as possible, cover and cook for 10 minutes. Do not remove the lid, but leave off the heat for a further 10 minutes to finish cooking in the steam.

While the rice cooks, smear the fish with ½ teaspoon sesame oil, a splash of mirin and another of soy. Coarsely chop the sushi ginger. When the rice is cooked, heat the last of the groundnut oil, and when nicely hot, cook the fish for 3–6 minutes a side, depending on thickness and how you like salmon cooked. Fold the ginger and thyme through the forked-up rice and serve the fish over the rice, drizzled with the remaining soy and sesame oil.

SWEDISH LOX PUDDING

SERVES 6 | **PREP** 30 MINUTES | **COOK** 45 MINUTES–1 HOUR

Smoked salmon layered with very thinly sliced potato, dill and spring onions, and a crisp crumb topping. Soft and creamy, smoked salmon transformed. Yum.

25g butter
125g spring onions
20g bunch of dill
200g smoked salmon
  trimmings
4 large King Edward, Desiree
  or similar potatoes,
  about 900g
400ml crème fraîche or
  whipping cream or 200ml
  crème fraîche mixed with
  200ml double cream
4 tablespoons fresh white
  breadcrumbs
salt and freshly ground
  black pepper

Use half the butter to smear a 5cm deep, 2.5-litre gratin dish. Keeping separate piles, trim and finely slice the spring onions. Strip the dill off the stalks and chop. Slice the salmon into chunky strips.

Peel and rinse the potatoes. Slice thinly as if making crisps – a mandolin makes short work of this – but don't rinse. Spread one third of them in the buttered dish. Season lightly with salt and pepper. Cover with half the onion, dill and smoked salmon. Top with half the remaining potatoes, the remaining onion, dill and salmon and season. Finish with the last of the potatoes.

Preheat the oven to 190°C, Gas Mark 5.

Heat the crème fraîche or cream in a small pan until pourable, then pour it over the pudding. Encourage it to sink through the layers, shaking the dish a couple of times. Settle the surface flat. Cover with a thin layer of breadcrumbs and dot with the last of the butter.

Bake for 45 minutes–1 hour until the cream is bubbling round the edges, the crumbs golden and a sharp knife gets no resistance when driven through the potatoes. Serve alone, followed with green beans or a crisp salad.

SALMON AND PRAWN FISH PIE

SERVES 4 | **PREP** 20 MINUTES, PLUS COOLING | **COOK** 1 HOUR

I can't believe it had never occurred to me before to use store-bought fillets of cooked fish to make fish pie. One day, as I stood in store considering poached salmon fillets and particularly enticing-looking Atlantic peeled prawns, my brain lit up. Bingo, posh fish pie with no hassle. It is worth, though, taking a bit of trouble with the white sauce, seasoning the milk with onion and bay, then adding a little Dijon mustard to the roux. Parsley or dill freshens the flavours, then all the pie needs is a topping of buttery mashed potato.

It will make the pie even more desirably distinctive to sprinkle gently fried breadcrumbs over the top. I added freshly grated Parmesan, too, baking the pie until crusty and filling the kitchen with delicious aromas. Serve with peas or upgrade with a mix of al dente sugar snap peas, green beans and mangetout.

1 small onion
1 bay leaf
400ml milk
2 poached salmon fillets
200g cooked Atlantic
  peeled prawns

Halve, peel and slice the onion, then place in a pan with the bay leaf. Add the milk and a generous pinch of salt and pepper and simmer for 5 minutes. Cover and leave for at least 20 minutes.

Remove the fish and prawns from their packaging and pat dry with kitchen paper. Break the salmon in chunks into a 1.5-litre, 5cm-deep gratin dish. Season with salt and pepper. Scatter prawns, then herbs over the top.

2 tablespoons finely chopped
dill or flat leaf parsley
800g potatoes
50g butter
1 tablespoon plain flour
1 teaspoon Grey Poupon
Dijon mustard
½ lemon
1 tablespoon crème fraîche
salt and freshly ground
black pepper

For the optional topping
2 tablespoons freshly grated
Parmesan cheese
25g fresh white breadcrumbs
25g butter

Peel, chunk and rinse the potatoes. Boil in salted water until tender. Drain and mash with half the butter and 100ml of the infused milk, whipping it until fluffy.

To make the sauce, melt the remaining butter in a small pan and stir in the flour, followed by the mustard. Add the remaining milk gradually, stirring constantly to make a smooth sauce. Simmer gently, stirring regularly, for 5 minutes. Taste and season with salt and lemon juice. Slacken with the crème fraîche. Pour the sauce over the fish. Leave to cool and set.

Preheat the oven to 200°C, Gas Mark 6. Place spoonfuls of mash round the edge of the dish, then fork across, making big swirls with the fork. Dredge with the Parmesan and crumbs stirred through the melted butter. Bake for 40 minutes, checking after 30, until the top is crusty.

SMOKED TROUT MAYO WITH CAPERS AND CHIVES
SERVES 2 | **PREP** 20 MINUTES | **COOK** 20 MINUTES

This is a lovely undemanding way of turning a pack of smoked trout fillets into an elegant accompaniment for asparagus and minted new potatoes. It could also be made with poached or hot smoked salmon instead of delicately flavoured trout, and is good with minted fresh peas instead of asparagus or piled into curls of lettuce.

400g new potatoes
few mint sprigs
knob of butter
400g British asparagus
2 tablespoons Hellmann's
mayonnaise
1 heaped teaspoon Dijon
mustard
1 lemon
2 smoked rainbow trout
fillets
1 tablespoon capers in
brine, drained
1 tablespoon snipped chives
salt

Scrape the potatoes and boil in salted water with the mint, saving a few choice leaves, until tender. Drain. Just before serving, toss with the butter and chopped reserved mint leaves.

Snap off the woody asparagus ends and boil the spears in plenty of salted water for 2–3 minutes until just tender. Drain and then rest on kitchen paper to blot.

Beat together the mayo, mustard and 1 tablespoon lemon juice in a mixing bowl. Break the fish into bite-sized pieces and fold through the dressing. Add the lightly squeezed capers (to eliminate vinegar) and most of the chives and mix again. Serve scattered with the last of the chives, accompanied by the hot minted potatoes and asparagus.

MACKEREL, HERRING AND SARDINES

Little hairy bones put people off this family of fish, particularly herrings. A lazy solution to boning mackerel fillets is cutting out the central line of bones in a long strip, as it rarely matters to have two pieces rather than one fillet. Sardines are easier, as the carcass can be eased off the little fish; the tricky devils are herring. It's wise to grill all these fish on foil, which can be used later to bundle away all the debris. All these fish can stand strong seasoning, but if very fresh, they need no seasoning at all. A can of sardines in olive oil is a useful standby, delicious on toast spread with Dijon mustard or topped with pesto, both with tomato salad and rocket. I often pop a packet of smoked mackerel into my basket. I love it with creamed horseradish and new potatoes, or broken into hot, short pasta, such as frilly campanelle, with a dollop of creamed horseradish and finely snipped chives. (In fact, I am going to have that for lunch.)

GRILLED MACKEREL AND BRAMLEY APPLE SAUCE WITH HORSERADISH

SERVES 2 | **PREP** 20 MINUTES, PLUS CHILLING | **COOK** 20 MINUTES

This harmonious combination of food was on the menu at Quo Vadis, at a lunch to celebrate the Brammy Awards, started 21 years ago to raise the profile of Bramley cooking apples. Tom Kerridge and I won chef and cookery writer awards. I went home via the fish shop to buy fresh mackerel fillets to make the dish again. A sharp apple sauce is a good alternative to gooseberries, a classic combo, and creamed horseradish suits fresh as well as smoked mackerel. The snap of watercress is a good accompaniment. Serve with boiled new potatoes or bread and butter.

1 Bramley apple, about 300g
1 tablespoon sugar
10g cold butter
4 mackerel fillets
1 tablespoon vegetable oil
4 tablespoons creamed horseradish
salt and freshly ground black pepper
flourishing bunch of watercress, to serve

Quarter, peel, core and chop the apple. Place in a lidded pan with 100ml water. Cover and cook over a medium heat for about 5 minutes until soft and fluffy. Beat in the sugar. Tip into a bowl, then beat in the butter to thicken. Leave to cool slightly, then chill.

Preheat the oven to 200°C, Gas Mark 6. Check the fish fillets for bones, using tweezers if necessary to remove. Line a small roasting tin with foil and lightly smear with the oil (to avoid the skin sticking). Lay out the fish and season with salt and pepper. Roast for 5–10 minutes until cooked through.

Serve the mackerel hot with cold apple sauce and creamed horseradish – at QV they came in ramekins – with a pile of watercress on the side.

BUTTERFLIED HERRING WITH GARLIC AND PARSLEY CRUMBS

SERVES 2 | **PREP** 15 MINUTES | **COOK** 15 MINUTES

Don't look away now, thinking you don't eat fresh herring. This way of cooking the fish we prefer to kipper or pickle might make you forget about those off-putting hair-like bones. The recipe works for neatly trimmed, boned sardines and pilchards, and anchovies, by pressing garlicky breadcrumbs over the flesh and baking until the fish is just cooked and the topping aromatic and crusty. Serve with new potatoes, flowering broccoli and lemon wedges.

2 tablespoons olive oil
6–8 herrings, butterflied, boned and trimmed
75g white bread without crusts
4 garlic cloves
75g bunch of flat leaf parsley
1 lemon
salt and freshly ground black pepper

Preheat the oven to 220°C, Gas Mark 7. Lightly oil a flat or shallow oven tray that can accommodate the fish in a single layer. Tear a similar-sized piece of clingfilm and place the fish on it, skin-side down.

Tear the bread into a food processor bowl and blitz to crumbs. Lightly crush, then peel and finely chop the garlic. Pick the leaves from the parsley and finely chop. Add the garlic and parsley to the crumbs and pulse to mix.

Season the fish with salt and pepper. Divide the crumb mix between the fish, pressing with your fingers to cover. Use a spatula to lift onto the prepared oven tray. Dribble with the remaining oil and bake on the top oven shelf for 8–12 minutes until the topping is golden and the fish cooked through. Serve with the lemon, cut into wedges.

TARTE FINE SARDINES

SERVES 4 | **PREP** 30 MINUTES | **COOK** 25 MINUTES

This is what I call assembly food. It's quite cheffy but easy to achieve, comprising a series of separately prepared foods that all come together at the last moment. The pastry is a quickly baked, thinly rolled sheet of puff pastry. Once cooled, it is cut into cookie-sized circles. These will be topped by slippery-soft, finely chopped fried onion and lightly cooked peeled and diced tomato. The finale is a couple of grilled sardine fillets hidden under a salad of small mixed leaves in a lime-flavoured vinaigrette. If that sounds like a lot of work, it isn't and all of it, except grilling the sardines, could be done in advance. If fresh sardines are off the radar, try fillets from a tin. The tarts make a lovely starter, but two followed by cheese and a pud would do me for supper.

flour for dusting
250g puff pastry
3 or 4 vine tomatoes, about 400g
2 medium onions
2 tablespoons olive oil
25g butter plus a knob for greasing
8 sardine fillets
handful of small mixed salad leaves
2 tablespoons ready-made vinaigrette (or see page 10 for homemade)
generous squeeze of lime
salt and freshly ground black pepper

Preheat the oven to 220°C, Gas Mark 7. Flour a work surface and roll the pastry out to approximately 30cm square, 2mm thick. Line a baking sheet with baking parchment rubbed with butter – a little underneath, too, so that it sticks to the sheet – then roll the pastry loosely round a rolling pan and lay out on the lined tin. Prick all over with a fork. Bake for 5–8 minutes until crisp and pale golden, flip and cook for a further minute or so. You want it crisp but not brown. Slip onto a wire rack to cool, then use a round cutter, approximately 11cm, to cut out 4 circles.

Meanwhile, boil the kettle. Pour boiling water over the tomatoes, count to 30, drain, skin and quarter. Scrape the seeds into a sieve over a bowl. Chop the flesh into small dice.

Halve, peel and finely chop the onions, then soften gently in a non-stick frying pan, stirring often, in 1 tablespoon of the olive oil. Crush the tomato seeds and add the juice to the onions. Simmer until sticky. Transfer to a bowl. Add the tomatoes to the pan, then the butter, salt and pepper and cook briefly until soft – the dice should still be discernible.

Lightly oil a sheet of foil on a grill pan. Lay out the sardine fillets, skin-side down. Grill for 2–3 minutes. Spread the onion mix over the pastry circles and top with the tomato, then the sardines, skin-side up. Cover with the leaves tossed in the vinaigrette flavoured with the lime juice and serve.

TOMATO AND PESTO SARDINES ON TOAST

SERVES 2 | **PREP** 15 MINUTES | **COOK** 5 MINUTES

When you're caught on the hop, desperate for something quick and vaguely healthy for supper, don't forget about canned sardines in olive oil. They make a great storecupboard supper on hot buttered toast with a smear of creamy Dijon mustard.

This variation on that theme makes the snack more substantial, giving it a summery twist with pesto instead of mustard and hiding everything under a chunky tomato salad. Dense-textured sourdough or ciabatta works best here, providing a good contrast of textures. Each mouthful is a wonderful mixture of sardines melting against hot, garlicky crusty toast with creamy pesto and the sweet acidity from tomatoes. A hint of freshly chopped parsley gives a grassy finish.

Another trick with canned sardines is to remove the backbones, then mash them smooth with their olive oil, plenty of black pepper and a generous squeeze of lemon juice. You then have a delicious sardine pâté to pile onto hot buttered toast or layer up, bruschetta-style, with tomatoes or watercress.

2 thick slices of sourdough
  or similar bread
1 garlic clove
2 tablespoons pesto
2 × 120g cans sardines in
  olive oil
1 very large or 2 medium
  vine tomatoes
2 tablespoons extra virgin
  olive oil
1 tablespoon chopped flat
  leaf parsley
1 lemon
salt and freshly ground
  black pepper

Toast the bread and peel the garlic. Rub one side of the toast with the garlic until most of it has disappeared. Spread generously with pesto. Split the sardines in the cans and remove the backbones, piling the sardines onto the toast as you go. Tip the oil in the cans over the top.

Core the tomato, cutting it out in a pointed plug shape, then slice into chunky wedges. Lay the wedges over the sardines, piling them up to entirely cover the fish. Splash the tomatoes with the extra virgin olive oil, then season with salt and pepper. Scatter the parsley over the top and serve with the lemon, cut into wedges.

TUNA

Lovely thick fillets of tuna only need a brief flash in the pan or on the griddle so that the middle stays dark and juicy. Tuna is a usefully versatile food to remember for easy, mid-week suppers. I like it Japanese-style, with noodles or rice and frilly pink so-called sushi ginger. It is also very good with guacamole. And don't forget sustainable canned tuna; it's a great storecupboard standby for instant pasta dishes and Salade Niçoise. The finest is white tuna, *bonito del norte*, which is often packed in olive or vegetable oil rather than brine. It is far more expensive than ordinary canned tuna, but there is no going back once you have tasted the difference, although yellowfin tuna chunks in sunflower oil are a reasonable alternative.

TUNA WITH GUACAMOLE

SERVES 2 | **PREP** 20 MINUTES, PLUS CHILLING | **COOK** 5 MINUTES

Tuna suits being cooked on the griddle, etching attractive scorch lines into the pale surface, giving onto moist, dark and almost raw fish in the middle. It's vital, as ever, but particularly in this instance, to get the griddle really hot before committing the fish and just leaving it long enough to sear before turning the fillets. The firm, meaty flesh goes very well with similarly dense avocado and can take the other spicy flavours of guacamole.

2 ripe avocados

3 limes

16 cherry tomatoes, about 150g

1 medium red onion

1 red bird's eye chilli

25g bunch of coriander

2 Cornish yellowfin tuna steaks, each at least 2cm thick

1 dessertspoon sunflower or groundnut oil

salt and freshly ground black pepper

Run a sharp knife round the length of the avocados. Twist apart, remove the stone and use a spoon to scoop all the flesh into a bowl. Squeeze over the juice of 1 lime. Season with salt and pepper. Mash coarsely whilst stirring to mix.

Chop the tomatoes and peel and finely chop the onion. Finely dice the chilli, discarding the seeds. Mix into the avocado. Taste and adjust the seasoning with pepper and lime juice. Stir in 2 tablespoons chopped coriander. Drape with clingfilm touching the food and chill until required.

Place a griddle over a high heat and leave for several minutes until very hot. Season the fillets on both sides with salt and pepper, smear with the oil, then cook for 1 minute on each side (turn by scraping a spatula under the fillets and lifting). Again cook briefly so that the middle retains its dark colour. Top with the guacamole and serve with remaining limes, cut into wedges, and the remaining sprigs of coriander.

SALADE NIÇOISE

SERVES 4 | **PREP** 20 MINUTES | **COOK** 15 MINUTES

To ensure everyone gets a fair share of everything, it makes sense to serve this in individual dishes or on a large platter. My latest version is light on lettuce but a generous combination of artichoke hearts, new potatoes, green beans, cherry tomatoes, black olives and cucumber, with hard-boiled egg, anchovy and good-quality canned tuna. Try a hint of dill along with the usual basil for a lovely mix of crunch and creamy, bland, salty and grassy.

400g new potatoes

4 eggs

200g green beans

150g cherry tomatoes

½ cucumber

1 oak leaf lettuce heart

1 garlic clove

1 tablespoon red wine vinegar

3 tablespoons olive oil

280g jar sliced artichoke hearts, drained

50g can anchovy fillets in olive oil, drained

about 10 basil leaves

few dill sprigs, optional

75g black olives, preferably Niçoise

300g can good-quality tuna, drained

salt and freshly ground black pepper

Scrape the potatoes, cut into even-sized chunks and cook in boiling salted water with the eggs, allowing about 10 minutes. Drain. Set aside to cool. Crack the eggs all over, then peel under cold running water.

Top and tail and halve the beans. Boil in salted water for 3 minutes. Drain. Halve the tomatoes round their middles. Peel the cucumber and slice very thinly. Separate the lettuce leaves, rinse and pat dry. Arrange a few choice leaves on a platter or in 4 wide bowls.

Peel, chop and then crush the garlic. Mix with the vinegar, olive oil and salt and pepper.

Pile the cooled potatoes, beans, tomatoes, cucumber, artichokes, anchovies, torn basil and dill, if using, over the lettuce, then add the black olives, halved eggs and broken tuna. Spoon over the vinaigrette and serve.

CRAB

I love crab. When I'm in Cornwall, where I can buy it live, freshly boiled or freshly picked, it's top of my shopping list. In London, where I live, I can buy boiled crab to pick myself but often treat myself to 100g pots of freshly picked Cornish white and brown crab meat (www.seafoodandeatit.co.uk for stockists) and 50/50 packs. This enterprising company also sell packs of crab legs, so there is nothing to stop you making these favourite recipes. Crab is never a cheap option, but the silky white meat and creamy brown is addictive and a versatile ingredient for quick meals. It loves chilli and South East Asian flavourings.

CORIANDER CHILLI CRAB CLAWS

SERVES 2 | **PREP** 15 MINUTES | **COOK** 20 MINUTES

Taste restaurant is a bright new star in St Agnes, my childhood Cornish stamping ground. My aunts, who lived there, would have loved the homemade fish cakes, steamed local mussels with white wine and garlic, and modern take on wild mushroom and spinach lasagne. The dish I wanted to make at home was the cracked crab claws in a Thai-style coriander, lime and chilli broth. I've adapted it using prepared crab claws from my London fishmonger, but freshly boiled crab would be even better. It's a greedy hands-on dish to serve as a chunky soup or over basmati rice cooked while the sauce simmers. Yum.

1 medium onion
1 tablespoon groundnut oil
1 garlic clove
1 red bird's eye chilli
1 kaffir lime leaf
¼ teaspoon dried chilli flakes
300ml fish stock or 300ml
   water and ¼ chicken
   stock cube
1 tablespoon Thai sweet
   chilli sauce
1–2 tablespoons Thai fish
   sauce (nam pla)
1 lime
knob of butter
10 generous coriander sprigs
10 cooked, cracked crab claws
salt

Halve, peel and finely chop the onion. Soften gently, stirring occasionally, in a medium pan in the oil with a pinch of salt. Peel and then crush the garlic to a paste, split, deseed and finely chop the chilli and mix both into the softening onion with the lime leaf and chilli flakes. Cook for a few minutes, then add the fish stock or 300ml water and crumbled stock cube. Simmer for 5 minutes.

Add the sweet chilli sauce and season to taste with nam pla and lime juice. Whisk in the butter. Add the coriander, and when wilted, slip the crab claws under the liquid. Heat through and serve or reheat later.

CRAB AND PEA PIES

MAKES 6 | **PREP** 30 MINUTES | **COOK** 20 MINUTES

I used a little pot of Cornish 50/50 crab for these lovely pies, but white crab meat will give a less assertive flavour. Imagine it now, biting into golden, flaky pastry giving onto a soft filling of crab mixed with pea purée and swirls of mayonnaise. I'm ashamed to say that I've been known to eat two on the trot but one is almost sufficient, particularly if served with salad or a mix of asparagus, green beans and new potatoes tossed with butter and mint.

125g frozen petits pois
4 spring onions
25g butter plus a knob
100g crab meat
1 tablespoon fresh white
  breadcrumbs
2 tablespoons Hellmann's
  mayonnaise
200g puff pastry
flour for dusting
1 egg
salt

Preheat the oven to 220°C, Gas Mark 7. Boil the peas until tender. Trim and finely slice the spring onions. Soften in the butter with a pinch of salt. Place the drained peas and softened spring onions in the bowl of a food processor and blitz a couple of times to mix and almost purée. Spread out in a bowl. Cool slightly, then top with the crab and crumbs, stir, add the mayo and lightly mix.

Lightly roll the pastry on a floured work surface and, using a 10cm cutter, stamp out 12 circles, re-rolling the trimmings. Line a baking sheet with buttered baking parchment. Whisk the egg. Lay 6 circles on the parchment and paint with a 1cm egg border. Pile in the crab, fit the lids, squashing lightly, and crimp with a fork. Paint all over with egg, make a central steam hole and bake for 15 minutes until puffed, crisp and golden.

CRAB AND PICKLED CUCUMBER LINGUINE

SERVES 2 | **PREP** 25 MINUTES, PLUS STANDING AND CHILLING | **COOK** 10 MINUTES

This pasta dish is a modified version of a salad that I first made when entertaining a crowd for my birthday. It's a simple but flavourful combination of white crab meat with sweet pickled cucumber, coriander and a hint of chilli. It is very good against the bite of al dente linguine. It is quick and easy to make, but the cucumber preparation does need to be thoroughly chilled. Both crab and cucumber could be made and kept safely in the fridge for up to 48 hours.

½ small cucumber
1 teaspoon sugar
1 tablespoon white wine
  vinegar
1 small red chilli
2 tablespoons lemon juice
2–3 tablespoons best olive oil
15g coriander
100g white crab meat
200g linguine
salt and freshly ground
  black pepper

Wash the cucumber and finely slice – a mandolin is ideal for this – place in a colander and sprinkle with 1 tablespoon salt. Leave for at least 20 minutes, preferably 30 or 40. Rinse thoroughly, squeeze dry, then squeeze dry again in a clean tea towel. Dissolve the sugar in the vinegar, mix in the cucumber, cover and chill for at least 40 minutes.

Trim and split the chilli, deseed and slice into batons, then into tiny dice. Mix into the lemon juice, then beat in sufficient olive oil to make a thick, creamy vinaigrette. Season with salt and black pepper. Mix in the finely chopped coriander (stalks and all) and crab meat. Cover and chill until required.

Boil the kettle and use the water to cook the linguine according to the packet instructions – about 10 minutes – until al dente. Drain and mix with the crab. Squeeze out any excess vinegar from the cucumber and stir into the pasta.

THAI CRAB CAKES WITH CUCUMBER RELISH

SERVES 2 | **PREP** 20 MINUTES | **COOK** 15 MINUTES

This mid-week treat for two could be stretched to three if served with oven frites and a few crisp salad leaves under the cucumber relish. The fragile little crab cakes firm up and create a gorgeous crisp shell in a hot oven.

1 small red chilli
100g white crab meat
100g brown crab meat
2 tablespoons Hellmann's
    mayonnaise plus extra
    to serve
3 teaspoons Thai fish sauce
    (nam pla)
50g bunch of coriander
100g fresh breadcrumbs
flour for dusting
1 egg
½ cucumber
1 tablespoon lime juice
2 tablespoons groundnut oil

Trim the chilli, halve it lengthways, scrape away the seeds and slice it into skinny batons, then tiny dice. Place the crab meat, mayo, 2 teaspoons of the fish sauce, most of the finely chopped coriander, most of the chilli and just over half the breadcrumbs in a mixing bowl. Mix. Working quickly, halve the mix and make 3 thick patties from each half. Dust with flour.

Beat the egg in a bowl and have the remaining crumbs on a large plate. Quickly turn one crab cake at a time through the egg and then place on the crumbs, turning to cover; 2 knives are useful to pat them into shape. Chill, clingfilm-covered.

Preheat the oven to 220°C, Gas Mark 7. Next make the relish. Peel the cucumber, halve lengthways, scrape out the seeds and finely slice. Place in a small bowl with the remaining fish sauce, remaining coriander, lime juice and remaining chilli. Stir to combine.

Pour the oil into the middle of a foil-lined small, shallow roasting tin. Smear both sides of the cakes with oil and roast for 15 minutes or until very crisp. Rest on kitchen paper and serve with the relish and a dollop of mayo.

CRAB, LIME AND AVOCADO SALAD

SERVES 2 OR 4 | **PREP** 15 MINUTES

Citrus fruit goes well with white crab meat, its tangy sharp zing cutting through the rich, creamy meat. Here it's matched with lime, little segments carefully cut from their skin. Avocado is another surprisingly good bedfellow for crab and, together with lime and peppery wild rocket, combine into a smart, healthy salad.

50g wild rocket
1 large or 2 small yielding
   avocados
2 limes
100g white crab meat
½ teaspoon clear honey
2 tablespoons best olive oil
freshly ground black pepper

Pile the washed, drained rocket in the middle of 2 or 4 plates. Halve the avocado lengthways, twist apart, remove the stone and carefully peel. Slice across the halves to make chunky, but not too chunky, curls. Scatter them over the rocket, tweaking to spread and semi-mix.

Use a small, sharp knife to peel 1 lime. Slice out the segments, leaving the membrane behind. Scatter the segments over the avocado and top with chunks of crab. Squeeze the discarded lime into a bowl and top up, if necessary, with juice from the second lime – you need 1 tablespoon of juice, maybe a tad more. Stir in the honey, plenty of freshly ground black pepper and beat in the olive oil. Taste, adding more lime if you think necessary. Splash the dressing over the salad. That's it.

CRAB, MAYO AND CHIPS

SERVES 2 | **PREP** 20 MINUTES | **COOK** 35 MINUTES

Freshly picked crab, the brown meat seasoned with vinegar, salt and pepper, the legs cracked, a bowl of homemade mayonnaise, crusty oven chips and cucumber and lettuce salad or pickled cucumber with dill, is a *Desert Island* dinner. When in Cornwall, a crab per person is a greedy option, but this is superior making-do.

500g medium–large potatoes
2 tablespoons sunflower oil
Maldon sea salt, to taste
2 egg yolks
2 teaspoons Dijon mustard
2 teaspoons lemon juice
about 200ml light olive oil or
   100ml olive oil and 100ml
   groundnut oil
50g brown crab meat
50g white crab meat
1–2 tablespoons wine vinegar
10 cooked, cracked crab claws
salt and freshly ground
   black pepper

Boil the kettle. Peel the potatoes. Slice into chip-sized pieces and rinse. Add to boiling salted water and boil for 5 minutes until just tender. Drain and cool. Preheat the oven to 220°C, Gas Mark 7. Toss the chips with the sunflower oil and spread out in a single layer on a shallow roasting tin. Season with salt. Roast for 20 minutes. Use a palette knife to turn. Roast for a further 10–15 minutes until crusty and golden. Drain on kitchen paper, toss with a twist of Maldon sea salt and pile in a bowl.

For the mayo, whisk or beat the yolks with the mustard, lemon juice, pinch of salt and 1 tablespoon of the olive oil until pale. Add the remaining oil in a trickle, whisking or beating continually until thick and glossy. Mix together the crab meats and season with salt, pepper and vinegar to taste. Pile into ramekins (portion control is a wise move) and arrange on a platter with the claws. Dive in.

PRAWNS AND BROWN SHRIMPS

When you're in a hurry, a bag of prawns is a useful option for a quick meal. They make a good curry, although it will taste better if stock is made with the shells and the prawns cooked from raw. They're great for salads, to bolster fish pie and in puff pastry turnovers.

Raw prawns should have their intestinal tract removed – it's the black line that runs down the inside curl of the prawn, easily removed by running a sharp, small knife down the line and swiping it away – but rarely spoils the flavour and is not harmful. It does make the prawns fan out attractively. I often slice larger prawns in half, to make them go further in couscous and other salads. I am addicted to little brown shrimps, first encountered on the coast in Brittany where you see them piled high in the market. They are eat-all, their crunchy little shells part of the treat.

Crayfish tails look like shaggy prawns and have a similar texture but stronger, fishier flavour and aroma. They are interchangeable with prawns in the following recipes.

PRAWN AND PINEAPPLE THAI SALAD

SERVES 2 | **PREP** 15 MINUTES | **COOK** 5 MINUTES

Quick, healthy, attractive and requiring very little work, so the perfect thing to knock up after a busy day at work. If you like crunchy food with attitude, you will love this.

200g green beans
1 small pineapple or 140g
    prepared fresh pineapple chunks
3 Little Gem lettuce hearts
160g cooked peeled king prawns
few coriander sprigs
salt

For the dressing
1 red bird's eye chilli
2 tablespoons groundnut or
    sesame oil
1 tablespoon Thai fish sauce
    (nam pla)
1 lime

Boil the kettle while you top and tail the beans. Cut the beans in half and cook them in boiling salted water for 2 minutes. Drain, splash with cold water and drain again.

Next make the dressing. Trim and split the chilli. Scrape away the seeds and slice into skinny strips, then into tiny dice. Don't forget to wash your hands with soapy water to get rid of the chilli juices that will burn your eyes and other tender parts of the body. Mix together the chilli, oil, fish sauce and juice from the lime.

Finish the salad by preparing the pineapple. If using a whole pineapple, peel the fruit, cut out the woody core and cut the flesh into thick slices and then into bite-sized chunks. Separate the lettuce leaves, rinse and shake dry. Arrange the lettuce in the middle of 2 plates, top with the beans and scatter over the pineapple and prawns. Spoon the dressing over the top and add the coarsely chopped coriander.

PRAWN, TOMATO AND BUTTERNUT MAFTOUL RISOTTO

SERVES 2 | **PREP** 20 MINUTES | **COOK** 30 MINUTES

Giant couscous, also known as maftoul and fregola, has taken over as my favourite quick dinner standby, filling in for pasta, regular couscous and risotto rice. It is so quick to cook and proving endlessly versatile. For this prawn risotto, the maftoul is quickly boiled, then simmered in stock and liquidized cherry tomatoes with diced carrot and butternut squash. Highly recommended.

100g giant couscous, maftoul
   or fregola
1 medium onion
1 tablespoon olive oil
200g butternut squash
100g carrot
150g raw peeled king prawns
150ml light chicken stock
175g cherry tomatoes
½ lemon
salt

Boil the kettle and use 1 litre of the water to boil the giant couscous in a saucepan for 8 minutes. Drain.

Meanwhile, halve, peel and finely chop the onion. Soften in the olive oil in a spacious, lidded frying/sauté pan, allowing about 10 minutes. Deseed the butternut and cut into small kebab-sized pieces. Scrape the carrot and dice small like Dolly Mixtures. Add the butternut and carrot to the onion, add a generous pinch of salt and cook, covered, stirring a couple of times, for 10 minutes.

Uncurl the prawns and trace the black line with a small, sharp knife. Swipe away the black. Add the giant couscous and stock to the vegetables, cover and simmer for 5 minutes.

Blitz the tomatoes in a food processor until smooth, then pass through a sieve into the risotto, scraping underneath so that nothing is wasted. Add the prawns, stirring over a very low heat for about 5 minutes until pink. Adjust the seasoning with salt and lemon juice.

SHRIMP AND CELERY GIGLI PASTA

SERVES 2 | **PREP** 15 MINUTES | **COOK** 15 MINUTES

Gigli is a pretty pasta, shaped like a cone with a frilly edge. It's perfect for this simple way of stretching 100g brown shrimps to make supper for two.

1 lemon
2 celery heart sticks
150g gigli or other frilly
   pasta, such as campanelle
150g frozen petits pois
10g butter
100g cooked brown shrimps
1 tablespoon finely
   chopped dill

Remove 1 tablespoon very finely grated zest from the lemon; a microplane grater is best for this. Halve the lemon and collect 1 tablespoon juice. Finely slice the celery into half-moons.

Cook the pasta until just al dente, then add the peas and cook for a further few minutes until the peas are tender. Add the celery, return to the boil and then drain.

Toss the pasta with the lemon zest and reserved juice and butter. Add the shrimps and dill. Toss again and eat this pretty, crunchy pasta treat.

LENTIL, POMEGRANATE AND SHRIMP SALAD

SERVES 4 | **PREP** 15 MINUTES | **COOK** 10 MINUTES

This is a jewellery box of a salad, a wonderful sparkling, brightly coloured mix of textures and colours to excite the palate. Every forkful will be different, little brown shrimps vying for your attention with glossy beetroot, jewel-like pomegranate seeds, peas and bamboo shoots, all glowing against the dark backdrop provided by the lentils.

The salad is underpinned with a dressing made with lemon juice, honey and nutty rapeseed oil. Spiky fronds of dill sharpen the look and the flavours. Perfect for a buffet-style meal piled into curls of lettuce, but delicious on its own, or maybe tumbled over baked potatoes.

150g frozen petits pois
400g boiled beetroot
1 lemon
1 teaspoon clear honey
2 tablespoons cold-pressed
    rapeseed oil
250g ready-to-eat Puy lentils
½ pomegranate (100g seeds)
120g canned sliced bamboo
    shoots
100g cooked brown shrimps
1 tablespoon chopped dill
salt

Cook the peas in boiling salted water until just tender. Drain, return to the pan and cover with cold water. Leave for a few minutes, then drain again. Peel the beets and cut into small kebab-sized dice. Toss with 1 tablespoon lemon juice and a generous pinch of salt.

Make the dressing in a serving bowl by dissolving the honey in 1 tablespoon lemon juice, then whisk in the oil. Stir the lentils through the dressing thoroughly, then add the pomegranate seeds and drained bamboo shoots. Toss thoroughly, add the beets and toss again. Now add the shrimps, peas and dill. Toss just before serving to avoid the lemon in the salad dulling the colour of the peas.

PRAWNS IN ALMOND TOMATO SAUCE

SERVES 4 | **PREP** 25 MINUTES | **COOK** 25 MINUTES

I do like using nuts to thicken sauces and here almonds and pine nuts are ground into a paste with parsley and garlic, then stirred into tomato cooked with onions. This thick, luscious cook-in sauce is versatile; try it for cooking diced cod or salmon, or tofu, if that's your thing, or blanched cauliflower florets. I like it with prawns, using cooked prawns for this relatively quick and easy supper. Sharpen the sauce with cayenne and lemon and the dish is done. Serve over couscous, rice or quinoa, or keep the dish light and summery with green beans tossed with new potatoes.

1 Spanish onion
3 tablespoons olive oil
900g vine tomatoes
½ teaspoon sugar
100g blanched almonds
100g pine nuts
4 garlic cloves

Boil the kettle. Halve, peel and finely chop the onion. Soften in the olive oil in a spacious frying/sauté pan. Pour boiling water over the tomatoes. After about 30 seconds, pierce with a knife and if the skin peels back drain the tomatoes. Cut out the core, quarter lengthways and scrape the seeds into a sieve placed over a bowl. Chop the tomato flesh and stir into the soft, lightly coloured onions. Season with salt, pepper and the sugar. Cook, uncovered, for 10 minutes, stirring often, until the sauce is thick but juicy.

small bunch of flat
   leaf parsley
¼ teaspoon cayenne pepper
juice of ½ lemon
400g cooked peeled prawns
   or shrimps
salt and freshly ground
   black pepper

Place the almonds, pine nuts and peeled garlic in the bowl of a food processor. Pick the leaves off the parsley and add them, too. Add 3 tablespoons of water from the tomato seeds pressed through the sieve and process the mixture to a thick paste. Scrape the paste into the tomatoes and cook together for a few minutes, adding a little more tomato water if the sauce is very thick. Stir in the cayenne. Taste and season with salt, pepper and lemon juice. Fold in the prawns or shrimps. Heat through and serve with whatever you fancy.

PRAWN CHAPCHAE

SERVES 2 | **PREP** 20 MINUTES | **COOK** 15 MINUTES

Years ago in my days as a restaurant critic, the publishing magnate-cum-poet Felix Dennis tipped me off about a Korean restaurant in Soho. Apart from the staggering collection of pickled ginseng in huge jars, I particularly remember eating *chapchae*, sometimes called *japchae*, for the first time. This lovely noodle dish is a great combination of crunch and slurp, salty and sweet, sour and spicy-hot with a hint of pickle, and I've been making versions of it ever since. Ideally you want cellophane noodles, but wheat or rice noodles are a good substitute. It makes the most of a small amount of seafood or meat and adapts perfectly with chicken, pork, lamb or steak, all cut into slivers. Try it, too, with minced meat or even monkfish and squid.

10g dried or 100g fresh
   shiitake mushrooms
100g dried glass, rice or
   stir-fry noodles
1½ tablespoons toasted
   sesame oil
1 teaspoon toasted
   sesame seeds
1 carrot
6 spring onions
25g fresh root ginger or
   pickled sushi ginger
2 tablespoons Kikkoman
   soy sauce
½ teaspoon sugar
¼ teaspoon dried chilli flakes
1 garlic clove
1 large shallot
1 tablespoon groundnut oil
160g raw peeled king prawns

If using dried shiitake, cover with boiling water to hydrate. Thinly slice fresh shiitake. Boil the noodles for 5 minutes, drain, rinse and toss with ½ tablespoon of the sesame oil and half the sesame seeds.

Slice the scraped carrot and trimmed spring onions into matchsticks. Peel, quarter and finely slice the ginger. Mix together the soy, sugar, chilli, crushed garlic and remaining sesame oil. Halve, peel and finely chop the shallot. Swirl the groundnut oil around a hot wok. Add the carrot and shallot and stir-fry for 2 minutes. Add the spring onions, prawns, ginger and mushrooms. Continue stir-frying for 1 minute. Add the soy sauce mixture and stir-fry for 30 seconds, then add the noodles. Scatter the remaining sesame seeds over the top and serve with chopsticks or fork and spoon.

GINGER PRAWNS WITH VIETNAMESE NOODLE SALAD

SERVES 4 | **PREP** 25 MINUTES | **COOK** 15 MINUTES

Here's a dish to wake up your taste buds. Full of vim and vigour, crunch and slippery noodles, this salad is an unexpected mix of cucumber and fennel with a sharp, zingy dressing. A hint of sweetness comes from using Thai chilli sauce rather than raw chilli. It gives the pale green and white ingredients an injection of red chilli that won't blow your head off.

This herby Vietnamese-style salad is delicious on its own and could be served with any number of other things apart from prawns; try lime-seasoned strips of fried chicken or fish.

300g raw peeled prawns
2 garlic cloves
15g fresh root ginger
2 tablespoons groundnut oil
150g vermicelli bean thread
    or rice noodles
150g cucumber
1 small fennel bulb,
    about 150g
10g coriander stalks and
    leaves
5g small mint leaves

For the dressing
1 garlic clove
1 tablespoon Thai fish sauce
    (nam pla)
2 tablespoons lime juice
1 tablespoon Thai sweet
    chilli sauce

For the garnish
2 tablespoons roasted salted
    peanuts or cashews
1 tablespoon Thai sweet
    chilli sauce

Run a knife down the inside curl of the prawns and wipe away the black veins. Peel and chop the garlic, and peel and grate the ginger. Crush the ginger and garlic together to make a paste, then stir with 1 tablespoon of the oil. Smear this over the prawns and set aside to marinate.

To make the salad, soak the noodles in cold water for 10 minutes until soft enough to cut into manageable lengths (approximately 8cm). Drain, cover with boiling water and leave for 15 minutes to soften.

Peel the cucumber, use a teaspoon to scrape out the seeds, then slice into thin half-moons. Trim and halve the fennel lengthways. Slice thinly across the halves. Chop the coriander. Drain the soft noodles.

For the dressing, peel, chop and crush the garlic to a paste. Mix with the remaining dressing ingredients. Add the noodles and mix thoroughly, then add the remaining salad ingredients and mint. Mix.

Place the nuts in a plastic bag, seal the end and bash with something heavy to crumb.

To complete the dish, heat the remaining oil in a non-stick frying pan or wok and stir-fry the prawns, tossing until uniformly pink and just cooked through. Give the salad a final toss, pile into the middle of 4 plates or bowls and top with the prawns. Scatter with the crushed nuts and a swirl of chilli sauce.

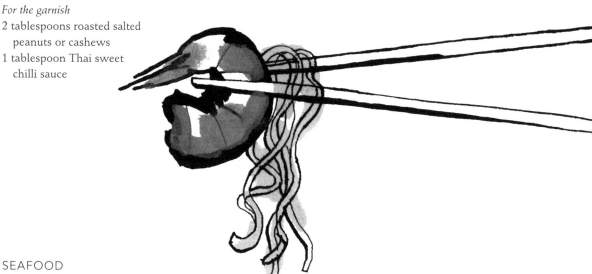

RED QUINOA SALAD WITH SAMPHIRE AND PRAWN KEBABS

SERVES 4 | **PREP** 20 MINUTES | **COOK** 20 MINUTES

It's mildly thrilling to watch quinoa cooking, the tiny balls coiling into life. I had wonderful black quinoa at Lima (www.limalondon.com), an exquisite Peruvian restaurant in Rathbone Place, near Charlotte Street in London, although red quinoa is the most exotic variety I've seen on sale. It looks very pretty with beetroot and verdant samphire, the salad topped with prawn kebabs and chilli-flavoured tomato vinaigrette. The recipe begins by finely chopping a couple of large chillies and covering them in olive oil. You won't need all of it for this recipe, but it can be kept, covered, in the fridge to use in any recipe requiring chilli. Alternatively, cheat with Thai chilli dipping sauce.

150g samphire
2 large red chillies, about 25g, deseeded
6 tablespoons best olive oil
100g red quinoa
250g boiled baby beetroot
1 lemon
Maldon sea salt, to taste
280g raw peeled king prawns
4 small vine tomatoes
1 teaspoon red wine vinegar
pinch of sugar
6 basil leaves
salt

Boil the kettle. Rinse the samphire. Place in a bowl and cover with boiling water and a stretch of clingfilm. Soak (for at least 10 minutes) until required. Trim and split the chillies, slice into skinny strips and then dice. Place in a jar and add the olive oil.

Rinse the quinoa and simmer, covered, for 10 minutes in 300ml water. Leave, covered, for about 15 minutes to soak up the liquid, taking the odd peak to watch them unfurl.

Peel and quarter the beets, then drench with lemon juice and season lavishly with Maldon sea salt. Run a knife down the inside of the outstretched prawns and swipe away the black thread. Divide the curled prawns between 18–24 wooden skewers (no need to soak in water, as the kebabs cook very fast).

Quarter the tomatoes. Scrape the seeds into a sieve over a bowl and crush the juice through the sieve. Add the vinegar, sugar and a pinch of salt. Whisk with 2 tablespoons of the chilli oil including about ½ teaspoon chilli. Stir in the tomato and shredded basil.

Heat a griddle. Just before cooking, use a pastry brush to smear with oil from the chillies. Cook the kebabs briefly on both sides, just until the prawns turn pink. Serve the quinoa topped with the beets and drained samphire. Add the kebabs and spoon over the vinaigrette. Kepow!

SQUID AND MUSSELS

Supermarkets sell small squid, cleaned up, with the tentacles tucked inside the sac. They sell it defrosted or frozen in 500g or 1kg bags and it's something I regularly buy for the freezer. These small squid defrost quickly but like all frozen seafood hold a lot of water. These bags used to be a little-known bargain, but although prices have crept up, they are still extremely good value. The sweet tender flesh is easy to cook well and immensely versatile. It suits fast or slow, steady cooking, never in between. I love it River Café-style, the sac opened out and etched with a narrow lattice on the inside, then quickly griddled and served with finely chopped chilli in olive oil and a rocket salad. It is also delicious stuffed.

I eat a lot of mussels in September through to February. Apart from being plentiful, they are incredibly good value, healthy and nutritious. Much as I love *Moules Marinière*, particularly Belgian-style with chips and mayo on the side, there is much fun to be had altering the seasonings.

SQUID, CHORIZO AND SWEET POTATOES

SERVES 3–4 | **PREP** 30 MINUTES | **COOK** 45 MINUTES

When I'm in Cornwall, I like to buy just-caught squid in Newlyn (contact Trelawney Fish for wholesale fresh Newlyn seafood on 01736 361793) for this forgiving stew. The combination of spicy chorizo with strips of creamy mild squid and chunks of golden sweet potato in thick tomato sauce is a winner. Serve it in bowls with crusty bread and butter, adding briefly boiled green beans for a fresh green crunch.

400g prepared squid
60g diced chorizo
1 tablespoon olive oil
1 medium red onion
2 garlic cloves
300g sweet potatoes
400g can chopped tomatoes
½ chicken stock cube
25g bunch of coriander or
   flat leaf parsley
salt and freshly ground
   black pepper

Remove the tentacles from inside the squid sacs. Trim the tentacles to remove the hard 'beak'. Halve the sacs lengthways, then slice across to make short, chunky ribbons, not rings. Stir-fry the chorizo in the olive oil over a medium heat in a spacious, lidded frying/sauté pan for 2 minutes.

Halve the onion, peel and finely chop. Peel and chop the garlic. Stir both into the crisping chorizo. Reduce the heat slightly and stir-fry for 5 minutes. Add a generous pinch of salt, cover and cook for a further 5–10 minutes.

Meanwhile, peel and dice the sweet potatoes. Boil in salted water for 5 minutes. Drain, saving a cup of the water.

Stir the squid into the onions whilst increasing the heat slightly, stirring as the pieces squirm and firm. Add the sweet potato, tomatoes, crumbled stock cube and reserved water. Season with salt and pepper, establish a steady simmer, cover and cook for 30 minutes. Stir occasionally to avoid sticking.

Season to taste, then chop the herbs and stir in just before serving.

CALAMARI PASTA WITH TOMATOES AND PEAS

SERVES 4 | **PREP** 25 MINUTES | **COOK** 15 MINUTES

Combining squid with tomatoes and peas is an inspired idea from Marcella Hazan's seminal 1973-published *The Classic Italian Cook Book*. Rather than stew them together slowly, as Ms Hazan does, in this dish everything is cooked quickly and pointed up with a little chilli and fresh coriander. Messicani pasta is particularly suitable. It's the one that looks like big, flat belly buttons, and when mixed with curls of cooked squid, the two look deceptively similar, although the tentacles take on a spooky reminder of what you're eating. The squid cooks and curls in garlicky olive oil with a hint of chilli; diced tomato and fresh coriander are added at the end. The peas are cooked with the pasta. Everything is tossed together with a lump of butter to unite and enrich the flavours. This combination has become a favourite in my house. Surprisingly delicious cold, it is a very good dish to make for a picnic or the lunch box.

500g small, prepared squid
5 vine tomatoes
400g messicani or campanelle pasta
300g frozen petits pois
large knob of butter
1 bird's eye red chilli
1 large garlic clove
3 tablespoons olive oil
50g bunch of coriander
salt and freshly ground black pepper

If the squid is frozen, slip it into a bowl of cold water and leave for about 20 minutes to defrost. Remove the tentacles from inside the sacs. Quarter the sacs lengthways. Trim the tentacles to remove the hard 'beak'.

Boil the kettle. Pour boiling water over the tomatoes in a bowl and count to 30. Drain, splashing with cold water, cut out the core, quarter and peel the tomatoes. Place a sieve over a bowl and scrape the seeds into the sieve. Dice the flesh. Crush the pip debris with the back of a spoon into the bowl. Add the flesh to the juice in the bowl.

Cook the pasta al dente according to the packet instructions in plenty of boiling salted water, adding the peas 5 minutes before the end of cooking. Drain and return to the pan with the butter. Toss and keep warm.

Trim and split the chilli, scrape away the seeds and slice into batons, then into tiny dice. Crack the garlic with your fist, flake away the skin, chop, then crush to a paste with a pinch of salt. Heat the oil in a spacious frying/sauté pan. Stir in the garlic and add the chilli and squid, tossing continually as the pieces curl and the tentacles kick. Add the tomatoes and their liquid and let everything bubble up. Mix the pasta and peas into the squid. Chop the coriander bunch. Check the seasoning and add the chopped coriander. Mix and serve.

BLACK RISOTTO

SERVES 4 | **PREP** 35 MINUTES | **COOK** 45 MINUTES

Black risotto is a Croatian speciality made with octopus or squid and its ink. It varies according to the cook but the best, I think, includes tomato and hard cheese, giving the risotto sweet piquancy and a creamy richness. I make it with squid and a couple of sachets of cuttlefish ink from my fishmonger. Last time I made it he'd just taken delivery of a huge box of freshly picked samphire and I couldn't resist buying rather a lot. After a 15-minute soak in boiling water, it made the perfect garnish for this dramatic, but forgiving, risotto.

2 medium onions
2 tablespoons olive oil
15g butter
2 garlic cloves
200g ripe tomatoes
500g prepared squid
150g samphire, optional
350g Arborio rice
250ml dry white wine
2 × 4g sachets *nero di seppia* (cuttlefish ink)
½ chicken stock cube
2 tablespoons freshly grated Parmesan cheese plus extra to serve
2 tablespoons chopped flat leaf parsley
salt and freshly ground black pepper

Boil the kettle. Trim, halve and finely chop the onions. Soften gently, stirring occasionally, in the oil and butter in a spacious frying/sauté pan.

Keeping separate piles, peel, finely chop and crush the garlic to a paste with a pinch of salt. Cut the core out of the tomatoes in a pointed plug shape, then finely chop or blitz in a food processor into passata. Slice the squid into small stamp-sized pieces. Halve or quarter the (large) tentacles. Pour boiling water over the samphire, if using, and leave, covered.

Stir the garlic into the softened onion and a few minutes later add the squid. Cook gently, stirring often, for about 15 minutes until very juicy and tender. Stir in the rice, then add the wine. Simmer for 5 minutes, then add the tomatoes and season with salt and pepper.

Dissolve the ink and stock cube in 750ml water from the kettle and add to the pan in one hit. Stir briskly, then occasionally as the rice soaks up the black liquid. Stir in extra water – 300–500ml – as required for creamy rice with a bite at the centre; about 20–25 minutes. Remove from the heat, stir in the grated Parmesan, cover and leave for 10 minutes before serving with the drained samphire, if using, parsley and extra Parmesan.

GINGER, CHILLI AND CORIANDER MUSSELS

SERVES 2 | **PREP** 30 MINUTES | **COOK** 15 MINUTES

This variation on *Moules Marinière* goes in a South East Asian direction, adding chilli and ginger to the onion and creamed coconut instead of white wine for the liquor to help steam open the mussels, and the almost soapy tang of coriander replaces the grassy snap of parsley. How much chilli you add is a matter of taste; the coconut softens the hit but it is hardly cooked, so watch out. The mussels look very pretty flecked with green and the soup at the end is glorious.

1kg cleaned mussels
1 small onion
1 garlic clove
1 small red bird's eye chilli
20g fresh root ginger
1 tablespoon groundnut or
   other flavourless oil
2 spring onions
50g coriander
160ml can creamed coconut

Check over the mussels, discarding any that are cracked or don't close when given a sharp tap.

Peel and finely chop the onion and garlic. Split the chilli lengthways, scrape away the seeds, slice into batons and finely chop. You will need a scant half teaspoonful for a hint of heat, more if you like it hot. Peel the ginger and slice into wafer-thin scraps. Heat the oil in a large, lidded pan, stir in the onion, chilli, ginger and garlic and allow to soften gently.

Meanwhile, trim and finely slice the spring onions. Holding the coriander in its bunch, slice finely, working up from the stalk end. Add the spring onion, stalk end of the coriander bunch and the coconut to the pot.

Increase the heat as high as possible, stir as the coconut heats up, then add the mussels. Stir a few times, cover and cook, shaking the pan a few times to encourage even cooking, for 3–4 minutes until all the mussels have opened. Tip into a warmed bowl and add the remaining coriander, stir once and serve.

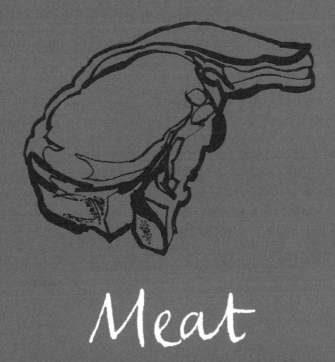

Meat

I'm increasingly contrary when it comes to buying and cooking meat. I want the best but can't always afford a fine organic, free-range chicken, thick fillet steak or joint of heritage pork, so I shop around for lesser-known cuts, like pig cheeks, skirt steak, lamb neck and chicken wings. I'm a champion of the so-called fifth quarter, or offal, to use its less attractive name. I'm particularly keen on the surprising versatility of chicken livers and lambs' kidneys. I like making a little meat go a long way and could probably fill a whole book with meatball recipes, several of which you'll find here. I'm also an aficionado of turning meaty sausages into risotto and cassoulet, matching them with gnocchi as well as mash. Most of the recipes in this section are quick, but others simmer away on the back burner while you get on with something else.

CHICKEN

Chicken is without a doubt our favourite after-work dinner, being easy to cook and endlessly versatile. I see no point in going into the pros and cons of organic and free-range as opposed to fast-grown birds, but will highlight a few points. Outdoor-reared, slow-growing birds have larger joints, the meat is denser and the flavour more pronounced. The price is noticeably higher. I favour thigh over breast, because it is muscly meat with a bouncy texture. Breast can end up stringy, dry and tasteless. Depending on what I'm cooking, I buy fillets – boned and skinned – or complete thighs. If I butcher the pieces myself, I save the bones and freeze them, building up my supply until I have enough to make stock. I also save cooked chicken bones and carcasses (adding leek trimmings, parsley stalks and leftover onion).

Spring chicken, or poussin, is a useful mid-week roast chicken for two, but leftover roast chicken often inspires my recipes. I also often buy cooked chicken for instant suppers; these gratins, pies, salads, fricassees, curries and rice dishes are my stock in trade. Minced chicken is also worth seeking out for meatballs, patties and burgers.

CHICKEN WITH FIGS IN RED WINE
SERVES 4 | **PREP** 25 MINUTES | **COOK** 1 HOUR 10 MINUTES

Figs grow wild with abandon in fields that edge the beach at Thanos, a favourite spot on the Greek island of Lemnos. Many end up in variations on this one-pot baked chicken dish. The chicken is imbued with figgy wine juices and buttery soft garlic. My recipe owes a debt to Susie Jacobs' *Recipes From A Greek Island*, one of my favourite books for real Greek cooking.

1 large whole chicken or
   4 chicken legs
1 heaped teaspoon ground
   coriander
1 teaspoon ground cumin
¼ teaspoon cayenne pepper
1 head of garlic
2 bay leaves
12 figs
250ml red wine
1 lemon
few flat leaf parsley sprigs
salt and freshly ground
   black pepper

Preheat the oven to 200°C, Gas Mark 6.

Cut the whole chicken into portions or joint the legs and remove skin. Mix the coriander, cumin and cayenne with a generous seasoning of salt and pepper and rub into the chicken pieces. Place in a heavy roasting dish.

Split the head of garlic and peel each clove, then tuck the cloves between the chicken with the bay leaves and figs. Pour over the red wine to submerge. Cover and cook in the oven for 45 minutes.

Grate the zest of the lemon over the top, add the lemon juice, turn the chicken, re-cover and cook for a further 15–25 minutes until garlic and chicken are thoroughly cooked. Sprinkle with the finely chopped parsley just before serving. This reheats well – I like it with new potatoes and green beans, while Ms Jacobs recommends saffron rice.

JON LEYNE'S LIME AND LEMON GRASS CHICKEN

SERVES 4 | **PREP** 15 MINUTES | **COOK** 40 MINUTES

Mishal Husain's moving tribute to colleague Jon Leyne on Radio 4 had me scribbling a shopping list. Her description of Jon's lime and lemon grass chicken, its citrusy brown broth with a mild chilli, gingery cumin tang, sounded so easy to make and so delicious, it would be criminal not to pass on the recipe. It's not the most beautiful dish, but the rice you need to serve with it will soak up the juices and taste unbelievably good.

800g skinned chicken
 thigh fillets
1 tablespoon sesame oil
2 teaspoons lemon zest
2 red chillies
2 lemon grass stalks
2 kaffir lime leaves, fresh
 or dried
2 teaspoons grated fresh
 root galangal or ginger
2 teaspoons ground cumin
1 tablespoon brown sugar
1 tablespoon lime juice
1 teaspoon tamarind paste
250ml coconut cream
250ml chicken stock
250g basmati rice

Open out the chicken fillets and slice in half through the width. Brown the pieces in batches in the hot sesame oil in a spacious pan that can accommodate the entire dish, transferring to a plate as you go.

Stir all the other ingredients, except the coconut, stock and rice, into the pan and cook for 2 minutes. Return the chicken and add the coconut cream and stock. Simmer, stirring a few times, for 30 minutes.

Meanwhile, rinse the rice under cold water until the water runs clean. Place in a pan with a good-fitting lid and cover with 375ml cold water. Bring to the boil and then immediately reduce the heat to very low. Cover and cook for 10 minutes. Turn off the heat and leave covered – do not remove the lid – for 10 minutes for the rice to finish cooking in the steam. Fork up the rice before serving.

Serve the chicken with the cooked basmati rice.

THAI MANGO CHICKEN SALAD

SERVES 4 | **PREP** 20 MINUTES | **COOK** 20 MINUTES

This is a vibrant, crisp, healthy salad with a pungent, sweet-sour chilli-flecked dressing. The crunch comes from lightly cooked green beans, finely sliced celery heart and cucumber, with sweet, fruity mango making a slippery, soft contrast. Juicy griddled chicken is tossed in at the last moment with mint and Thai basil or coriander to turn this colourful salad into a main dish.

200g green beans
2 medium red onions
1–2 red bird's eye chillies, deseeded
1 celery heart
½ cucumber
6–8 skinned chicken thigh fillets
1 tablespoon vegetable oil
1 teaspoon sugar
3 tablespoons Thai fish sauce (nam pla)
1 tablespoon soy or oyster sauce
2 limes
1 ripe mango
15g Thai basil or coriander
15g mint
salt

Boil the kettle. Halve the trimmed beans. Boil in salted water for 2 minutes. Scoop out of the pan into a colander. Splash with cold water.

Meanwhile, halve, peel and very finely slice the onions. Place in a bowl and just cover with boiling water. Leave for 10 minutes. Drain. Finely chop the chillies. Finely slice the celery bundle, wash and shake dry. Peel the cucumber, halve lengthways, scrape out the seeds and slice into skinny half-moons.

Place a griddle over a medium heat. When very hot, lay the chicken, oiled and salted, skin-side down, on the griddle. Cook without moving for 5 minutes, turn and cook for a further 5 minutes, juggling thereafter to cook thoroughly. Rest for 5 minutes.

Dissolve the sugar in the fish sauce, then stir in the soy or oyster sauce and lime juice. Add the onion and chilli. Peel the mango and cut into chunky slices, discarding the stone. Chop the basil or coriander and mint leaves. Mix the celery, cucumber and beans into the dressing. Add the herbs and chunky-cut chicken. Toss and eat.

CHICKEN CHASSEUR

SERVES 4 | **PREP** 30 MINUTES | **COOK** 1 HOUR

It was Judy Murray's confession on Desert Island Discs that she ate Chicken Chasseur with chips every night when she read French and Business Studies at Edinburgh University that had me scribbling a shopping list. Made properly, this old favourite is really, really good. My recipe is adapted from *The Prawn Cocktail Years* written with Simon Hopkinson. Serve with chips or new potatoes.

8 skinned chicken thigh fillets
plain flour for dusting
6 shallots, about 150g
200g button mushrooms
15g butter
1 tablespoon vegetable oil
400ml dry white wine

Roll the chicken thighs in flour seasoned generously with salt and pepper. Peel and finely chop the shallots. Wipe and quarter the mushrooms.

Heat the butter and oil in a roomy, heavy-based casserole dish and gently brown the chicken. Remove to a plate. Add the shallots to the pan and sweat until golden before adding the mushrooms. Cook for 5 minutes, stirring once or twice, and add the wine. Stir as it comes up to the boil, then return the chicken with the thyme and bay leaf. Establish a gentle simmer,

4 thyme sprigs
1 bay leaf
4 tomatoes
squeeze of lemon juice
2 tablespoons finely chopped
 flat leaf parsley
salt and freshly ground
 black pepper

cover the pan and cook for 10 minutes. Remove the lid and cook for about 35 minutes until the sauce reduces slightly and turns syrupy.

Meanwhile, place the tomatoes in a bowl and cover with boiling water. Count to 30, drain, splash to cool, cut out the core in a pointed plug shape, quarter, peel, deseed and dice.

Remove the thyme and bay from the dish and add the lemon juice and salt and pepper to taste. Mix in the tomatoes and cook for 5 more minutes. Stir in the parsley and serve.

GREEN PEA CHICKEN

SERVES 4 | **PREP** 20 MINUTES | **COOK** 30 MINUTES

You are never far from something good to eat if there is a bag of peas in the freezer. When I say peas, I actually mean petits pois. They always deliver the sweetness of young peas and never disappoint as ordinary frozen peas often do. Whenever inspiration is flagging or I'm stuck for a quick cooking solution, it's frozen petits pois that often come to the rescue. Take this simple twist on what was heading towards a relatively ordinary stewy sort of chicken supper. It started, as so many dishes do, by softening onion in butter, but this time I used finely sliced spring onion with lemon zest. In went the chicken, and as it gently cooked in the buttery juices, the aromas smelt increasingly of peas. In a flash of inspiration, frozen peas and spinach were transformed into a bumpy bright green purée to stir into the chicken. It looked stunning and tasted fresh and spring-like, delicious with new potatoes.

165g spring onions
1 small lemon
50g butter
400g skinned chicken
 thigh fillets
200ml chicken stock
300g frozen petits pois
100g young spinach
1 teaspoon mint sauce
salt and freshly ground
 black pepper

Trim and finely slice the spring onions, including as much green as possible. Remove the zest from half the lemon and finely chop. Melt the butter in a spacious sauté pan over a medium–low heat and stir in the onion and lemon zest. Season with salt and pepper, cover and cook gently, stirring once or twice, for 5–6 minutes to soften.

Cut the chicken into kebab-sized pieces. Stir the chicken into the wilted onion, turning as the pieces change colour, adjusting the heat so that the chicken cooks gently and remains juicy.

Bring the stock to the boil in a medium pan and add the peas. Boil for 2–3 minutes, then crush the spinach under the liquid and cook for a further minute or so until the spinach wilts. Add the mint sauce. Liquidize with a hand held electric blender or tip into a food processor and blitz briefly so that the mixture has a bumpy texture rather than working to a smooth purée. Stir into the chicken, taste and season with salt and pepper. Warm through and serve.

GRIDDLED CHICKEN, ROAST AUBERGINE AND YOGHURT

SERVES 2 | **PREP** 20 MINUTES | **COOK** 45 MINUTES

I love pile-up food. This translates as layers of food, each cooked separately, resulting in a pile of different textures, combining creamy with crunchy, hot with cold. Chicken is often the starting point because it's friendly to so many different flavours. Here I've beaten thigh fillets into little escalopes and left them in a simple lemon juice and olive oil marinade while aubergines and tomatoes are roasted soft and squashy. The chicken is griddled crusty on the outside but juicy and tender within. All these ingredients are piled haphazardly in the middle of the dinner plates, then topped with garlicky, lemony Greek yoghurt dressing. The finale is a sprinkling of toasted pine nuts and grassy flat leaf parsley. It's a great way of bringing excitement to a mid-week chicken supper; the veg and yoghurt, even chicken, could be prepared in advance.

2 ripe vine tomatoes
3 tablespoons olive oil
4 skinned chicken thigh fillets
1 lemon
2 medium aubergines
1 garlic clove
300g natural yoghurt (I like
   sheep's milk yoghurt)
2 tablespoons toasted
   pine nuts
1 tablespoon chopped
   flat leaf parsley
Maldon sea salt

Preheat the oven to 180°C, Gas Mark 4. Halve the tomatoes round their middles. Place on a foil-lined shallow baking tray. Smear the cut surfaces with a little of the olive oil and place on the bottom shelf in the oven before it comes up to temperature.

Open out the chicken pieces, cut into 3 roughly equal pieces and place, with space between them, on a sheet of clingfilm approximately 30cm square. Cover with a second sheet. Use a rolling pin or similar to gently but firmly bash all over to flatten and almost double in size.

Halve the lemon. Remove the top piece of clingfilm from the chicken and squeeze half the lemon over. Splash with 1 tablespoon olive oil. Turn to smear both sides. Return the second sheet of clingfilm.

Trim and quarter the aubergines lengthways, then arrange on a second shallow baking tray. When the oven comes up to temperature, smear the cut surfaces with 1 tablespoon olive oil and place the tray on the top shelf. Bake for 35 minutes or until the aubergine pieces are soft to the prod.

Crack the garlic and flake away the skin, then chop and crush to a paste. Stir it into the yoghurt with a squeeze of lemon and the remaining oil.

Heat a griddle for several minutes until very hot. Salt half the chicken on one side. Press, salt-side down, onto the hot griddle and cook for 3–4 minutes to make a crusty seal. Turn and repeat once or twice again until cooked through. Keep warm while you cook the second batch. Remove the tomatoes from the oven at the last minute, by which time they should be squashy and juicy.

Serve the chicken interlaced with aubergine and tomato, topped with the yoghurt, pine nuts and parsley.

CHICKEN CHILLI WITH CHOCOLATE

SERVES 4 | **PREP** 35 MINUTES | **COOK** 50 MINUTES

Chili con carne suits being made with chicken, although it's a faff to chop it into small pieces. It speeds up the cooking while a square or two of dark chocolate unites the sauce, resulting in a silky rich texture. Serve over rice, adding the usual garnish of soured cream plus diced or sliced avocado, a squeeze of lime, chopped coriander and a dribble of sweet chilli sauce.

75g rashers streaky bacon

2 medium onions

2 tablespoons olive oil

1 bay leaf

500g skinned chicken
   thigh fillets

1 small lemon

½ teaspoon dried oregano

1 teaspoon ground cumin

1 teaspoon cayenne pepper

1 teaspoon plain flour

1 tablespoon tomato purée

400ml chicken stock

200ml red wine

25g dark chocolate (minimum
   70% cocoa solids)

400g can haricot beans

salt

To serve

4 tablespoons soured cream

2 avocados

1 lime

1 tablespoon chopped
   coriander

1 tablespoon Thai sweet
   chilli sauce

Chop the bacon into small pieces. Peel and finely chop the onions. Stir both into the hot olive oil in a spacious, heavy-based pan with the bay. Cook, stirring often, for 15 minutes.

Cut the chicken into skinny ribbons and then into 5mm cubes. Zest half the lemon in small scraps. Scoop the contents of the pan into a sieve, draining the oil and juices back into the pan. Add the chicken and quickly brown. Add the oregano, cumin, cayenne, flour and ½ teaspoon salt whilst stirring briskly. Add the lemon zest and all the juice, tomato purée, stock and wine. Return the drained onion to the pan, stir in the chocolate and simmer gently, covered, giving the odd stir, for 20 minutes.

Taste and adjust the seasoning. Stir in the drained beans. Reheat now, later or tomorrow and serve topped with the soured cream, stoned, peeled and diced avocados, lime juice, coriander and chilli sauce.

HARISSA CHICKEN WINGS WITH BLACK VENUS RICE

SERVES 4 | **PREP** 15 MINUTES, PLUS MARINATING | **COOK** 35 MINUTES

I love gnawing on crusty roast chicken wings and these are briefly marinated in spicy harissa and yoghurt. They go extremely well and look very enticing arranged around a platter piled with black rice. The latter glistens gloriously when tossed with a dressing of balsamic vinegar and olive oil, its nutty grains enhanced by peas and succulent fillets of sun-drenched tomatoes. Quick, easy and impressive.

1 tablespoon rose harissa
2 tablespoons thick
   natural yoghurt
3 tablespoons olive oil
25–30 trimmed chicken wings
300g Biona Black Venus Rice
   or other black rice
200ml frozen petits pois
190g sun-drenched tomatoes
   in oil
1 tablespoon balsamic
   vinegar
1 lemon
salt

Mix together the harissa, yoghurt and 1 tablespoon of the olive oil in a mixing bowl. Add the chicken wings, stirring to coat thoroughly. Cover with clingfilm and chill for at least 15 minutes and up to several hours.

To cook, preheat the oven to 220°C, Gas Mark 7. Line a shallow roasting tin/tins with foil. Lay out the wings and roast for 15 minutes. Carefully drain off the juices and turn the pieces, then return to the oven for a further 15 minutes until very crusty.

Meanwhile, rinse the rice and place in a pan with 600ml water. Bring to the boil, reduce the heat to low, cover and cook for 35 minutes. Leave to absorb any remaining water and finish cooking in the steam.

Cook the peas in boiling salted water until tender. Drain.

Scoop the tomatoes out of the oil and cut the pieces in half. Mix the balsamic and remaining olive oil into the rice, then fold in the peas and tomatoes. Pile onto a platter and edge with the chicken wings and the lemon, cut into wedges.

ORANGE AND APRICOT CHICKEN PILAF

SERVES 3–4 | **PREP** 20 MINUTES, PLUS MARINATING | **COOK** 30 MINUTES

Pilaf is a forgiving dish and this one, made with the remains of a roast chicken, is a feast of textures and flavours. The chicken is marinated with marmalade and orange juice while the rice cooks with onion, orange zest, chilli flakes, fennel seed and cardamom. Sweet and tangy, spicy with bursts of aniseed and cardamom, serve it with a dribble of mango chutney. I have also made this with pheasant and it is a dish to remember when you are facing leftover Christmas turkey.

250–400g cooked chicken
1 orange
1 tablespoon marmalade
1 medium onion
8 soft dried apricots
25g whole blanched almonds
1½ tablespoons groundnut oil
6 green cardamom pods
¼ teaspoon fennel seeds

Tear the chicken into bite-sized pieces. Remove the orange zest with a fine grater. Squeeze the juice into a bowl and stir in the marmalade. Add the chicken, turning to thoroughly smear. Cover and chill for a minimum of 20 minutes.

Halve, peel and finely chop the onion. Quarter the apricots. Stir-fry the almonds in ½ tablespoon of the oil in a spacious, lidded frying/sauté pan until evenly golden. Tip onto a fold of kitchen paper. Add the remaining oil and onion. Cook, stirring often, with a pinch of salt until slippery soft and lightly coloured.

¼ teaspoon chilli powder
200g basmati rice
350ml chicken stock
salt

Extract the cardamom seeds and bash using a pestle and mortar or something heavy to pulverize, add the fennel seeds, bash again and add to the onion with the chilli. Rinse the rice under cold water until the water runs clean, then stir it in with the orange zest and apricots, then add the stock. Bring to the boil, reduce the heat to very low, cover and cook for 10 minutes. Leave, still covered, off the heat for 10 minutes.

Fold in the chicken and orange mix and the almonds. Leave, covered, for 5 minutes before serving.

MOMO WITH WATERCRESS RAITA
SERVES 4 | **PREP** 30 MINUTES, PLUS CHILLING | **COOK** 10 MINUTES

Momo are highly spiced Nepali meatballs steamed in thin pastry wrappers. I used Chinese dim sum wrappers for mine, but the little meatballs are healthier and just as good without the wrapper. I served them with garlicky watercress and cherry tomato raita, but other options would be a chilli-hot roast tomato sauce, or piled over a crisp salad with fresh mint and a Thai-style dressing made with equal quantities of Thai fish sauce (nam pla) and lime juice and a splash of sweet chilli sauce.

500g minced chicken
bunch of spring onions
2 large garlic cloves
30g fresh root ginger
½ teaspoon freshly grated
    nutmeg
½ teaspoon turmeric
2 teaspoons ground cumin
½ teaspoon cayenne pepper
    plus extra for garnishing
2½ tablespoons groundnut oil
25g coriander
180g packet dim sum/wanton
    wrappers, optional

For the watercress raita
1 garlic clove
450g Greek yoghurt
1 tablespoon lemon juice
1 tablespoon olive oil
50g watercress
8 cherry tomatoes

Spread the mince out in a mixing bowl. Finely chop the trimmed spring onions and peeled garlic. Peel and grate the ginger. Scatter the onion, garlic and ginger over the mince with the nutmeg, turmeric, cumin, cayenne, 1½ tablespoons of the groundnut oil and the finely chopped coriander. Mulch together, working as if making dough. Cover and chill for 30 minutes–1 hour.

Make the raita by peeling and crushing the garlic to a paste, then beating it into the yoghurt with the lemon juice and olive oil. Chop the watercress, then fold into the yoghurt with the quartered tomatoes. Garnish with cayenne.

Quarter the sticky momo mix and, with wet hands, make 10 meatballs from each quarter. If using wrappers, place one on a flat hand, add a meatball, run a wet finger round the rim, making a 1-cm damp border, and bring all sides to the centre, pinch together and press down to seal.

Brush a steamer with the remaining oil and steam the wrapped or unwrapped meatballs in 2 batches, covered, for 10 minutes. Serve with the raita.

LIME PICKLE CHICKEN CURRY WITH POTATOES AND SPINACH AND CUCUMBER RAITA

SERVES 4 | **PREP** 20 MINUTES | **COOK** 35 MINUTES

Indian lime pickle is always fearsomely hot and can be used like a cook-in sauce to conjure a very passable faux curry. This home-alone supper was so quick and easy, I scaled up the ingredients and made it again for friends. This time I served it with warm Indian bread to scoop up the golden sauce and made cucumber raita with creamy yoghurt to soften the heat and occasional bursts of bitter lime peel.

750g new potatoes
2 medium onions
2 tablespoons vegetable oil
8 skinned chicken thigh fillets
4 heaped dessertspoons
  lime pickle
200g young spinach
1 lime
salt

For the cucumber raita
1 garlic clove
450g Greek yoghurt
1 tablespoon lemon juice
1 tablespoon olive oil
½ cucumber
1 tomato
pinch of cayenne pepper

Scrape the potatoes. Leave small ones whole, halve medium ones and chunk large ones. Boil in salted water until tender. Drain.

Halve and peel the onions, then slice down the halves, making skinny half-moons. Heat the oil in a spacious frying/sauté pan over a medium heat and toss the onions constantly for about 5 minutes to wilt slightly. Reduce the heat and leave to soften while you slice across the width of the chicken fillets into chunky strips.

Stir the chicken into the onions and stir-fry briskly until all the pieces change colour. Reduce the heat again and stir in the pickle and 150ml water. Simmer, stirring often, for about 15 minutes until the curry is thick and creamy, adding extra water if dry.

Meanwhile, make the raita by crushing the garlic to a paste, then beating it into the yoghurt with the lemon juice and olive oil. Peel and split the cucumber and use a teaspoon to remove the seeds. Chop into small dice. Chop the tomato. Stir both into the yoghurt. Garnish with cayenne pepper.

Fold the potatoes into the curry, then the spinach, stirring until the potatoes are covered in sauce and the spinach wilted. Season to taste with salt and lime juice. Eat now with the raita or reheat later.

ROAST CHICKEN LEGS WITH PEA PURÉE AND ASPARAGUS

SERVES 4 | **PREP** 15 MINUTES | **COOK** 40 MINUTES

This way of fast-roasting chicken joints, either whole legs, thighs or drumsticks, is a favourite with me. The pieces are oiled and lavishly dusted with Maldon sea salt flakes, ending up with very crisp skin and moist, juicy flesh. Sometimes I lay the joints over rosemary or thyme or slices of lemon. This works particularly well with lemony mashed potato or hummus, but no extra flavours are needed with creamy pea purée and lightly cooked English asparagus. This simple feast is easy to scale up or down and looks as good as it tastes.

400g British asparagus
2 tablespoons olive oil
4 chicken legs
Maldon sea salt, to taste
300g frozen petits pois
1 tablespoon crème fraîche,
    thick yoghurt, mascarpone
    or creamy goats' cheese
salt

Preheat the oven to 220°C, Gas Mark 7. Prepare the asparagus by snapping off the woody ends or trimming then peeling the ends with a potato peeler.

Lavishly oil the chicken legs and line up, skin-side uppermost, in a small roasting tin. Leave a little space between them. Season the skin with Maldon salt. Roast for 40 minutes. Rest while you complete the recipe.

Boil a full kettle. Half-fill a spacious pan with kettle water, add salt and boil the peas until tender. Scoop into a food processor. Re-boil the water, add the asparagus and boil for 2–4 minutes, depending on the fatness of the stalks; you want them just tender to the point of a knife. Scoop into a colander. Add 1 tablespoon of the asparagus cooking water and crème fraîche, yoghurt, mascarpone or goats' cheese to the peas and blitz to make a smooth purée. Serve the chicken next to the purée topped with the asparagus.

PORK, BACON AND HAM

I eat a lot of minced pork, rarely on its own, usually Chinese-style mixed with chicken or prawns. For meatballs it needs help to avoid being dry but, like all pork, can take any flavour you care to throw at it. Occasionally I might treat myself to a pork chop, simply grilled or griddled, the curl of fatty skin that runs down the side snagged to avoid the chop buckling as it cooks. I like it with apple or rhubarb sauce. Like most people, I'm addicted to belly pork, particularly the big fat rashers that look like Desperate Dan's breakfast. Pig cheeks are another economical cut that is perfect for stews. Aptly named tenderloin or pork fillet is the lean, tender fillet steak of the pig. It cooks quickly or very slowly; in between it will be tough and dull, so versatile for kebabs, stews or flash-fry dishes.

Gammon steaks are perfect for comforting suppers, quickly fried or grilled, with a creamy parsley sauce, butter-tossed carrots and mash, or with a white onion sauce, the chopped onions softened in water, and plenty of seasoning, then liquidized with a splash of cream. I like this combination with boiled potatoes crushed into chopped garlic, softened in olive oil, mixed with a handful of watercress that wilts against the hot potatoes. Another good thing to serve with a grilled or fried gammon steak is a mound of shredded sprouts, stir-fried with quite a lot of nutmeg, carved in chunky scraps with a small, sharp knife.

A bacon sarnie, upgraded into a BLT, is a favourite home-alone supper and so are variations on carbonara made with add-on peas or broad beans. A pack of decent ham and another of Parma or Serrano ham have instant supper written all over them.

TERIYAKI PORK MEATBALLS, RICE AND WILTED PAK CHOI

SERVES 4 | **PREP** 20 MINUTES | **COOK** 30 MINUTES

Seasoning meatballs with gingery, soy-flavoured teriyaki sauce is a simple but very effective idea. If you're short on time, opting for ready-made sauce speeds things up. The meatballs remain light and delicate by adding breadcrumbs and beaten egg. I've specified trendy panko breadcrumbs, but I tend to make my own, drying the bread first in the oven for about 10 minutes at 150°C, Gas Mark 2, then blitzing in the food processor. I've made these meatballs twice lately, the first time, for a meal in a hurry, piled into a quickly toasted tortilla fold with pan-fried spring onions, the latter wilted until floppy and sweet. This way, with rice and stir-fried pak choi with a hint of chilli in the oil, makes a more traditional meal.

For the teriyaki sauce
15g fresh root ginger
4 tablespoons soy sauce
4 tablespoons mirin
1 tablespoon sake, vodka
    or gin
1 teaspoon sugar or
    3 tablespoons ready-made
    teriyaki sauce

For the meatballs, pak choi and rice
250g basmati rice
500g pak choi
500g minced pork
50g panko breadcrumbs or
    50g breadcrumbs made
    with oven-dried white
    bread (see introduction)
2 shallots, about 80g
4 tablespoons groundnut oil
1 egg
½ teaspoon dried chilli flakes

Begin with the teriyaki sauce. Peel and finely grate the ginger into a small pan. Add all the other ingredients and simmer gently, swirling the pan until the sugar dissolves, until reduced to about 3 tablespoons. Leave to cool and thicken.

Rinse the rice until the water runs clean, place in a lidded pan with 375ml water and bring to the boil. Immediately reduce the heat to very low, clamp on the lid and cook for 10 minutes. Turn off the heat and leave, uncovered, for 10 minutes.

Separate the pak choi leaves and halve lengthways. Crumble the pork into a mixing bowl and scatter the crumbs over the top.

Peel and finely chop the shallots. Soften gently in 1 tablespoon of the oil in a frying pan. Scatter over the meat and add the cooled teriyaki sauce and beaten egg. Mix thoroughly with a fork. Pinch off sufficient mix to form into walnut-sized balls, aiming for at least 32. Wipe out the frying pan, add 2 tablespoons oil and gently fry the balls, in batches, until crusty and cooked through.

Heat the remaining oil in a wok, swirling it round the pan, then add the pak choi, tossing constantly to wilt, adding the chilli after a couple of minutes. Fork up the rice and serve topped with the wilted pak choi and meatballs.

THAI-STYLE MEATLOAF

SERVES 8 | **PREP** 25 MINUTES | **COOK** 1 HOUR 10 MINUTES

A solve-all, feed-the-five-thousand dish that can be served hot, sliced in the dish, or cooled, covered and chilled to eat later or tomorrow. Slice over rice noodles, use for Thai salads or noodle dishes or pile into wraps or on toast. Very yum, very useful.

2 medium onions
3 tablespoons groundnut oil
2 garlic cloves
2 small red chillies, deseeded
30g fresh root ginger
1 small lemon
90g bunch of coriander
50g couscous
2 eggs
1 tablespoon Thai fish sauce
   (nam pla)
500g minced chicken
500g minced pork
salt

Preheat the oven to 180°C, Gas Mark 4. Halve, peel and finely chop the onions. Soften in 2 tablespoons of the oil in a spacious sauté pan.

Peel, finely chop and crush the garlic to a paste with a pinch of salt. Finely chop the chillies. Peel and grate the ginger. Zest half the lemon. Stir the garlic, chillies, ginger and lemon into the slippery, soft onions. Stir-fry for a couple of minutes.

Boil the kettle. Starting at the stalk end, finely chop the coriander. Add the stalks to the pan, stirring until they wilt before turning off the heat. Pour 125ml boiling water over the couscous, cover and leave for 5 minutes to hydrate. Fork up to loosen the grains.

Whisk the eggs in a mixing bowl with the fish sauce. Add the chicken and pork, the onion mixture, hydrated couscous and the rest of the coriander. Mix and mulch with your hands.

Grease a 1-litre gratin dish with half the remaining oil. Pat the mixture into the dish, making a slight mound. Smear with the remaining oil. Drape with a piece of baking parchment. Cook in the oven for 1 hour.

PORKY PIE

SERVES 4 | **PREP** 30 MINUTES | **COOK** 55 MINUTES

Not a fib, but French-style shepherd's pie using minced pork (preferably Gloucester Old Spot) instead of lamb. The distinguishing mashed potato sandwich is laced with apple, while a buttery, cheesy crumb coating should result in a crusty layer all over the pie. The pork filling is cooked in milk flavoured with tarragon, bacon and onion.

800g floury potatoes
1 small Bramley cooking
   apple, about 260g
50g butter
3 medium onions
1 tablespoon sunflower oil
4 rashers smoked streaky
   bacon
500g decent minced pork
1 dessertspoon plain flour
150ml milk

Peel, chunk, rinse and boil the potatoes in salted water until tender. Scoop into a bowl, leaving 4 tablespoons cooking water in the pan. Add the quartered, cored, peeled and chunked apples. Cover and boil for 5–8 minutes until soft. Return the potatoes to the pan, through a mouli-legume, or mash, with 40g of the butter, beating to disperse the apple.

Halve, peel and finely chop the onions. Soften them, stirring often, in the hot oil in a spacious frying/sauté pan for about 10 minutes until glossy but hardly coloured.

Chop the bacon, increase the heat slightly, add to onions and fry until crusty, then brown the pork with the onion. Stir in the flour and add the milk, stirring until thick and creamy. Stir in the tarragon and salt and pepper to taste.

1 tablespoon chopped
  tarragon
30g fresh white breadcrumbs
20g finely grated Parmesan
  cheese
salt and freshly ground
  black pepper

Preheat the oven to 190°C, Gas Mark 5. Smear a 1.5-litre gratin dish with the remaining butter. Mix the crumbs and cheese, add half to dish and swirl to encourage it to stick to the butter. Add half the mash, smooth, add the meat, smooth, and finish with the mash. Fork the surface and add the remaining crumbs. Bake for 30 minutes or until crusty.

MARMALADE PORK MEATBALLS WITH TOMATO AND ORANGE SAUCE
SERVES 4–6 | **PREP** 25 MINUTES | **COOK** 35 MINUTES

Spicy pork sausages and bitter-sweet, chunky-cut Seville orange marmalade is a particularly good combination. It inspired these herby meatballs, roasted briefly, then finished in a fresh orange and tomato sauce. I turned the combo into a faux risotto and served it with cooked giant couscous (Sardinian fregola). Alternatively, serve over pasta or rice.

2 medium onions
1½ tablespoons olive oil
25g fresh breadcrumbs
2 tablespoons soured cream
500g minced pork
2 teaspoons dried sage
2 tablespoons Seville orange
  marmalade
10g flat leaf parsley
600g tomatoes
25g butter
1 juicing orange
sugar, to taste
salt and freshly ground
  black pepper
giant couscous, rice or pasta,
  to serve

Halve, peel and finely chop the onions. Soften in 1 tablespoon of the olive oil in a spacious frying pan with a pinch of salt.

Stir the crumbs into the cream in a cup. Place the pork in a mixing bowl. Season with salt and pepper. Scatter the sage over the meat and add the marmalade. Chop the parsley leaves and add half. Add the creamy crumbs and softened onion. Mix thoroughly. Form into a ball and then into quarters.

Line a shallow roasting tin with foil smeared with the remaining oil. With wet hands, form 12 small balls from each quarter, rolling in your hands, transferring to the prepared tin. Chill, covered, until required.

Chop the tomatoes. Melt most of the butter in the empty frying pan, stir in the tomatoes and the juice from the orange (100ml) and simmer, stirring often, for 10–15 minutes until sauce-like. Pass through a sieve to catch pips etc, scraping under the sieve, too. Season to taste with salt and sugar. Beat in the remaining butter.

Preheat the oven to 200°C, Gas Mark 6. Roast the balls for 15 minutes. Rest for 5 minutes, then tip the balls and juices into the sauce. Reheat when ready, served with the remaining parsley.

PORK AND GREEN OLIVE EMPANADAS

MAKES 16–20 | **PREP** 30 MINUTES | **COOK** 30 MINUTES

Puff pastry is perfect for these moreish little pasties. Minced pork is given a sweet and sour note with sultanas, diced cornichons and pimento-stuffed green olives, with a hint of chilli, garlic, lemon and coriander. They are particularly good hot from the oven, eaten alone or with salad, but reheat well and make a great snack with a beer or will be appreciated in the picnic basket with a bag of cherry tomatoes.

2 medium onions

1 tablespoon olive oil

2 large garlic cloves

20 pimento-stuffed green olives, about 100g

10 cornichons

50g coriander

500g minced pork

½ chicken stock cube

1 lemon

2 tablespoons sultanas

½ teaspoon dried chilli flakes

2 tablespoons fresh white breadcrumbs

2 × 320g sheets puff pastry

1 egg

butter for greasing

salt

Halve, peel and finely dice the onions. Soften in a spacious frying/sauté pan in the oil with ½ teaspoon salt. Peel and chop the garlic, then crush to a paste with ¼ teaspoon salt. Quarter lengthways and chop the olives and cornichons. Chop the coriander.

Stir the garlic into the onions, then brown the meat. Crumble the stock cube and juice from the lemon over the top, stirring as it bubbles away. Add the sultanas and chilli and simmer, stirring, for 5–8 minutes until moist rather than wet. Stir in the olives, cornichons and coriander. Stir in the breadcrumbs (to absorb the excess fat). Spread out in a bowl/plate to cool; pop in the freezer if you're in a hurry.

Preheat the oven to 220°C, Gas Mark 7. Unfurl the pastry and cut 8 × 9cm circles from each sheet. You may be able to re-roll the offcuts and make 4 more. Paint a beaten egg border, add a spoonful of filling and press the edges to seal. Make steam holes with a fork, paint with egg and arrange on a buttered baking parchment-lined baking sheet. Bake for 15 minutes until puffed and golden.

LEMON AND PARSLEY PORK WITH BEANS

SERVES 4 | **PREP** 30 MINUTES | **COOK** 1 HOUR

Belly pork delivers strong porky flavour in stews like this. Here the porkiness is counter-balanced by lemon zest and juice, garlic, a hint of chilli and bay, creamy haricot blanc beans and grassy fresh green beans. It's a harmonious combination, the white beans thickening the juices and masses of chopped parsley taking up the slack.

As always, belly pork is fatty, so care has to be taken to strain as much out of the dish as possible. It could, if it suited your plans, be started today and finished tomorrow. That way, the solidified fat can be lifted off after 24 hours in the fridge. Potatoes, boiled or mashed, are a good accompaniment.

4 large garlic cloves
2 Spanish onions
1½ tablespoons rapeseed oil
900g belly pork joint
    or rashers
generous pinch of dried
    chilli flakes
2 lemons
2 bay leaves
500ml light chicken stock
300g green beans
80g bunch of flat leaf parsley
400g can haricot beans
salt and freshly ground
    black pepper

Peel the garlic and slice into thin rounds. Halve the onions, peel and finely slice. Heat the oil in a spacious frying/sauté pan over a medium–low heat and add the garlic, stirring until pale golden. Scoop out of the pan onto a saucer. Add the onions, increase the heat slightly and fry, tossing regularly, for 10 minutes until wilted and lightly coloured. Scoop the onions into a sieve, draining back into the pan.

Use a sharp, thin-bladed knife to remove the pork skin and its layer of fat in one slice. Cut the meat into kebab-sized chunks, trimming the excess fat. Brown the pork in batches, transferring to a lidded pan that can accommodate the entire dish.

Add the onions, chilli, garlic and finely grated lemon zest to the meat, season with salt and pepper and add the bay and juice from the lemons. Bubble up before adding the chicken stock. Establish a gentle simmer, cover the pan and cook for 45 minutes.

Top and tail and halve the green beans. Boil in salted water for 2 minutes, then drain. Finely chop the parsley leaves. When the 45 minutes is up, remove the lid, add the drained and rinsed white beans and simmer, uncovered, for 15 minutes. Taste and adjust the seasoning before stirring in the parsley and green beans.

PORK CHOPS WITH RHUBARB

SERVES 2 | **PREP** 20 MINUTES | **COOK** 25 MINUTES, PLUS RESTING

The tart, fresh flavour of rhubarb is a surprisingly good partner for pork. In this quick and simple dish, the chops are cooked on the griddle and the rhubarb stewed with butter and sugar to take the edge off its sharpness. It makes an interesting alternative to apple sauce, our usual choice with pork chops.

Serve with the first early new potatoes or try my speedy baked potatoes – halve the potatoes lengthways, cut a wide, 5mm-deep lattice, smear with oil and add a sprinkle of Maldon sea salt. Place on a foil-lined tray and bake, without waiting for the oven to come up to temperature, at 220°C, Gas Mark 7. They will be ready in 20–30 minutes.

2 pork loin chops
200g rhubarb
25g butter
2 tablespoons sugar
1 tablespoon groundnut
  or sunflower oil
Maldon sea salt

Prepare the chops by cutting down the rind in 3 or 4 places right to the meat, so that when the chops cook they don't buckle. Season both sides with sea salt, rubbing salt into the rind. Set aside.

Cut the rhubarb stalks into pieces approximately 3cm long. Rinse and shake dry. Place in a saucepan with 3 tablespoons cold water, bring to the boil, add the butter and sugar and cook, covered, with the heat reduced to very low, for about 10 minutes until tender.

To cook the chops, smear both sides with the oil. Heat a griddle pan for several minutes until very hot. Lay out the chops, press down with a spatula and cook thus for 2 minutes. Turn and repeat. Reduce the heat and cook for a further 3–5 minutes on each side until cooked through. Transfer to warmed plates and leave to rest for 10 minutes before serving surrounded by the rhubarb sauce.

PORK RAGU

SERVES 4 | **PREP** 20 MINUTES | **COOK** 45 MINUTES

Pork fillet is such a lean, quick-cook cut of meat, but it's never occurred to me before to make ragu with it. One evening, when I had four hungry mouths to feed and *Wolf Hall* to watch, I found myself making ragu for a pasta supper in front of the TV. My it was good, and quick, too, jollied along with copious draughts of red wine.

1 medium onion
1 garlic clove
1½ tablespoons olive oil
2 celery sticks
2 carrots, about 175g
few fresh thyme sprigs
400g pork fillet
150ml milk
200ml red wine
400g can chopped tomatoes
250ml chicken stock
400g casarecce, fusilli, penne
   or large macaroni
salt and freshly ground
   black pepper
chunk of Parmesan cheese,
   to serve

Halve, peel and finely chop the onion and garlic. Soften both over a medium–low heat in the oil in a heavy-based, lidded pan that can hold all the ingredients.

Trim and finely chop the celery (peeled first if very fibrous). Scrape and finely dice the carrots. Strip the leaves from the thyme sprigs. Stir all these ingredients into the onions and add a generous pinch of salt and several grinds of pepper. Cover and sweat, stirring occasionally.

Meanwhile, slice the pork into skinny ribbons, then into tiny dice. Stir the pork into the softening vegetables to brown. Add the milk and cook for a few minutes, then add the red wine and let it bubble away, giving the occasional stir, followed by the tomatoes and stock. Adjust the heat, semi-cover and leave to simmer, stirring occasionally, for 30 minutes.

Remove the lid, increase the heat slightly and simmer until thick and creamy. Taste and adjust the seasoning before stirring into the pasta, cooked al dente according to the packet instructions. Serve with the Parmesan for people to grate over the top themselves.

PORK SATAY WITH PICKLED CUCUMBER NOODLES

SERVES 4 | **PREP** 30 MINUTES, PLUS MARINATING AND STANDING | **COOK** 15 MINUTES

Don't wait for barbecue weather to cook these kebabs, as a hot griddle indoors will do just as well. The lean meat is cubed slightly smaller than usual for kebabs and the oil in the lime marinade helps stop it drying out. What you're after is crusty on the outside but juicy and tender on the inside.

The satay sauce is a cheat recipe using peanut butter and coconut cream with a few other Thai seasonings. Although cans of coconut cream are small – usually 160ml – you are unlikely to use all of it, but save the leftovers for another recipe.

Noodles of any type go perfectly with this, but I like the chewy texture of egg noodles. They're sharpened with a Thai-style dressing and crisp slivers of pickled cucumber. Finish the meal with melon balls tossed with lime juice and shredded mint.

600g pork fillet
1 garlic clove
1 lime
2 tablespoons groundnut oil
3 tablespoons Thai sweet chilli sauce
1 small cucumber
2 teaspoons salt
1 tablespoon rice wine vinegar
1 tablespoon Thai fish sauce (nam pla)
250g medium egg noodles
2 tablespoons toasted sesame oil

For the peanut sauce
4 tablespoons crunchy peanut butter
1 tablespoon Thai fish sauce (nam pla)
160ml can coconut cream
2 tablespoons Thai sweet chilli sauce
1 tablespoon soy sauce
1 lime
1 tablespoon chopped coriander

Soak 20 wooden skewers in cold water until required.

Cut the pork into small kebab-sized chunks. Peel, chop and crush the garlic to a paste and mix with the juice from 1 lime, the groundnut oil and 1 tablespoon of the sweet chilli sauce. Mix thoroughly with the meat, cover and chill for 30 minutes.

Peel the cucumber, split lengthways, scrape out the seeds with a teaspoon and slice into chunky half-moons. Spread out in a colander, sprinkle with the salt and leave for 20 minutes. Rinse and squeeze dry in a tea towel. Mix in a bowl with the rice wine vinegar, the remaining sweet chilli sauce and the Thai fish sauce.

Next make the peanut sauce by gently heating the peanut butter with the fish sauce, 100ml of the coconut cream, chilli sauce, 2 tablespoons water, the soy sauce and lime juice to taste. Add extra water if too thick.

Thread the pork onto the skewers and cook for 2–4 minutes on each side on a hot griddle or barbecue coals at the white ash stage.

While the kebabs are cooking, cook the noodles according to the packet instructions, drain and toss with the toasted sesame oil and then with the cucumber mixture and coriander.

Serve the noodles and kebabs with a dollop of the peanut sauce.

CARAWAY PORK WITH SWEET–SOUR RED CABBAGE

SERVES 4 | **PREP** 25 MINUTES | **COOK** 55 MINUTES–1 HOUR 20 MINUTES

The sweet and sour, tender caraway-flavoured pork provides a good change of texture to juicy stewed cabbage with occasional chunks of apple. The dish is served borscht-style with a dollop of soured cream and garnish of chives. It reheats perfectly and keeps, covered, in the fridge for 48 hours.

1 medium–large onion
1 tablespoon sunflower oil
1 teaspoon caraway seeds
400g pork fillet
½ red cabbage, about 750g
3 russet or Cox apples, about 300g
1 tablespoon balsamic vinegar or pomegranate molasses
2 tablespoons cider vinegar
175ml cider or apple juice
4 tablespoons soured cream
2 tablespoons finely snipped chives or flat leaf parsley
salt and freshly ground black pepper

Preheat the oven to 170°C, Gas Mark 3.

Halve, peel and finely chop the onion. Soften in the oil in a flameproof lidded casserole over a medium heat. Lightly pound the caraway to release its pungency and stir into the onion.

Cut the pork into slim kebab-sized pieces, discarding the sinew. Quarter the cabbage and cut out the hard white stalk, discarding the outer damaged leaves. Slice thinly across the quarters. Quarter the apples, cut out the core and peel. Slice each piece in 3.

Stir the pork through the softening onion, stirring as it firms and changes colour. Stir in the balsamic, then the cider vinegar and cider or apple juice. Stir the cabbage and apple into the meat and season generously with salt and pepper, then drape a sheet of greaseproof paper over and touching the food. Hold firm with the lid.

Cook in the oven for 45 minutes. The cabbage will have wilted and the meat should be tender but still with resistance to the bite; cook for a further 15–25 minutes if necessary. Serve with the soured cream and chives or flat leaf parsley.

PAELLA ON A STICK

SERVES 2–4 | **PREP** 30 MINUTES, PLUS SOAKING AND MARINATING | **COOK** 15 MINUTES

I am rarely without chorizo, relying on this spicy sausage to bring flavour and interest to so many modest dishes. It always goes well with pork and here, along with red peppers and an olive oil and lemon marinade with thyme, it's almost paella on a stick.

Serve the kebabs with rice laced with peas and a scoop of garlicky pesto or quickly blitz several garlic cloves with a big bunch of parsley and a splash of olive oil. Stir this paste into the rice at the last moment. Accompany with garlic bread, chilled beer or a Spanish red, and bingo, you have a feast.

340g free-range pork
   escalopes or fillet
1 small lemon
2 tablespoons olive oil
few thyme sprigs
150g Iberico chorizo sausage
2 Romano red peppers

Soak 16 wooden skewers in cold water until required.

Slice the pork into strips approximately 7 × 2cm. Remove 2 strips of zest from the lemon and squeeze 1 tablespoon of the juice into a mixing bowl. Whisk in the olive oil, then stir in the thyme and zest, giving both several prods to release their flavour. Add the meat, twisting it around to thoroughly coat. Cover and chill for a minimum of 40 minutes, longer if possible.

Run a sharp knife down the length of the chorizo sausage and peel away the rubbery skin. Cut into chunky slices. Cut the peppers into pieces about the size of a large stamp, discarding the seeds. Thread the skewers with strips of pork interspersed with chorizo and pepper.

Cook over barbecue coals at the white ash stage or on a very hot griddle, turning after 3–4 minutes when the meat has formed a seal and the pepper is scorched and juicy and cooking for a further 3–4 minutes.

PULLED CHICKEN, HAM AND LEEK PIE

SERVES 3–4 | **PREP** 15 MINUTES, PLUS COOLING | **COOK** 50 MINUTES

Here is a modest way of turning cooked chicken into a comforting mid-week treat.

1 trimmed leek, about 200g
25g butter plus extra
   for greasing
1 dessertspoon plain flour
100ml dry white wine
150ml milk
200–300g cooked chicken
100g breaded or pulled ham
320g ready-rolled puff pastry
flour for dusting
1 egg
salt

Slice the leek into 5mm-thick rounds. Rinse. Melt the butter in a wide-based, lidded pan over a medium heat. Stir in the leek, add a generous pinch of salt, cover, reduce the heat slightly and cook for 6–8 minutes until very soft.

Sift the flour over the top and stir until disappeared. Add the wine, stirring as it thickens. Cook for a couple of minutes, then add the milk and simmer briefly until thick. Turn off the heat. Tear the chicken and ham over the top in bite-sized pieces. Mix thoroughly, then leave to cool.

Preheat the oven to 220°C, Gas Mark 7.

Unfurl the pastry and lightly roll on a floured surface to slightly increase the size. Line a baking sheet with baking parchment and smear with butter. Etch a line across the middle of the pastry. Pile the cold filling onto half the pastry. Paint a 1cm border with beaten egg on the 3 edges, fold over the pastry and seal with a fork. Paint with egg. Carefully lift onto the parchment. Fork a few air holes. Bake for 25–35 minutes until crusty and golden.

HAM HOCK AND BROAD BEAN RISOTTO

SERVES 2, GENEROUSLY | **PREP** 30 MINUTES | **COOK** 35 MINUTES

I always bother to peel broad beans after cooking. I think it's worth the effort to reveal the bright green beans inside the dull rubbery shells. Their creamy distinctive flavour goes extremely well with chunks of salty ham, lovely in this beguiling risotto with mint, ricotta and Parmesan.

500g broad beans, about
　150g shelled beans
1 chicken stock cube
2 shallots, about 50g
40g butter
200g Arborio rice
splash of dry white wine
1 teaspoon Dijon mustard
90g pulled ham hock or torn
　English ham
2 tablespoons ricotta or
　mascarpone
1 tablespoon freshly grated
　Parmesan cheese plus extra
　to serve
15 mint leaves
salt

Boil the kettle. Shuck the beans. Add a generous pinch of salt and the beans to 1 litre boiling water. Boil for 1 minute. Scoop the beans onto a plate to cool.

Dissolve the stock cube in the bean water, then cover to keep hot. Halve, peel and finely chop the shallots. Melt the butter in a spacious sauté pan over medium–low heat. Stir in the shallot and stir-fry for 6–8 minutes until soft but uncoloured. Add the rice and stir-fry for 2 minutes, then add the wine and Dijon, stirring as the wine evaporates. Stir in the ham and a third of the hot stock. Simmer, stirring occasionally, until the liquid is absorbed into the rice.

Nick the straight side of the cooling, wrinkling bean casings with your thumbnail and pinch out the beans inside.

Add another third of the stock to the rice, continuing as before, then add the beans and remaining stock. Simmer, stirring constantly, until the rice is thick and creamy. Stir in the ricotta or mascarpone and Parmesan. Cover and leave for 5 minutes. Stir in the mint and serve with more Parmesan.

HAM, POTATO AND CELERY GRATIN

SERVES 3–4 | **PREP** 25 MINUTES | **COOK** 50 MINUTES

Fenland celery is grown in rich peaty soil and is so highly rated that it has its own PGI (protected geographical indication), our *appellation contrôlée*. The stalks grow pale and wide, the flavour mellow yet powerful and tangy, the tall plant instantly recognizable by its hand-trimmed pointed root. Its season runs from October to the end of December, so look out for it then and try it in gratins like this with potato and ham in a creamy, lemony sauce under a crisp breadcrumb and Parmesan crust. Bliss.

350g Charlotte or similar waxy potatoes
400–600g bunch of celery
55g butter
30g plain flour
1 dessertspoon Dijon mustard
100ml milk
½ lemon
120g thickly sliced English ham
25g fine fresh white or panko breadcrumbs
20g freshly grated Parmesan cheese
salt and freshly ground black pepper

Boil the potatoes until tender. Drain and leave to cool.

Boil a full kettle. Trim the celery leaves and set aside. Peel the stalks with a potato peeler if very fibrous. Cut the stalks into pieces approximately 2 × 10cm. Rinse. Measure 1.5 litres boiling water from the kettle into a spacious saucepan. Add 1 teaspoon salt, place over a high heat and return to the boil. Add the celery. Simmer, covered, for 8 minutes. Drain, reserving 450ml cooking water. Spread the drained celery in a mixing bowl. Finely chop the leaves.

Melt 45g of the butter in the celery pan. Off the heat, stir in the flour and then the mustard. Add the celery stock, stirring over a medium heat as it simmers and thickens. Add salt to taste. Stir in the milk and lemon juice. Simmer gently, stirring often, for 5 minutes.

Preheat the oven to 200°C, Gas Mark 6. Tear the ham into bite-sized pieces. Scatter the leaves, ham, thickly sliced peeled potatoes and plenty of black pepper over the celery, pour on the sauce and mix. Transfer to a 1.5-litre gratin dish. Scatter with the crumbs mixed with the Parmesan. Dot with the remaining butter. Bake for 25–35 minutes until crusty and bubbling round the edges.

PULLED HAM HOCK AND PEA PASTA WITH HERBS
SERVES 3–4 | **PREP** 15 MINUTES | **COOK** 15 MINUTES

Whenever I see pulled ham hock on sale – it's sold in an eye-catching red 180g double pack – I pile it into my shopping basket. It's such a useful standby; perfect for quickie pasta suppers like this one, but ideal, too, for sandwiches and gratins. These chunky pieces of well-flavoured ham get mixed with my other favourite standby of frozen petits pois. Binding all the ingredients is silky Greek yoghurt with honey, which might sound odd but the flavours work well with a last-minute squeeze of lime to lend a sweet-sour finish.

350g fusilli, penne or other
  short pasta
200g frozen petits pois
180g pulled ham hock or
  thick sliced ham
150g Greek yoghurt
1 lime
2 tablespoons snipped chives
1 tablespoon shredded
  marjoram or basil
salt and freshly ground
  black pepper

Cook the pasta in plenty of boiling salted water according to the packet instructions. Add the petits pois for the last few minutes of cooking.

While that is going on, pick over the ham hock, discarding any fat and gristle. If using sliced ham, tear it into bite-sized scraps.

Drain the pasta and peas and tip into a warmed serving bowl (or back into the pan). Add the ham, yoghurt, juice from half the lime and the herbs. Season with freshly ground pepper, toss and serve with extra lime juice to taste; I told you it was a quickie.

GAMMON AND PINEAPPLE NOODLES
SERVES 2 | **PREP** 20 MINUTES | **COOK** 20 MINUTES

I was listening to Radio 4 one day as I pondered what to do with a gammon steak when an item came up about maple syrup. There on the table sat a pineapple and, bingo, I found myself reinventing a period piece from the Sixties. Juicy pineapple, slivers of gammon, hint of chilli and sweet maple syrup morphed into sauce for egg noodles. Sounds mad but just you try it.

1 medium onion
1 tablespoon sunflower oil
1 small red chilli
½ small pineapple, about
  200g, peeled
300g gammon steak
1 tablespoon maple syrup
200g egg noodles
salt

Halve, peel and finely chop the onion, then soften gently with a pinch of salt in the oil in a spacious frying/sauté pan. Trim, split, deseed, finely slice and chop the chilli, then stir into the softening onion.

Cut out the woody core of the pineapple, then slice approximately 3mm thick and cut into bite-sized triangles. Slice the gammon into strings approximately 5mm thick, 1cm wide and 4–5cm long.

Stir the gammon into the softened onion, increase the heat slightly, and stir-fry until all the pieces firm and darken. Add the maple syrup and toss a few times, then add the pineapple and stir-fry for 3–4 minutes until the sauce is turning very juicy.

Meanwhile, cook the noodles according to the packet instructions. Drain and mix into the sauce. Serve immediately.

PIG CHEEKS, FENNEL AND ORANGE

SERVES 4 | **PREP** 25 MINUTES | **COOK** 1 HOUR

Whilst visiting my son Henry in the Black Mountains, I often shop in Abergavenny where I found inexpensive pig cheeks. These lean nuggets are perfect for kebabs or slow-cooked dishes like this intriguing stew, hauntingly flavoured with fennel seed and orange. I served it over brown rice topped with finely sliced runner beans to soak up the gorgeous juices.

3 medium onions
2 tablespoons olive oil
1 teaspoon fennel seeds
½ teaspoon dried chilli flakes
12 pig cheeks
1 tablespoon plain flour
200ml dry white wine
2 juicing oranges
400ml light chicken stock or
    ½ chicken stock cube
salt

Halve, peel and chop the onions. Heat the oil in a spacious, lidded, heavy-based pan and stir in the onions. Stir-fry over a high heat until beginning to wilt and colour, then reduce the heat. Lightly pound the fennel seeds using a pestle and mortar and stir into the wilting onions with the chilli and a generous pinch of salt.

Use a sharp knife to slice off the membrane that covers one side of the cheek, as if skinning a fish. Chop into bite-sized pieces. Stir the pieces into the onion, increase the heat and brown thoroughly. Stir in the flour and add the white wine, stirring as it bubbles and thickens.

Remove 3 long strips of orange zest, tear into scraps and add to the pan. Add the orange juice and stock or cube dissolved in 400ml boiling water. Simmer, covered, giving the odd stir, for 45 minutes or until the meat is very tender. Serve now or reheat later.

FENNEL, BACON AND GREEN OLIVE PASTA

SERVES 2 | **PREP** 15 MINUTES | **COOK** 25 MINUTES

This is one of those scratch-round-the-fridge suppers that turned out so well that I want to pass on the recipe. I happened to have baby fennel, but a single large bulb is just dandy and so is celery sliced into bite-sized chunks. Green olives and cornichons, with a final flourish of coarsely grated Parmesan and knob of butter, make the dish.

150g penne, casarecce or
    other short pasta shapes
50g butter
1 medium onion
6 rashers smoked streaky
    bacon
1 tablespoon olive oil
4 baby fennel bulbs,
    about 200g
8 pitted green olives
8 cornichons
salt
Parmesan cheese, to serve

Boil the kettle and use the water to cook the pasta until al dente, according to the packet instructions. Drain and toss with 1 tablespoon of the cooking water and half the butter.

As the pasta cooks, halve, peel and finely chop the onion. Chop the bacon. Melt half the remaining butter in the olive oil in a spacious, lidded sauté/frying pan. Stir in the onion with a pinch of salt, then add the bacon. Cook briskly, giving an occasional stir, while you halve the fennel lengthways (or quarter a large bulb) and slice across the pieces to make 5mm-thick slices. Stir the fennel into the softening onion and crisping bacon, reduce the heat, cover and cook for 15 minutes, giving occasional stirs.

Slice the olives into 3 rounds. Chop the cornichons. Stir both and the drained pasta into the veg. Stir, heat through, add the remaining butter and serve with grated Parmesan.

BORLOTTI BEAN, BACON AND PORK FILLET

SERVES 2 | **PREP** 25 MINUTES | **COOK** 45 MINUTES

This is one of those useful get-ahead suppers, a lovely borlotti bean and white wine pork stew, thick and sloppy, brimming with bacon, shallots, carrots and mushrooms. It's a mindless dish to make and one that will sit happily in the fridge for 24 hours without spoiling, ready to be heated up and turned into a restaurant-style supper in minutes.

The pork, a piece of fillet, is cooked separately and served in chunky slices over the top. If you prefer, the stew would be very good with pork chops or crusty pork sausages. I got the idea for the dish after enjoying something similar at the Chelsea Arts Club. It's a dish that transcends the seasons but in the summer, when borlotti beans are in season, it could be made with fresh beans instead of the standby canned beans I used. No need for an accompaniment, but green beans of some sort would go well as a side dish or tucked under the meat.

75g rashers rindless smoked
  streaky bacon
2 shallots
100g closed-cup small
  mushrooms
2 carrots, about 150g
1 garlic clove
250g pork fillet
2½ tablespoons sunflower oil
1 teaspoon plain flour
150ml white wine
1 bay leaf
few thyme sprigs
400g can borlotti or
  cannellini beans
1 tablespoon chopped
  flat leaf parsley
salt and freshly ground
  black pepper

Boil the kettle. Slice the bacon into chunky strips. Peel and finely chop the shallots. Wipe the mushrooms clean and slice into 4 pieces. Scrape the carrots and dice. Boil the carrots in 250ml water from the kettle with a pinch of salt for 5 minutes. Drain and save the water. Peel, chop and then crush the garlic with a pinch of salt. Smear the pork with ½ tablespoon of the sunflower oil.

Heat 1 tablespoon of the oil in a sauté pan and fry the bacon until the fat begins to melt. Reduce the heat slightly and stir in the shallots and garlic. Cook, stirring often, for 5 minutes, then stir in the mushrooms, tossing for a few minutes until damp-looking. Add the flour, stirring until disappeared, then add the wine, bay leaf and thyme. Let it bubble up, stirring to thicken, before adding the carrot water. Simmer for 5 minutes. Taste and adjust the seasoning with salt and pepper.

Tip the beans into a sieve, rinse with water, shake dry and add to the stew. Simmer gently for 10 minutes.

While the stew cooks, heat a non-stick, heavy frying pan with the last of the oil. When very hot, brown the pork all over, turning after a minute or so when a crust has formed to avoid tearing the meat. Reduce the heat and cook for 10 minutes, turning once.

Transfer the pork to a chopping board. Rest for 5 minutes, then slice thickly, 4 or 5 slices a portion. Reheat the beans, stir in the parsley and serve topped with the pork.

SAUSAGES

Bangers and mash is one of my Desert Island dishes, but the sausages have to be meaty and cooked crusty and the mash buttery and fluffy. I usually serve it with peas, sometimes with gravy, sometimes with fried onion and sometimes with apple sauce, but always with mustard. Decent, meaty sausages make instant meatballs that are perfect with pasta, mash, lentils and beans, soft polenta, even in risotto. They can be enriched with red wine and balsamic vinegar.

I tend to stick with fat, meaty sausages, usually pork, but ring the changes with cocktail sausages, chipolatas and occasionally frankfurters and black pudding. Chorizo, technically a sausage, usually flavours other dishes – with chicken or white fish – but there is one recipe here with gnocchi and chestnuts where it stars.

RED WINE SAUSAGE MEATBALLS WITH SPINACH PASTA
SERVES 2 | **PREP** 20 MINUTES | **COOK** 20 MINUTES

This is a blessedly comforting and intensely flavoured way of turning a few sausages into a pasta supper. The sausages morph into meatballs and are cooked in red wine and balsamic vinegar, then tossed with spinach and pasta.

2 medium onions
1 tablespoon sunflower oil
350g meaty chipolatas
250ml red wine
1 tablespoon balsamic
    vinegar
200g penne rigate or other
    short pasta
150g young spinach
large knob of butter
salt

Boil the kettle. Halve, peel and finely chop the onions. Heat the oil in a spacious frying/sauté pan, stir in the onions and gently soften, stirring regularly, until slippery soft.

Meanwhile, run a knife down the chipolatas and peel away the skin. Make 5 balls from each chipolata, rolling firm between your palms. Add the sausage to the softened onion. Increase the heat slightly and shake the pan to move them around as they brown all over.

Add the wine and let it cook briskly, stirring regularly until syrupy, the sausage balls red. Add the balsamic.

Co-ordinate cooking the pasta in boiling salted water from the kettle according to the packet instructions. When tender, drain and return to the pan with the spinach and butter, stirring as it wilts. Tip into the sausage balls, toss and serve. Yum.

BANGERS AND MASH, BALSAMIC ONIONS AND APPLE SAUCE

SERVES 3–4 | **PREP** 25 MINUTES | **COOK** 35 MINUTES

Time for fluffy, buttery mashed potato with crusty, meaty pork sausages. In this version, there is no gravy but dark, caramelized onion goo instead, with a sharp apple sauce – and don't forget a pot of your favourite mustard.

9–12 decent pork sausages
3 tablespoons sunflower oil
3 medium onions
1 tablespoon balsamic
   vinegar
900g King Edward or similar
   potatoes
75g butter
100ml milk
whole nutmeg for grating
1 Bramley cooking apple
squeeze of lemon
1 tablespoon sugar
salt

Fry the sausages in 1 tablespoon oil over a low heat, turning every so often, until crusty and done to your liking. Mine took 30 minutes, co-ordinating neatly with everything else. If preferred, grill or roast them.

Halve, peel and finely slice the onions. Heat the remaining oil in a second frying pan and add the onions. Cook briskly, tossing constantly, for 5 minutes. Reduce the heat to medium–low and cook for 20–30 minutes, stirring often, until slippery soft. Add the balsamic vinegar and 2 tablespoons water. Let it bubble away. Turn off the heat.

Meanwhile, peel, chunk and rinse the potatoes. Boil in plenty of salted water until tender. Drain. Melt 50g of the butter, in the milk, in the pan, then pass the potatoes through a mouli-legume or ricer, or mash, into the hot liquid. Beat until light and fluffy. Add half the remaining butter and a generous grating of nutmeg. Cover with a tea towel.

Quarter the apple, peel, core and chunk into a pan. Add a squeeze of lemon and 4 tablespoons water. Cook, covered, for 5–10 minutes until soft and fluffy. Beat in the sugar and remaining butter until smooth. Tip into a bowl to cool. Serve the beaten mash topped with the hot onion, sausages and cold apple sauce on the side.

SAUSAGES WITH TOMATO LENTILS

SERVES 4 | **PREP** 15 MINUTES | **COOK** 45 MINUTES

Quite by chance I caught the end of an episode of *Italy Unpacked* just as Giorgio Locatelli was frying plump Italian sausages for this simple dish. He'd already cooked some lenticchie grown locally in the foothills of the distant Apennine Mountains that could be glimpsed through the open window. Next up was homemade passata and the cooking aroma was palpable. Andrew Graham-Dixon, clearly in need of a glass of red, could hardly contain himself and neither could I. The next morning I was out early with my shopping list and here is the result.

250g lenticchie di
   Castelluccio or Puy lentils
½ chicken stock cube
1–2 tablespoons olive oil
12 meaty pork and herb
   sausages
3 shallots or 1 medium
   onion, about 150g
400g passata or 400g can
   chopped tomatoes
salt
best olive oil, to serve

Agitate the lentils in water to wash before placing in a pan with 900ml water and the crumbled stock cube. Cook at a gentle simmer, covered, for 30–40 minutes until tender and most of the liquid absorbed. Season to taste with salt.

Meanwhile, heat the oil in a heavy-based pan over a medium heat and brown the sausages thoroughly. Scoop out of the pan. Peel and finely chop the shallots or onion, then stir into the pan, reducing the heat slightly, stirring regularly as they soften. Return the sausages and passata or liquidized chopped tomatoes, cover, reduce the heat and cook gently, stirring now and then, for about 20 minutes until cooked through. Spoon the lentils into the pan, stir, check the seasoning, cook for a few minutes and then serve immediately or later with a swirl of best olive oil. Thanks Giorgio.

GNOCCHI WITH CHORIZO AND CHESTNUTS

SERVES 4 | **PREP** 15 MINUTES | **COOK** 30 MINUTES

A warming dish inspired by gnocchi with a crumble of meaty Italian sausage served at the River Café. Theirs is flavoured with sage in a thin, intensely savoury juice. Both are delicious.

1 large red onion
1 tablespoon olive oil
knob of butter
100g chorizo piquant,
   preferably whole sausage
200g whole peeled, boiled
   chestnuts
½ chicken stock cube
175ml red wine
200g passata or 227g can
   chopped tomatoes
500g potato gnocchi
salt and freshly ground
   black pepper

Boil the kettle. Halve, peel and chop the onion. Soften gently in the olive oil and butter with a generous pinch of salt in a heavy-based pan that can hold the entire dish.

Meanwhile, run a sharp knife down the chorizo, peel away the skin and quarter lengthways. Break into small chunks. Break the chestnuts into 3 or 4 pieces. Dissolve the stock cube in 250ml boiling water.

Stir the ragged chorizo into the onion, cooking until the fat begins to run and colour the onion. Add the wine and let it bubble up and virtually disappear. Add the stock and return to the boil, then add the tomato. Simmer for 10 minutes and taste and adjust the seasoning. Stir in the chestnuts and continue cooking.

Add the gnocchi to boiling salted water. When all the gnocchi has risen to the surface, scoop into the chorizo mixture. Simmer for a further few minutes and serve. This reheats perfectly.

SAUSAGE AND MUSHROOM CASSOULET

SERVES 4 | **PREP** 15 MINUTES | **COOK** 25 MINUTES

You'll find no goose in this cassoulet-inspired stew but sausages and mushrooms cooked with red onion, green lentils and haricot beans. They combine into a great comfort supper. It's stunningly easy to make. Serve in bowls and pass the mustard.

500g cocktail or chipolata
    sausages
3 tablespoons olive oil
1 large red onion
2 garlic cloves
8 medium closed-cup
    mushrooms
1 bay leaf
1 teaspoon thyme leaves
300ml red wine
squirt of tomato ketchup
400g can haricot beans
400g can green lentils
squeeze of lemon
salt and freshly ground
    black pepper

Smear the sausages with 1 tablespoon of the olive oil and grill, turning as they get crusty, ensuring they cook through.

Meanwhile, halve and peel the onion. Slice down the halves to make chunky half-moons. Peel and chop the garlic. Wipe the mushrooms and cut them into quarters.

Heat the remaining oil in a spacious frying pan over a medium heat and soften the onion, adding the garlic after 5 minutes. When the onion is sloppy, add the mushrooms, bay leaf and thyme, season generously with salt and pepper and continue to cook for a further 5 minutes. Add the wine and ketchup and let it bubble up, then reduce the heat to a simmer.

Tip the haricot and lentils into a sieve, rinse under cold running water, shake dry and add to the pan. Season again and cook for 5 more minutes or until the mushrooms are done to your liking and the stew juicy rather than wet. By now the sausages should be ready. Stir them into the stew, taste and season with pepper and a squeeze of lemon.

BLACK PUDDING, POMMES PURÉE AND APPLE SAUCE

SERVES 2 | **PREP** 20 MINUTES | **COOK** 25 MINUTES

This way of serving breakfast black pudding, thickly sliced and fried until crusty, makes a good supper with a tart apple sauce and French-style mashed potato. The latter is more sauce than mash, best made with unsalted butter and waxy potatoes. Serve with Dijon mustard and a chive garnish.

1 Bramley apple, about 300g
1 tablespoon sugar
60g butter
300g large Charlotte potatoes
75ml hot whole milk
250g black pudding
1 tablespoon sunflower oil
1 tablespoon snipped chives
salt

Quarter, peel and core the apple. Chop into a small pan. Add 4 tablespoons water, cover and boil for 5 minutes. Beat in the sugar and 10g of the butter. Cool.

Boil the unpeeled potatoes until tender. Drain. Spear with a fork and use a small, sharp knife to whip off the skin. Return to the pan, cover and leave for 5 minutes. Pass through a mouli-legume or ricer (do not use a food processor) or mash super-smooth. Return to the pan. Shave the remaining butter over the top and use a wooden spoon to beat thoroughly until smooth and glossy. Have ready the hot milk and add gradually, beating constantly with the wooden spoon, until pale, fluffy and runnier than British mash. Taste and season with salt.

Slice the pudding 1cm thick in long, diagonal slices. Fry in the hot oil until very crusty. Serve with the hot purée, cold sauce and chive garnish.

SAUSAGE AND BROAD BEAN RISOTTO

SERVES 3–4 | **PREP** 20 MINUTES | **COOK** 30 MINUTES

This is my idea of perfect week-night food; easy to shop for, only a few ingredients, simple to cook and comforting yet light and interesting to eat. Broad beans give the dish a summery note whilst making it look pretty and rather elegant. And as a bonus it works well reheated the next day with a little extra liquid.

Any pork sausages are good here, but choose high meat content, preferably organic, so that they don't weep fat as they fry. Because the sausages are unzipped and the meat broken into meatball-sized pieces, it's a loaves and fishes kind of dish. Quantities feed two handsomely but will stretch to three, even four, unless you have humungous appetites. A final shower of Parmesan gives extra umami.

6 meaty pork sausages
1 tablespoon sunflower oil
1 large red onion
200g shelled fresh or frozen
  broad beans
1½ chicken stock cubes
15g butter
200g Arborio rice
1 dessertspoon Dijon
  mustard
freshly grated Parmesan
  cheese, to serve

Boil the kettle. Run a sharp knife down the sausages and peel away the skin. Break into 5 or 6 equal pieces per sausage. Heat the oil in a lidded sauté pan over a medium heat and thoroughly brown the sausage pieces, turning after a couple of minutes when a seal has formed.

While the sausages cook, trim, halve and peel the onion. Slice, then chop into small pieces.

Half-fill a medium pan with boiling water from the kettle, return to the boil and add the beans. Boil for 2 minutes and scoop out of the pan as they rise to the surface into a colander to drain, then spread out on a plate to cool. Dissolve the stock cubes in 1 litre of the boiling water.

Add half the butter to the pan, and when melted, add the onion, reducing the heat slightly and stirring occasionally for 3–4 minutes as the onion softens. Stir in the rice, continuing until glossy, then add the mustard, stirring briskly. Add a ladleful of stock and stir as it bubbles into the rice, then continue thus, stirring regularly, until the rice is thick and creamy with a slight bite at the centre – about 20 minutes. Remove from the heat.

Remove the bean skins by pinching one side of the beans with a thumbnail pressed against your index finger, then gently squeeze out the bright green bean as the rice cooks. Stir the remaining butter and beans into the risotto, cover and leave for 5 minutes before serving with Parmesan.

GRATIN OF SAUSAGES AND APPLE

SERVES 2–4 | **PREP** 20 MINUTES | **COOK** 40 MINUTES

I've been cooking versions of this comforting sausage supper for more years than I care to recall. The idea comes from Sue Miles, a cook at the sharp end of the restaurant revival in the late Eighties who died prematurely in 2010. We worked together at *Time Out* in the early days of the magazine and earned very little. I'd asked Sue for a cheap and cheerful supper idea and this is what she came up with.

It's important, I discovered after several disasters, to use decent meaty sausages and virtually cook them before layering up with the apples. You can use any apples you like. Cookers flop and make the dish juicier, while eaters retain their shape. Similarly, you can make it with most hard cheeses. I prefer the strong flavour of mature Cheddar, but mild Gruyère makes a good crust.

1 tablespoon sunflower oil

500g meaty pork sausages or chipolatas

2 tablespoons lemon juice

1 Bramley cooking apple or 2 Cox apples, about 200g

50g fresh white or wholemeal breadcrumbs

100g mature Cheddar or Gruyère cheese

1–2 tablespoons English or Dijon mustard

25g butter

1 tablespoon finely grated Parmesan cheese

Heat the oil in a frying pan and brown the sausages thoroughly, allowing at least 15 minutes, continuing until virtually cooked. Drain on kitchen paper. While the sausages fry, pour the lemon juice into a bowl. Quarter, peel and core the apples. Slice thinly across the quarters directly into the lemon juice. In a second bowl, mix together the breadcrumbs and half the grated Cheddar or Gruyère.

Preheat the oven to 200°C, Gas Mark 6.

Diagonally slice the sausages into 2 or 3 pieces. Leave chipolatas whole. In a 24 × 18 × 4cm gratin dish, make 2 sausage layers, beginning with apple, then sausage, smearing the underside of the sausage with mustard as you go, ending with apple. Don't be too neat about this, snuggling the sausages up close. Top with the breadcrumbs mixed with cheese, then finish with the remaining grated Cheddar or Gruyère and slivers of butter. Dust the top with the Parmesan. Pop in the oven and cook for about 25 minutes until the top turns into a golden carapace.

POACHED FRANKFURTERS
WITH CARAWAY SAUERKRAUT

SERVES 4 | **PREP** 20 MINUTES | **COOK** 50 MINUTES

There is something about the bouncy texture and subtly assertive sweet flavour of frankfurters that can be surprisingly delicious. Here they are poached, potée-style, with bacon and onions, adding caraway-flavoured sauerkraut, its sharpness mellowed with white wine and chicken stock. By adding chunks of potato, too, the result is a hearty meal-in-a-bowl with a good mix of textures and beguiling flavours. It reheats perfectly and is served with a generous garnish of chopped flat leaf parsley to give colour and freshness.

1 small onion
½ tablespoon sunflower oil
2 garlic cloves
4 rashers rindless smoked
   streaky bacon
2 teaspoons caraway seeds
10 beechwood smoked
   frankfurters
350g sauerkraut
150ml dry white wine
1 chicken stock cube
25g bunch of flat leaf parsley
salt and freshly ground
   black pepper

Trim, halve, peel and finely chop the onion. Soften in the oil in a spacious, lidded frying/sauté pan over a medium heat. Cook the onion for about 10 minutes, stirring occasionally.

Crack the garlic, flake away the skin and slice into thin rounds. Chop the bacon. Lightly crush the caraway seeds using a pestle and mortar. Rinse and then slice the frankfurters into bite-sized chunks, approximately 2cm wide.

Boil the kettle. Stir the garlic into the onion and cook for a couple of minutes until golden at the edges before adding the bacon. Cook, giving the odd stir, for about 5 minutes until beginning to crisp, then add the caraway and the rinsed, drained sauerkraut. Stir thoroughly, then add the wine and let it bubble away into the sauerkraut.

Add the frankfurters, ½ teaspoon salt and the stock cube dissolved in 500ml boiling water. Bring to the boil, then reduce the heat slightly, cover and simmer for 30 minutes.

Taste the liquid and adjust the seasoning with salt (it's unlikely that you'll need more) and freshly ground black pepper. Serve the soupy stew immediately or reheat later with the finely chopped flat leaf parsley.

POACHED PAK CHOI SAUSAGES
WITH CORIANDER NOODLES

SERVES 2 | **PREP** 15 MINUTES | **COOK** 25 MINUTES

Only bother to make this with really meaty sausages, at least 70% meat. They are poached in a lemon grass, Thai fish sauce (nam pla) and lime-seasoned broth flavoured with spring onions, then finished with pak choi. Everything is spooned over medium egg noodles with coriander and served with the most fearsomely hot chilli sauce you can lay your hands on. Just a dash mind.

1 litre chicken stock
1 lemon grass stalk
1 tablespoon Thai fish sauce
   (nam pla)
25g fresh root ginger

Simmer the stock for 10 minutes with the lemon grass, bashed to release the flavour, nam pla, thinly sliced ginger and finely chopped, deseeded chilli.

Trim and cut the spring onions into 3cm lengths. Leave the sausages whole or slice on the diagonal into 3 pieces (easier for eating). Trim the pak choi, quarter lengthways and separate the leaves. Chop the coriander (stalks and all).

1 red bird's eye chilli
bunch of spring onions
6 Cumberland pork sausages
3 pak choi, about 235g
25g coriander
1 lime
2 nests medium egg noodles,
   about 200g
salt
thick chilli sauce, to serve

Boil the kettle. Adjust the stock seasoning with lime juice and salt. Add the sausages and spring onions and simmer for 10 minutes. Add the pak choi, pushing it under the liquid and simmer for a further 5 minutes.

Meanwhile, cook the noodles according to the packet instructions using water from the kettle. Drain and mix with the coriander. Divide between deep bowls and spoon the sausages and broth over. Offer chilli sauce and fork and spoon.

MARMALADE HOT DOGS WITH LEMON ROAST SWEET POTATOES

SERVES 4 | **PREP** 15 MINUTES | **COOK** 45 MINUTES

Stuck for a way to liven up Bonfire Night sausages? Here's a twist on that old trick of smearing them with marmalade. These sausages are part-cooked alongside thick slices of sweet potato and finished in a generous dousing of marmalade. The sweet, fluffy but crusty-edged golden potatoes are in total contrast to the tangy, meaty sausages freshened by a top-knot of piquant sun-drenched tomatoes. Smoky campfire marmalade (radnorpreserves.com) provides bonfire flavour without poking in the ashes.

4 sweet potatoes, about
   200g each
3 tablespoons rapeseed oil
16–24 meaty pork chipolatas
4 tablespoons marmalade
1 lemon
190g sun-drenched tomatoes
   in oil
salt

Preheat the oven to 200°C, Gas Mark 6. Peel the potatoes and slice thickly, about 1cm.

Heat a roasting tin that can hold the pieces in a single layer with 2 tablespoons of the oil for 2 minutes. Turn the sweet potato pieces through the hot oil and cook in the oven for 20 minutes or until the base is crusty. Turn and return to the oven for a further 10–15 minutes until cooked through.

Meanwhile, line a second roasting tin – shallow is best – with foil, shiny side up, smear with the remaining oil and lay out the sausages. Roast for 20 minutes until turning crusty and golden. Drain off any excess fat, turn and cook for a further 10 minutes. If necessary, drain again. Spoon the marmalade over and return to the oven for a further 10 minutes until really crusty and the marmalade melted and sauce-like.

Pile the sweet potato on a plate or platter, add a squeeze of lemon, the sausages and sauce and top with the drained tomatoes.

LAMB

Lamb is such a versatile meat and very hard to cook badly. I am very keen on minced lamb, turning it into meatballs, patties and ragu-style sauce for pasta and gratins, using a wide range of seasonings to ring the changes. Lamb loves aubergine, rosemary, red wine and vinegars, but is just at home with tomatoes and spinach, peas and mint. Fruit is often teamed with lamb, in curries and stews that simmer away on the back burner while you get on with something else.

My favourite cut is lamb neck fillet for kebabs and stews, but for a quick after-work supper, I'm very partial to crusty grilled chops with a dollop of garlicky hummus. Half a shoulder of lamb is a good mid-week roast, using leftovers to make variations on shepherd's pie.

POLENTA WITH LAMB RAGU

SERVES 4 | **PREP** 25 MINUTES | **COOK** 1 HOUR

Lamb ragu tastes rich and unctuous but cooks quickly. Instead of spooning it over pasta or baked potatoes (my favourite), try it this way over slabs of crusty griddled or fried polenta.

1 medium onion
1 garlic clove
2 medium carrots
2 celery sticks
4 tablespoons olive oil
500g minced lamb
250ml red wine
150ml milk
¼ teaspoon grated nutmeg
250ml passata or 400g
   can tomatoes, puréed
   and sieved
250g quick-cook (1 minute)
   polenta
salt and freshly ground
   black pepper

Peel and dice the onion, garlic and carrots. Finely chop the trimmed celery. Heat half the oil in a heavy-based pan, stir in the onion and cook for 5 minutes before adding the carrots, celery and garlic. Season generously with salt and pepper, then reduce the heat, cover and cook for 10 minutes.

Increase the heat and add the lamb, stirring as it browns. Add the wine and cook, stirring occasionally, until juicy rather than wet. Repeat with the milk, stirring often, then add the nutmeg and tomato. Once boiling, turn the heat very low and gently simmer, uncovered, for 30–35 minutes. It should be a thick, cohesive sauce. Season to taste.

For the polenta, add 1 teaspoon salt to 1 litre vigorously boiling water. Using a long-handled wooden spoon, stir in the polenta and turn the heat very low. Stir constantly until very thick and shrinking from the pan sides. Pour onto a baking sheet or plate. Leave to go cold.

When ready to serve, heat a griddle or heavy frying pan until very hot. Cut slices or triangles of polenta, smear with the remaining oil and griddle or sear for 3–5 minutes on each side until deeply etched, crusty and golden. Spoon over the ragu and serve.

SLIPPER MOUSSAKA

SERVES 4–6 | **PREP** 35 MINUTES | **COOK** 1¼ HOURS

A cute name for a cute dish; the slipper being half an aubergine. Usefully, the three component parts – roasted aubergine halves, minced lamb and thick white sauce – are made at the same time, but could be done hours apart. The aubergine is cut with a deep, wide lattice to encourage even cooking and allow the flesh to sag apart ready to be filled with the mince, highly seasoned with oregano and parsley, red wine and tomato. Once the slippers are filled, the sauce sits on top and an egg yolk stops it sliding off. The finale is a generous grating of Parmesan. They need about half an hour in a hot oven, but could be kept on hold, covered, in the fridge for 24 hours.

Slippers suit being served with a Greek-style salad accompaniment. I recommend wedges of vine tomato, lightly cooked green beans, black olives, feta and mint, with a dressing of one part balsamic vinegar to three parts fruity olive oil mixed with garlic crushed to a paste with a little salt.

3 decent-sized aubergines, about 900g

3 tablespoons olive oil

1 Spanish onion

2 garlic cloves

2 vine tomatoes, about 100g

250g minced lamb

100ml red wine

1 teaspoon dried oregano

2 tablespoons chopped flat leaf parsley

2 tablespoons fresh white or wholemeal breadcrumbs

25g butter

25g plain flour

300ml milk

whole nutmeg for grating

1 egg yolk

3 tablespoons freshly grated Parmesan cheese

salt and freshly ground black pepper

Preheat the oven to 200°C, Gas Mark 6. Trim and halve the aubergines lengthways. Cut a wide, 1cm-deep, lattice in the cut surface without puncturing the skin. Arrange on a shallow roasting tin and smear the lattice with half the olive oil. Roast for 25 minutes or until soft. Set aside to cool.

Meanwhile, halve, peel and finely chop the onion. Crack the garlic with your fist, flake away the skin, chop and crush to a paste with a pinch of salt. Heat the remaining oil in a spacious, lidded frying pan and stir in the onion and garlic. Cook briskly for 5 minutes, then reduce the heat, add 2 tablespoons water, cover and cook for 10 minutes until wilted.

Quarter the tomatoes and blitz into passata in a food processor. Crumble the meat over the onions and stir-fry to brown. Add the wine and allow to bubble away. Season with salt, pepper and the oregano, then add the passata and half the parsley. Transfer to a saucepan, cover and leave to simmer for 20 minutes, giving the odd stir, until thick and dry. Stir in the breadcrumbs and spoon into the aubergine halves.

To make the topping, melt the butter in a small pan and stir in the flour, then add the milk gradually whilst stirring briskly to make a smooth, thick sauce. Add a generous pinch of salt and grated nutmeg and cook gently for 5 minutes. Cool slightly, then beat in the egg yolk. Spoon down the middle of the slippers. Dredge with the Parmesan and bake for 25 minutes.

LAMB KHORESH WITH PLUMS AND MINT

SERVES 4 | **PREP** 30 MINUTES | **COOK** 1¼ HOURS

Khoresh is Iranian stew, generally made with lamb and seasonal fruit, with humungous amounts of gently softened onion and fresh herbs. Plums proved a good choice with lamb neck fillet flavoured by saffron with a small bunch of mint. It sounds unlikely, but the slight sourness of British plums with intense minty back flavour is extremely good with saffron lamb. Serve with couscous or rice to mop up the gorgeous juices, adding a top-knot of creamy yoghurt for luxury.

4 medium–large onions,
  about 500g
50g butter
800g lamb neck fillet
1 tablespoon olive oil
¼ teaspoon saffron threads
1 small lemon
300ml chicken stock
500g British plums
25 mint leaves
300g thick natural yoghurt
salt and freshly ground
  black pepper

Halve, peel and finely slice the onions. Soften gently, stirring occasionally, in the butter with ½ teaspoon salt, covered, in a flameproof, lidded casserole.

Slice the meat into 2cm-thick medallions. Quickly brown the meat in the olive oil in a frying pan. Add the meat and saffron to the sloppy, hardly coloured onions. Add juice from half the lemon and the stock. Cover and simmer gently for 45 minutes.

Season with salt, pepper and lemon juice to taste. Slice the plums off the stones in big pieces. Add to the pan with most of the chopped mint. Simmer, uncovered, for a further 20 minutes. Serve with a dollop of yoghurt and the last of the mint.

BALSAMIC LAMB WITH BEANS AND PEAS

SERVES 2 | **PREP** 20 MINUTES | **COOK** 25 MINUTES

Syrupy balsamic vinegar gives a mellow, sweet-sour, rich winey flavour and dark colour to all kinds of dishes. It's particularly good with onions and lamb, here combined in a simple stir-fry. Separately cooked peas and beans bring bright freshness to the dish. This is good alone or with potatoes, noodles or rice.

200g lamb neck fillet
3 tablespoons thick balsamic
  vinegar such as Belazu
  or 6 tablespoons 'thin'
  balsamic vinegar
1 medium onion
1 tablespoon olive oil
100g fine green beans
100g frozen petits pois
salt and freshly ground
  black pepper

Trim the fat and sinew from the lamb and slice thinly, no thicker than 2mm, not worrying if untidy. If using a thin as opposed to syrupy balsamic vinegar, quickly simmer in a small pan until syrupy and reduced by half. Place the meat in a dish, add 2 tablespoons of the vinegar and mix to thoroughly coat.

Halve, peel and thinly slice down the halves of the onion to make little half-moons. Heat the olive oil in a spacious frying/sauté pan and stir-fry the onion for 10–15 minutes until slippery soft.

Trim and snap the beans in half, then cook with the peas in boiling salted water until just done. Drain.

Add the remaining vinegar to the onion and stir-fry for a few more minutes, then increase the heat and add the lamb and juices. Stir-fry until all the pieces are brown. Add the greens, toss, season to taste and serve.

LAMB WITH MINTED CRUSHED PEAS AND POACHED GARLIC

SERVES 4 | **PREP** 20 MINUTES | **COOK** 30 MINUTES

My local Sunday farmers' market is small, changes slightly but is always a good balance of hardcore meat, fish, fruit and vegetables, bread and cheeses, and occasional oddballs, like the guys who make Moroccan pancakes. I never shop with a list but buy what's plentiful and just in season.

One Sunday, I bought a small boned leg of lamb with thoughts of a classic summer barbecue, the lamb butterflied and eaten with new potatoes and peas cooked with mint. At the veg stall, I found the peas and early broad beans, obviously just-dug new potatoes and beetroot, and couldn't resist pale green new season garlic and the very last of the English asparagus.

It was too hot to fire up the barbecue, so I put a spin on my original plan by poaching the garlic in olive oil with balsamic vinegar and used the oil to season the lamb. Once rested, the lamb was thickly sliced and piled over peas crushed with mint, those delicious new potatoes, buttery nuggets of garlic and homemade mint sauce. Yum.

2 heads of new season garlic

6 tablespoons olive oil

2 tablespoons thick balsamic vinegar, such as Belazu

1 small butterflied leg of lamb or 4 lamb leg steaks

1kg new potatoes

small bunch of mint

400g shelled peas or frozen petits pois

2 teaspoons English mint sauce

salt

For the mint sauce

20 mint leaves

1 teaspoon sugar

3 tablespoons cider vinegar

Separate the garlic cloves from the heads and peel. Place in a small pan and cover with the olive oil. Simmer gently, swirling occasionally, for 10 minutes. Add the balsamic and cook for a further 5–10 minutes until butter-soft.

Cut steaks across the width of the butterflied lamb (or leave whole) and smear both sides with the oil from the garlic.

Scrape the potatoes and boil in salted water with the mint. Drain and keep warm. Cook the peas. Drain and crush with a potato masher – you want them bruised and cracked, not smooth. Mix with the mint sauce. Keep warm.

Heat a griddle for a few minutes until very hot. Season one side of the steaks with salt. Lay salt-side down on the hot griddle and cook for 3–5 minutes, depending on the thickness and how you like your lamb. Season the exposed side, turn and repeat. Leave to rest for 5 minutes. Slice thickly across the width of the steaks.

For the sauce, finely chop the mint and place in a jug with the sugar and 1 tablespoon boiling water. Leave for a moment, then stir in the vinegar.

To serve, pile the steak over the crushed peas. Add any juices. Serve with the garlic, potatoes and mint sauce.

POMEGRANATE LAMB MEATBALLS WITH AUBERGINE SAUCE

SERVES 2–3 | **PREP** 30 MINUTES | **COOK** 1 HOUR

Lebanese food is high on my list of favourite cuisines, not least for the delicious ways with aubergine and minced lamb. The other night, when I was all set to make smoky, creamy Moutabal to serve with crusty little lamb meatballs flavoured with allspice, fresh coriander and toasted pine nuts, I plucked Claudia Roden's magnificent *Arabesque* book from the shelf. As I flicked past the beautiful photos, I came across an intriguing recipe for aubergine sauce in the section on Turkish food. The aubergine is roasted (or grilled whole), mashed and then stirred into a thick white sauce flavoured with nutmeg and grated Gruyère. My little meatballs sat proudly on top of the delicious sauce with a zig-zag of pomegranate syrup and handful of fresh pomegranate seeds.

For the sauce
1 large aubergine, about 250g
25g butter
1 tablespoon plain flour
300ml milk
whole nutmeg for grating
2 tablespoons grated
  Gruyère cheese

For the meatballs
1 medium onion, about 150g
1 large garlic clove
2 tablespoons olive oil
1 tablespoon pine nuts
250g good-quality minced
  lamb
½ teaspoon ground allspice
1 tablespoon finely chopped
  coriander
1 tablespoon pomegranate
  syrup
3 tablespoons fresh
  pomegranate seeds
salt and freshly ground
  black pepper

Preheat the oven to 220°C, Gas Mark 7. Pierce the aubergine a few times and place on a small foil-lined roasting tin. Bake, turning once, for 30–40 minutes until saggy and the flesh obviously soft. Using tongs or an oven glove, hold the stalk and use a sharp knife to slash lengthways into quarters, then leave to drain in a colander.

Meanwhile, for the meatballs, peel and grate the onion, then squeeze dry. Crack the garlic, peel, finely chop and crush to a paste with a pinch of salt. Heat 1 teaspoon of the oil in a frying pan and stir-fry the pine nuts golden. Tip onto kitchen paper to drain and wipe out the pan. Quickly fry the onion and garlic in ½ tablespoon of the oil. Crumble the meat into a mixing bowl. Scatter the allspice, onion, pine nuts and coriander over the top. Season with salt and pepper, then mix and mulch with your hands into a ball. Pinch off a little mixture and roll between your hands into approximately 30 cherry tomato-sized balls. Transfer to a plate as you go. Chill, covered, until required.

Scrape the aubergine flesh off the charred skin and chop finely. Melt the butter in a small saucepan and stir in the flour. Add the milk gradually, stirring to make a thick, smooth sauce. Simmer for 5 minutes, then season to taste with salt and freshly grated nutmeg. Stir the aubergine and cheese into the sauce.

Quickly fry the meatballs in a spacious non-stick frying pan in the remaining hot oil, working in batches. Serve the meatballs over the hot sauce with a zig-zag of pomegranate syrup and a scattering of seeds.

SPINACH AND SWEET POTATO SHEPHERD'S PIE

SERVES 2 | **PREP** 20 MINUTES | **COOK** 50 MINUTES

When there is leftover Sunday roast lamb, or chicken, to contemplate, here's a great spin on a national favourite. The meat is flavoured with thyme, onion, parsley and lemon, and hidden under a layer of buttery spinach topped with golden sweet potato mash. Nutmeg and lemon charge the fluffy mash, while Parmesan with breadcrumbs give it a crisp, salty finish.

400g sweet potatoes
25g butter
1 lemon
1 medium onion
1 tablespoon sunflower oil
3 thyme sprigs
200g leftover roast lamb
    or chicken
2 teaspoons plain flour
few flat leaf parsley sprigs
150g young spinach
whole nutmeg for grating
1 tablespoon fresh white
    breadcrumbs
1 tablespoon freshly grated
    Parmesan cheese
salt and freshly ground
    black pepper

Peel, chunk and boil the potatoes in salted water until tender. Drain, saving 150ml water, return to the pan and mash with half the butter and 1 tablespoon lemon juice.

Meanwhile, halve, peel and finely chop the onion. Soften in the sunflower oil in a spacious frying/sauté pan. After a couple of minutes, add the thyme leaves stripped from the stalks and a generous pinch of salt. Stir often.

Pick over the meat, discarding fat and gristle, and chop into small pieces. Season with salt and pepper. Stir the meat into the softened onion. Dust with the flour, stirring until disappeared, then stir in the potato water, stirring vigorously as the gravy thickens. Season with lemon juice, salt and pepper to taste. Chop the parsley, stir into the mix and spoon into a gratin dish or dishes.

Preheat the oven to 200°C, Gas Mark 6. Briefly sweat the spinach in the remaining butter. Season lavishly with freshly grated nutmeg. Pile it over the meat, then top with the mash. Fork up and dust with the crumbs mixed with the Parmesan. Bake for 30 minutes until crusty.

POTATO AND ROSEMARY LAMB KEBABS WITH HUMMUS

SERVES 4 | **PREP** 25 MINUTES, PLUS SOAKING AND MARINATING | **COOK** 30 MINUTES

A blast of early summer prompted barbecue frenzy and this meal-on-a-stick is a new favourite. The lamb is cut into smaller-than-usual pieces, so cooks quickly. I aim for crusty edges, leaving the inside pink and moist, whilst interspersed oiled potatoes get an interesting roastie-cum-baked finish. When outside cooking is off-limits, cook these on a hot griddle. I like lamb kebabs with hummus and usually make my own because I prefer garlicky, Lebanese-style hummus that is creamy with olive oil. It takes about six minutes using canned chickpeas and a food processor, and is sure to become a habit.

4 lamb leg steaks
2 large garlic cloves
1 large lemon
4 tablespoons olive oil
3 rosemary sprigs
500g small new potatoes
salt

For the hummus
400g can chickpeas
2 garlic cloves, preferably
　new season
1 lemon
¼ teaspoon ground cumin
shake of Tabasco sauce
1 tablespoon tahini, optional
about 150ml olive oil

Soak 16 wooden skewers in cold water for at least 1 hour.

Cut the lamb into small kebab-sized pieces. Crack the garlic with your fist and flake away the skin. Remove 2 strips of lemon zest, then squeeze the juice into a mixing bowl. Whisk in the oil and add the zest, garlic and rosemary. Mix in the lamb. Cover with clingfilm and chill for 1 hour.

Scrub or scrape the potatoes and boil in salted water until just tender. Drain.

To make the hummus, drain the chickpeas. Place in the bowl of a food processor with the peeled and crushed garlic, a generous squeeze of lemon juice, the cumin, a generous seasoning of salt and black pepper, the tahini, if using, Tabasco and 2 tablespoons of the olive oil. Blitz to roughly chop, scraping down inside the bowl a couple of times. With the motor running, add the remaining olive oil in a steady stream. Continue until very smooth, adding extra olive oil or lemon juice for the texture you favour; I like it thick but creamy. If it shows signs of splitting, add 1 tablespoon warm water gradually, with the motor running. Taste and fine-tune the seasoning.

Thread the meat and potatoes onto the skewers. Cook over barbecue coals at the white ash stage or on a very hot griddle for about 15 minutes, turning after 2–3 minutes. Serve with a generous dollop of the hummus.

CUMIN LAMB CHOPS WITH MOUTABAL

SERVES 2 | **PREP** 20 MINUTES | **COOK** 25 MINUTES

Treating lamb chops like escalopes, pounding them thin and cooking them quickly on a griddle or barbecue, is an idea from chef Theo Randall. Dusting them with cumin creates a haunting flavour that goes well with creamed aubergine. Grilling aubergines, then mashing the smoky flesh with garlic, lemon and olive oil gives a silky, fluffy texture that is compulsive. I like this with new potatoes.

4 lamb chops or cutlets
½ tablespoon olive oil
1 teaspoon ground cumin
1 aubergine, about 250g
2 garlic cloves
2 lemons
3–4 tablespoons best olive oil
salt and freshly ground
    black pepper

Place the chops or cutlets on a chopping board, cover with clingfilm and pound gently with a rolling pin until evenly thin, about 5mm. Smear with the ½ tablespoon olive oil, dust with most of the cumin and set aside.

Pierce the aubergine a few times and place under a hot grill, turning regularly, until the skin is scorched and saggy. Hold by the stalk over a sieve, quarter to the base and leave to drain. Scrape the flesh off the skin and place in a food processor bowl with the coarsely chopped garlic, juice of half a lemon, pinch of cumin, salt, pepper and 1 tablespoon of the best olive oil. Pulse, adding sufficient olive oil to make a fluffy purée. Adjust the seasoning with salt and lemon.

Heat a griddle or barbecue to white ash stage and cook the lamb for 1 minute a side for juicy pink meat. Rest briefly, salt, then serve with a lemon wedge.

LAMB KOFTA WITH APRICOTS

SERVES 4 | **PREP** 25 MINUTES | **COOK** 1 HOUR 20 MINUTES

Often I crave curry but I rarely want one to blow my head off. Kormas tend to be gently spiced and this one has a creamy sauce, the stewing juices thickened and softened by creamed coconut. Serve with yoghurt and mango chutney, and rice or Indian bread, or both.

2 medium onions
1½ tablespoons coconut
    or groundnut oil
20g fresh root ginger
2 large garlic cloves
½ teaspoon ground cumin
1 teaspoon chilli powder
10 green cardamom pods
800g lamb neck fillet
12 dried apricots, about 100g
7.5cm piece of cinnamon stick
½ teaspoon garam masala
25g creamed coconut
salt and freshly ground
    black pepper

Peel and finely chop the onions, then cook in the oil, stirring often, in a spacious, lidded pan for about 15 minutes until glassy and pale. Peel, finely slice and chop the ginger and garlic. Stir both into the onion, stirring for 2 minutes, then stir in the cumin, chilli and cardamom, stirring for 1 minute.

Cut the meat into kebab-sized pieces. Brown amongst the onions. Add the apricots, cinnamon, 250ml water and ½ teaspoon salt. Simmer for 5 minutes, then reduce the heat, drape a sheet of greaseproof paper over and touching the food and secure with the lid. Leave to simmer gently but steadily for 45 minutes.

Stir in the garam masala and crumbled creamed coconut, adding black pepper and salt to taste. Cover and cook for a further 15 minutes or until the meat is very tender. Serve now or reheat later.

HARISSA LAMB WITH POMEGRANATE MOLASSES AND BEETROOT

SERVES 4 | **PREP** 30 MINUTES | **COOK** 1 HOUR

This almost-tagine requires briefly marinating diced lamb in fiery harissa with yoghurt, then stewing it in tomato sauce sweetened with musky pomegranate or grape molasses. Both, once the preserve of specialist food shops, are now widely available and virtually interchangeable. A bottle will keep for ages and the syrup is a good way of adding interest to savoury and sweet dishes. In this stew, lemony beetroot colours everything a deep magenta, making it hard to distinguish meat from beet. Serve with couscous, bulgur or rice, with green beans and extra yoghurt.

750g butterflied lamb
   shoulder
1 tablespoon harissa
2 tablespoons natural
   yoghurt (I like sheep's
   milk yoghurt), plus extra
   to serve
3 medium onions
25g butter
400g boiled beetroot
1 lemon
½ chicken stock cube
227g can chopped tomatoes
1 tablespoon pomegranate
   or grape molasses
salt

Trim the excess fat and slice the lamb into kebab-sized pieces. Mix the harissa and yoghurt in a mixing bowl, add the meat and toss to coat.

Halve, peel and finely slice the onions. Melt the butter in a spacious, lidded frying/sauté pan and stir in the onions with ½ teaspoon salt. Cover and cook gently, stirring once or twice, until soft, sloppy and hardly coloured.

Boil the kettle. Peel and dice the beets into bite-sized chunks. Toss with the lemon juice and a generous pinch of salt. Dissolve the stock cube in 250ml boiling water. Add the meat to the onions, increase the heat and brown thoroughly, then add the stock, tomatoes and molasses. Adjust the heat so that the food simmers steadily, cover and cook for 30 minutes.

Add the beets and juices and cook for 15 more minutes or until lamb is very tender. Taste, adjust the seasoning and serve now or reheat later.

LAMB AND SPINACH MEATBALLS
WITH GINGER NOODLES

SERVES 4 | **PREP** 30 MINUTES | **COOK** 25 MINUTES

Lemon grass, soy and ginger broth provide bright, clean flavours for poaching plump little spinach-specked meatballs that bob amongst snowy white rice noodles. I prefer tagliatelle-style noodles or cheat with ready-soaked vermicelli-thick noodles.

100g dried tagliatelle-style
    rice noodles
2 tablespoons fresh white
    breadcrumbs
2 tablespoons milk
2 shallots, about 70g
25g butter
50g frozen spinach
300g minced lamb
1 lemon grass stalk
10g fresh root ginger
1½ chicken stock cubes
200g green beans
1 tablespoon soy sauce
salt and freshly ground
    black pepper

Soak, then agitate the noodles in boiling water. Mix the breadcrumbs into the milk. Halve, peel and finely chop the shallots. Melt the butter in a frying pan and gently soften the shallots, stirring often. Add the spinach, stirring to encourage it to unravel, continuing until wilted. Drain, squeeze dry and then tip onto a work surface and chop.

Crumble the lamb into a mixing bowl. Scatter clumps of soaked crumbs, then spinach over the lamb and season generously with salt and pepper. Mix with a fork and work into a ball, then break in half to make 18 small balls from each half, rolling between damp hands to avoid sticking. Chill, covered, until required.

Boil the kettle. Bash the lemon grass to release its flavour. Peel the ginger and slice into thin scraps or batons. Simmer both in 1 litre boiling water with the crumbled stock cubes while you top and tail the beans. Add the beans and boil for 2 minutes, then add the soy and meatballs and simmer for 10 minutes until they are firm and cooked through.

Drain the noodles in a colander and reheat by pouring a kettle of boiling water over them. Place in bowls and top with the meatballs and broth.

LIVER AND KIDNEYS

The fifth quarter is the quaint name for offal, and liver and lambs' kidneys are two favourites for quick, healthy, easy dishes. Calves' liver is the Rolls Royce, but lambs' liver is far cheaper with a firmer texture and stronger flavour; both suit flash-frying.

Chicken livers are still remarkably good value and immensely versatile once you get the hang of them. These slippery little devils must be picked over and any stringy bits pulled away and the occasional lump of fat removed. I love them dusted with flour and quickly fried in garlicky oil to form a thin crust while the inside remains pink and creamy. They can be piled onto thick doorsteps of buttered toast or sat on a mound of slippery onions atop fluffy mashed potato. They slip and slide deliciously with pasta and go well with mushrooms, and can take strong seasoning.

It is still possible to buy lambs' kidneys in their suet, and roasting them thus over a thick slice of bread spread thickly with mustard, cooking until the suet melts and the bread crisps, is the superb but unhealthily indulgent way of eating them. They are worth discovering for kebabs, devilled on toast, in sauces and with Mediterranean vegetables.

PAPPARDELLE WITH CHICKEN LIVERS AND TOMATO
SERVES 4 | **PREP** 15 MINUTES | **COOK** 20 MINUTES

I keep a tub of chicken livers in the freezer for dishes like this favourite pasta supper. The combination of buttery pasta with a rosemary-flavoured tomato sauce and tender chicken livers is moreish in the extreme. With garlic bread it's a useful storecupboard supper to know about.

400g chicken livers
2 plump garlic cloves
1 small onion
1 teaspoon rosemary leaves
2 tablespoons olive oil
175ml red wine
400g can chopped tomatoes
400g pappardelle
knob of butter
salt and freshly ground
　　black pepper
freshly grated Parmesan
　　cheese, to serve

Rinse the livers and pat dry with kitchen paper. Remove any stringy membrane or discoloured parts. Lightly crush the garlic with the flat of a knife and flake away the skin. Peel the onion and chop very finely. Finely chop the rosemary until it resembles green dust.

Heat the oil in a large frying pan over a medium heat. Add the garlic and stir-fry for a few seconds without letting it brown. Add the onion and cook gently for 5 minutes until soft. Add the livers and rosemary and cook for a couple of minutes until the livers are browned all over. Remove the livers to a plate.

Turn up the heat, add the wine and stir vigorously as it bubbles, reducing it by half. Add the tomatoes and cook briskly for 10 minutes until the sauce becomes jammy. Taste for salt and pepper. Stir the livers back into the sauce.

Meanwhile, cook the pasta according to the packet instructions in plenty of salted water until tender but firm to the bite. Drain the pasta and toss with the butter in a warmed serving bowl. Stir the sauce into the pasta. Serve with freshly grated Parmesan.

LIVER, BACON, MASH, ONION AND GRAVY

SERVES 2 | **PREP** 20 MINUTES | **COOK** 25 MINUTES

Sublime comfort grub, the cooking neatly co-ordinated.

2 large potatoes, about 350g
40g butter
generous splash of milk
2 medium onions, about 300g
4 tablespoons sunflower or
    groundnut oil
2 tablespoons balsamic
    vinegar
200g lambs' liver
plain flour for dusting
4 rashers streaky bacon
salt
Dijon mustard, to serve

Peel, quarter and chunk the potatoes. Rinse and boil in salted water for 10–15 minutes until tender. Drain. Melt 25g of the butter in the milk in the potato pan, return the potatoes and mash, or pass through a mouli-legume/ricer, then whip with the remaining butter. Keep warm.

While the potatoes boil, halve, trim, peel and finely slice the onions. Heat 2 tablespoons of the oil in a frying pan, and when very hot, stir in the onions, stirring constantly for a few minutes as they colour and shrink. Reduce the heat slightly and stir often as they soften and turn golden, adjusting the heat so that they don't crisp. When shrivelled and tender, add 1 tablespoon of the balsamic vinegar and let it bubble away into the onions.

Check over the liver, cutting off the fat etc. Pat dry with kitchen paper and dust with flour, shaking off the excess. Grill the bacon until crisp on both sides. In a second frying pan, heat 1 tablespoon oil and quickly fry half the liver. I like it pink in the middle, so allow about 30 seconds a side, depending on the thickness. Transfer to a hot plate and repeat with the second batch.

Add the remaining balsamic vinegar to the pan, swirl it around and add about 100ml water, stirring vigorously to scrape up the flour left in the pan to thicken the gravy. Serve the mash topped with the hot onions, crisp bacon, liver and gravy. Pass the Dijon.

LIVER WITH GARLIC AND PARSLEY

SERVES 2 | **PREP** 15 MINUTES | **COOK** 10 MINUTES

The idea of frying liver with a splash of vinegar might sound strange, but when it's finished with finely chopped garlic and quite a lot of flat leaf parsley, the flavours are vibrant and interesting. It's funny how we forget favourite recipes for years on end, but then something stirs the memory and there it is again, just as good as ever. I used to cook this once a week, finding the recipe in *Poor Cook* by Caroline Conran with delightful line drawings by Susan Campbell.

4 very thin slices of calves'
   or lambs' liver
plain flour for dusting
2 garlic cloves
10g bunch of flat leaf parsley
2 tablespoons vegetable oil
4 tablespoons red wine
   vinegar

Trim the liver, cutting out any sinews running through or edging the meat. Dust with flour and shake off any excess. Peel and finely chop the garlic. Finely chop the parsley and tumble it over the chopped garlic and chop the two together a few times to thoroughly integrate.

Have ready 2 warmed dinner plates. Heat most of the oil in a frying pan placed over a medium heat, swirling it around the pan. Cook the liver for 30–45 seconds a side so that it is just cooked through. Transfer to the warmed plates.

Reduce the heat slightly and add the garlic and parsley mixture to the pan, having added the remaining oil if the pan seems dry. Stir constantly for a few seconds then add the vinegar. It will seethe and bubble furiously. Stir to scrape up any bits stuck to the bottom of the pan and pour the juices over the liver. Eat immediately.

KIDNEYS, TOMATOES AND COURGETTES

SERVES 2 | **PREP** 25 MINUTES | **COOK** 25 MINUTES

I'm hooked on lambs' kidneys not least because they are incredible value. This fresh and vibrant way of cooking them with intense small vine tomatoes and small courgettes suits their bouncy texture and gentle flavour. The recipe is very quick and straightforward; the only fiddle is peeling the tomatoes.

300g miniature new potatoes
1 medium onion, about 125g
25g butter
1 teaspoon flavourless
   oil such as groundnut
   or sunflower
8 lambs' kidneys
250g small vine tomatoes
200g small courgettes
1 tablespoon chopped
   flat leaf parsley
salt and freshly ground
   black pepper

Boil the potatoes in salted water until tender. Scoop into a colander, reserving the water, and leave to cool slightly.

Halve, peel and finely chop the onion. Melt half the butter in the oil in a spacious frying pan and stir in the onion. Add a generous pinch of salt and cook, stirring occasionally, for about 10 minutes until the onion is wilted but hardly coloured.

By now the potatoes will be cool enough to handle, so quickly remove their skins. Slice the kidneys into 4 or 5 even-sized pieces, avoiding the white core. Place the tomatoes in a bowl.

Trim the courgettes and slice into 4 diagonal slices. Re-boil the potato water and add the courgettes. Boil for 2 minutes. Scoop into a colander and pour the boiling water over the tomatoes. Count to 30, drain and deftly remove the skin. Chop.

Stir the kidneys into the softened onion, increase the heat slightly and keep stirring until evenly coloured. Add the tomatoes and cook briskly, stirring, as they break down to make a sauce. Stir in the remaining butter, then the courgettes and potatoes. Heat through, check the seasoning, stir in the parsley and serve.

DEVILLED KIDNEYS ON TOAST

SERVES 2 | **PREP** 10 MINUTES | **COOK** 10 MINUTES

I sometimes like to treat myself to lambs' kidneys for supper. Three or four cut into slices and quickly fried with soft onion make a delicious, easy meal. Devilled on toast with peppery watercress makes a great light supper, but take care not to over-cook or they turn unattractively rubbery.

8 lambs' kidneys
2 tablespoons plain flour
2 teaspoons English mustard
    powder
1 teaspoon cayenne pepper
¼ chicken stock cube
2 teaspoons Worcestershire
    sauce
Tabasco sauce, to taste
50g butter
1 teaspoon sunflower oil
2 thick slices of bread
bunch of watercress
salt and freshly ground
    black pepper

Boil the kettle. If necessary, remove the thin, opaque skin covering the kidneys. Halve the kidneys lengthways, then use a small, sharp knife to cut out the white core. Mix together the flour, mustard, cayenne and a generous seasoning of salt and pepper and add the kidneys. Toss thoroughly, then scoop out of the flour, shaking off the excess.

Dissolve the stock cube in 150ml boiling water and add the Worcestershire sauce and a shake of Tabasco. Melt half the butter with the oil in a frying pan. When sizzling, add the kidneys, tossing constantly for a maximum 2 minutes, until plump and browned.

Meanwhile, make the toast.

Scoop the kidneys out of the pan to a plate, then add the stock, stirring as it reduces and thickens, continuing until reduced to a few tablespoons. Stir the kidneys through the sauce and serve over the toast, spread with the remaining butter, with watercress on the side. Totally yum.

BEEF

I don't eat steak that often, but when I do, I like to know where it's come from and how it's been reared. The best value is skirt – *onglet* and *bavette* in France – which I buy regularly in 500–600g pieces from my local farmers' market and butcher. For a steak supper, I oil it, salt it and slap it on a smoking griddle for a few minutes a side, then let it rest for double the cooking time before slicing across the grain. This is excellent with salsa verde and oven chips. I dice it for chilli con carne, ragu, pasties and pies, and cut large pieces for relatively speedy daubes and other stews.

When there is time, or when I am cooking today for tomorrow, I prefer clod, shin, chuck or blade for stews – all hard-worked parts of the beast that need long, slow cooking. For an occasional treat, I'd recommend rump or sirloin, and for a very special occasion, a large, 600g, heavily marbled bone-in rib-eye chop, enough for two big appetites with leftovers for a second meal.

I buy organic, free-range minced beef.

STEAK AND MUSHROOM SANDWICH

SERVES 2 | **PREP** 15 MINUTES | **COOK** 15 MINUTES

A good steak sandwich, when the meat is juicy and tender with plenty of flavour, the bread crusty and fresh and the condiments to your taste, is a treat indeed. This version, made in stages during the men's Wimbledon finals and remembered again as I sat glued to the Olympics, turned out exceptionally well. I used skirt steak, bought in a large piece from my butcher, but any steak is suitable. It's a sandwich to eat fast and furiously, and you will need paper napkins to mop your chin.

300g skirt or thick steak
   of choice
1 tablespoon groundnut oil
2 portobello or other large,
   flat mushrooms
1 tablespoon olive oil
large handful of young
   spinach
1 ciabatta loaf
butter for spreading
Maille or Grey Poupon Dijon
   mustard, to taste
Maldon sea salt

Heat a griddle over a medium heat until searingly hot. Pat the meat dry with kitchen paper and smear with groundnut oil. Season generously with sea salt, pressing it into the steak. Place on the hot griddle, pressing down with a spatula. Leave untouched for 2 minutes, turn to cook the other side, then repeat for 1–2 minutes a side depending on how rare you like it – skirt must be cooked rare. Remove to a board and leave to rest for 8 minutes.

Meanwhile, wipe and slice the mushrooms, then fry in the hot olive oil over a medium heat, turning the slices as they turn juicy and dark. Add the spinach, fold a couple of times as the leaves wilt and remove from the heat.

Split the loaf lengthways and cut in half. Butter the cut surfaces and quickly toast on the hot griddle. Smear with mustard. Slice the steak across the grain, cutting chunky slices. Dribble any meat juices over the top, add the mushrooms and spinach, clamp tight and halve the sandwiches. Eat.

THAI BEEF SALAD

SERVES 2 | **PREP** 20 MINUTES | **COOK** 15 MINUTES, PLUS RESTING

A good way to make one steak feed two.

250g thick sirloin or
  rump steak
1 tablespoon groundnut oil
1 tablespoon Maldon sea salt
½ teaspoon sugar
2 tablespoons lime juice
1 tablespoon Thai fish sauce
  (nam pla)
1 shallot or small red onion
1 red bird's eye chilli
10cm length of cucumber or
  1 small/Lebanese cucumber
6 cherry tomatoes
1 Little Gem lettuce heart
handful of rocket or mixed
  leaves
few coriander sprigs
10 mint leaves
1 tablespoon toasted
  sesame oil
1 teaspoon soy sauce

Rub the steak with the groundnut oil. Spread the salt out on a plate. Heat the griddle or heavy frying pan for several minutes until scorchingly hot. Press the steak into the salt on one side and cook, salt-side down, for 5–6 minutes until crusty. Salt the exposed side and repeat. Rest on a plate for 10 minutes.

Dissolve the sugar in the lime juice and fish sauce in a mixing bowl. Halve, peel and finely slice the shallot or onion and stir into the bowl. Finely chop the chilli, discarding seeds, and add that, too.

Peel the cucumber and thinly slice on the slant. Halve the tomatoes. Separate the lettuce, rinse and shake dry. Add all the salad ingredients – cucumber, tomatoes, lettuce, rocket or mixed leaves, coriander and mint – to the bowl and toss thoroughly. Transfer to a platter.

Slice the steak thinly across the width, smear with the toasted sesame oil and soy sauce, then pile over the salad, adding any meat juices.

JAPANESE STEAK STIR-FRY WITH RICE

SERVES 2 | **PREP** 15 MINUTES, PLUS CHILLING | **COOK** 25 MINUTES

Here is a very good reason to search out skirt steak. Buy it in a single piece from a butcher or farmers' market and chill in the freezer to make the thin slicing required easier. The stir-fry is just onions and steak, but in a recognizably Japanese broth made with dashi. This pungent stock can be bought in sachets or made by boiling kombu, or cheat with light chicken stock.

250g skirt or other
    lean steak
200g basmati rice
2 medium onions
2 tablespoons toasted
    sesame oil
300ml dashi or light
    chicken stock
50ml soy sauce
50ml sake
50ml mirin
pinch of sugar
10g pickled sushi ginger

Chill the steak in the freezer for at least 20 minutes while you prepare everything else, then slice into very thin slivers across the steak.

Rinse the rice thoroughly. Place in a pan with 350ml cold water and bring to the boil, then reduce the heat to very low, cover and cook for 10 minutes. Leave without removing the lid for 10 minutes. Fork up vigorously to loosen the grains.

Halve, trim and peel the onions, then slice down the halves into thin slivers. Heat the oil in a wok or spacious frying pan, stir in the onions and cook briskly to begin with, then reduce the heat and cook, stirring often, until wilted, lightly coloured and nuttily aromatic.

Heat the dashi with the soy, sake and mirin in a small pan. Increase the heat under the onions, add the steak and quickly stir-fry. Add the sugar, toss again and then add the stock. Simmer for 2 minutes. Place the rice in bowls, spoon over the contents of the pan, add the torn ginger and eat.

STEAK, POTATO AND ONION PIE

SERVES 4 | **PREP** 30 MINUTES | **COOK** 1 HOUR

For this pasty pie, lean shaggy skirt steak is chopped up small and mixed with diced onion and new potatoes, all held in puff pastry with plenty of seasoning. Be sure, though, that the edges are securely sealed and don't forget air holes, both of which help avoid leakage. Serve hot or cold.

knob of butter
2 × 320g ready-rolled puff
    pastry sheets
400g skirt or lean stewing
    steak
350g new potatoes
1 medium–large onion,
    about 165g
1 egg
salt, freshly ground black
    pepper and white pepper

Lightly butter a shallow roasting tin or baking sheet and line with baking parchment. Rub the parchment with butter and lay out one sheet of pastry.

Dice the steak in small pieces. Scrape or scrub the potatoes and dice slightly smaller than the steak. Halve, peel and finely chop the onion. Mix together with a generous seasoning of salt, black pepper and white pepper.

Preheat the oven to 200°C, Gas Mark 6. Whisk the egg. Pile the mixture in the middle of the pastry and spread evenly within a 2cm border. Paint with beaten egg. Lay the second sheet of pastry over the top. Press the edges. Paint the whole thing with egg wash, then roll the edges forward and crimp with a fork. Egg wash again. Make a few air holes with the tines of a fork and etch a pattern if you fancy it using a small, upturned knife.

Bake for 15 minutes, then reduce the temperature to 150°C, Gas Mark 2 and bake for a further 45 minutes until crusty and golden.

SHIITAKE AND STEAK MISO NOODLES

SERVES 2 | **PREP** 15 MINUTES | **COOK** 20 MINUTES

One of my favourite storecupboard standbys is a pack of miso soup paste sachets, preferably one with sea vegetables. Not only do they make the best sort of instant soup, when made up with less liquid they give oriental flavour to noodle dishes like this one. Unless you are big meat eaters, one decent-sized steak will feed two generously, merging with slippery red onion and shiitake mushrooms to make plenty of texturally interesting sauce for the noodles. It's an all-in-together dish, the steak and vegetables stir-fried in a wok or similarly large pan, the softened noodles stirred in right at the end. Thai fish sauce adds piquancy, while soy sauce lends its salty savour, the latter added to taste to balance the flavours.

1 large red onion
1 large garlic clove
100g shiitake mushrooms
200g rump or sirloin steak
1 tablespoon sunflower or
    groundnut oil
100g wide udon noodles
1 sachet miso soup paste
    with sea vegetables
1 tablespoon Thai fish sauce
    (nam pla)
2 tablespoons soy sauce plus
    extra to serve
200ml chicken stock
100g green beans, optional
salt

Halve, peel and finely slice the onion. Crack the garlic with your fist, flake away the skin, finely chop and sprinkle with a pinch of salt. Crush to a juicy paste with the flat of a knife. Halve the mushrooms. Smear the steak with a little of the oil.

Heat a griddle for 2–3 minutes until very hot. Prepare the noodles according to the packet instructions. Salt one side of the steak and slap down on the hot griddle. Cook, pressing down with a spatula for good contact, for 2 minutes. Salt the exposed side, turn and repeat. Transfer to a chopping board and leave to rest for 5 minutes.

Heat the rest of the oil in a wok or spacious sauté pan and cook the onion, tossing until wilted. Add the mushrooms and garlic, tossing for a couple of minutes, then add the miso soup paste, fish sauce, soy sauce and stock. Simmer briskly, stirring constantly, for a few minutes to reduce and consolidate the sauce.

Trim the steak and slice thinly across the width. Stir the drained noodles into the sauce, followed by the steak and juices. Stir again to heat through and mix thoroughly, then serve in bowls with the bottle of soy sauce.
A few green beans, halved and blanched, is a good addition.

BEEF PIES WITH MUSHROOM DUXELLE

SERVES 4 | **PREP** 30 MINUTES, PLUS CHILLING AND COOLING | **COOK** 50 MINUTES

These little pies were so good, I promptly made more. I was after a way to stretch a small amount of minced beef into a meal for six and it was sufficient to give the pies a rich flavour. It merged with a thick mushroom duxelle. The pies are surprisingly satisfying, great with mashed potato and greens.

200g plain flour plus extra
   for dusting
pinch of salt
85g butter
25g lard
3 large red onions
1 tablespoon olive oil
250g good-quality minced beef
1 teaspoon chopped thyme
½ tablespoon tomato purée
1 tablespoon fresh
   breadcrumbs
4 tablespoons chicken stock
200g mushrooms
1 garlic clove
1 egg, beaten

Using a food processor, blitz the flour, salt and 75g of the chunked butter and the lard into crumbs. With the machine running, add sufficient cold water (3–5 tablespoons) to make a ball. Chill in a plastic bag for 30 minutes.

Peel and grate the onions, then cook, stirring, in the remaining butter and ½ tablespoon oil in a frying pan until soft. Scoop out of the pan with a slotted spoon. Add the remaining oil to the pan and brown the meat. Stir in the thyme, tomato purée, breadcrumbs and stock. Simmer to amalgamate before adding the wiped mushrooms finely chopped with the garlic, tossing constantly until dark, juicy and shrunken. Return the onions to the pan, stir to mix, then tip into a bowl to cool. Preheat the oven to 220°C, Gas Mark 7.

Flour a work surface. Divide the pastry equally into 6, then roll out 6 circles to line a non-stick 6-cup muffin tin, with 1cm overhang, plus 6 lids. Line the tins and fill with the cooled mixture, wet the edge of the lids and crimp to seal. Make a central air hole and brush with egg. Bake for 10 minutes, then reduce the oven temperature to 180°C, Gas Mark 4 and cook for a further 25–35 minutes until golden. Run a knife around the inside edge, remove and eat.

STEAK AND STOUT STEW

SERVES 4 | **PREP** 20 MINUTES | **COOK** 1½–1¾ HOURS

This is a simple, delicious stew made with inexpensive skirt steak. It's sliced into chunky strips that break apart in gratifyingly tender lines when it's done. Red onion, a beer, a bundle of herbs and flour to thicken the juices are all it takes. Serve with sweet potatoes roasted in their skins.

3 large red onions
15g butter
3 tablespoons sunflower oil
4 thyme sprigs
1 bay leaf
800g piece of skirt steak
2 tablespoons plain flour
500ml pale ale
salt and freshly ground
   black pepper

Preheat the oven to 150°C, Gas Mark 2. Halve, trim, peel and slice the onions. Using a spacious, ovenproof, lidded casserole, soften them, covered, in the butter melted in 1 tablespoon oil with ½ teaspoon salt. Bundle the thyme and bay with string and add to the pot.

Meanwhile, slice the meat into thumb-sized strips, cut down the meat grooves. Roll the pieces through the seasoned flour and brown in batches in the remaining oil in a frying pan, transferring to a plate after each batch. Stir the meat into the soft onions, stirring briskly whilst adding the beer to knock the flour off the meat to thicken the gravy. Bring to the boil as you stir, then turn off the heat. Drape a sheet of greaseproof paper over and touching the food and secure it with the lid. Cook for 1¼–1½ hours or until the meat is very tender. Remove the herbs. Eat now, or reheat later or tomorrow.

TERIYAKI BEEF AND NOODLES

SERVES 2 | **PREP** 15 MINUTES | **COOK** 15 MINUTES

Steak leftovers went into this wonderful way of making a little steak go a long way. Skirt isn't suitable, but sirloin is a good alternative to expensive rib-eye, which would be my first choice. Whichever steak you choose, searing and resting it before slicing turns this into a super-quick dish.

200g leftover griddled rib-eye
    or sirloin steak or 200g
    rib-eye or sirloin steak
2 tablespoons sunflower
    or groundnut oil
1 medium onion
2 sheets egg noodles
200g green beans
150g frozen petits pois
1 tablespoon teriyaki sauce
1 tablespoon dry sherry
1 tablespoon soy sauce
Maldon sea salt

If using leftover steak, trim away the fat and slice across the width in 5mm-thick slices. If starting from scratch, heat a griddle or heavy-duty frying pan for several minutes until smoking. Smear the steak lightly with oil and, just before cooking, season one side with Maldon sea salt. Slap, seasoned-side down, on the griddle, pressing with a spatula to make good contact for a crusty surface. Cook for 2 minutes, then season the exposed side, turn and cook the other side. Repeat. Set aside to rest and cool.

To complete the dish, halve, peel and slice the onion. Heat the remaining oil in a spacious frying pan and fry the onion over a low heat, stirring often, until soft and golden. While the onion sizzles, cook the noodles according to the packet instructions. Drain and keep warm.

Top and tail the beans. Cook beans and peas separately in boiling water, drain separately and keep warm. Add the teriyaki, sherry and soy to the slippery, golden onion. Allow to bubble up, then stir in the slices of steak, drained noodles and peas. Toss thoroughly, smearing everything with the dark brown savoury juices. Serve over, with or mixed with the beans.

BURGUNDY POTATO SALAD WITH STEAK

SERVES 2, GENEROUSLY | **PREP** 20 MINUTES | **COOK** 20 MINUTES

Here's an excellent way of turning one steak into a generous dinner for two. I made it one holiday with leftover steak, waxy French potatoes and chives from the garden in Burgundy where I was staying. It could be part of an al fresco spread, but needs little else apart from a few salad leaves.

750g new potatoes
1 sirloin steak
1 tablespoon red wine
    vinegar
1 tablespoon Dijon mustard
2 tablespoons olive oil
3–4 tablespoons sunflower oil
    plus extra for oiling
3 tablespoons finely
    sliced chives
salt and freshly ground
    black pepper

Scrub the potatoes, to remove the skins, and boil in salted water until tender.

Oil the steak with olive oil, season on one side and cook for 2–4 minutes on a hot griddle or heavy frying pan. Season the exposed side, turn, repeat and rest for 5 minutes before slicing thinly across the width.

Place the vinegar in a salad bowl, season with salt and pepper, stir in the mustard, then whisk in the olive oil and sufficient sunflower oil to make a thick, creamy emulsion. Whisk in a dribble of warm water to slacken.

Drain and leave the small potatoes whole, halve the medium potatoes and chunk the large ones, cutting directly into the dressing. Stir well. Leave for a few minutes for the dressing to soak into and flavour the potatoes, then fold in the steak. Add most of the chives and toss thoroughly to mix. Give a final twist of black pepper and sprinkle over the last of the chives.

CHORIZO BEEF SLIDERS WITH ASIAN SALAD

SERVES 4 | **PREP** 25 MINUTES | **COOK** 10 MINUTES

Hellofresh.co.uk is a bit like my column in *The Times* except they do the shopping, delivering a box with everything needed to make three or five meals a week for two, four or six people. Being a chorizo fan, I love their idea of mixing a little chopped chorizo into a beef burger. This is my interpretation with a crisp, healthy Asian fridge-tidy salad to go with it. Instead of buns, I went for garlicky bruschetta on the side.

75g Iberico chorizo sausage
500g prime minced beef
1 generous tablespoon
    tomato ketchup
50g coriander
1½ tablespoons rapeseed oil
salt and freshly ground
    black pepper

For the salad
1 fennel bulb
1 lime
2 small red onions
2 carrots
200g cucumber
1 tablespoon Thai fish sauce
    (nam pla)
2 tablespoons Thai sweet
    chilli sauce
1 tablespoon toasted
    sesame oil
1 tablespoon toasted
    sesame seeds

For the bruschetta
4 thick slices of sourdough
    bread
2 garlic cloves
6–8 tablespoons best olive oil

Run a knife down the chorizo, cutting through the skin. Peel away and discard. Finely chop the chorizo. Mix the mince, chorizo, ketchup, half the chopped coriander, 1 tablespoon rapeseed oil and a generous seasoning of salt and pepper. Knead into a ball, divide into quarters, then make 4 small burgers from each quarter, patting gently but firmly. Smear lightly with the remaining oil. Chill, covered with clingfilm, until required.

Trim and halve the fennel lengthways, cut out the core and slice finely across the halves. Separate the pieces into a mixing bowl. Toss with lime juice. Trim, peel, halve and finely slice the onions. Toss with the fennel. Scrape the carrots and slice into whiskers about 6cm long. Halve the cucumber lengthways, scrape out the seeds with a teaspoon and slice into thin batons, each with skin. Add the carrots and cucumber to the fennel and toss with the nam pla, chilli sauce and sesame oil. Add the sesame seeds and remaining coriander.

Cook the sliders on a preheated griddle or barbecue at the white ash stage for 3–4 minutes a side for medium rare. Serve with the salad, adding the toasted bread rubbed with garlic and splashed with the best olive oil.

TAGLIATELLE WITH BEEF AND RED WINE RAGU

SERVES 4 | **PREP** 20 MINUTES | **COOK** 1¼ HOURS

Making ragu with diced rather than minced beef was inspired by a stupendous version I enjoyed at The Brackenbury restaurant on the Hammersmith Shepherd's Bush borders run by a team of ex-River Café folk. They use ox cheek and anchovy and it takes 4 hours; mine is far faster but similarly sublime.

400g diced skirt, chuck
   or other trimmed
   braising steak
2 tablespoons olive oil
1 medium onion
100g celery
1 garlic clove
1 teaspoon chopped thyme
pinch of dried chilli flakes
100g chestnut mushrooms
150ml red wine
400g can chopped tomatoes
350g tagliatelle or pappardelle
25g butter
salt and freshly ground
   black pepper
freshly grated Parmesan
   cheese, to serve

Preheat the oven to 170°C, Gas Mark 3.

Season the meat with salt and pepper. Brown in the hot oil in a medium-sized casserole. Scoop into a sieve over a bowl.

Peel and finely dice the onion, celery and garlic. Add all to the pan with the meat juices, thyme and chilli and gently soften, tossing regularly, for about 5 minutes.

Wipe the mushrooms and pulse in a food processor to finely chop. Add to the pan, tossing until dark and juicy. Coarsely chop the meat and return to the pan. Add the wine and bubble up for a couple of minutes. Stir in the tomatoes. Drape over a sheet of baking parchment to touch the food and secure with the lid. Bake for 1 hour or until the meat is very tender. Taste and adjust the seasoning.

Cook the pasta according to the packet instructions, drain and toss with butter, then with the sauce. Serve with grated Parmesan. If preferred, cook the ragu over a very low direct heat.

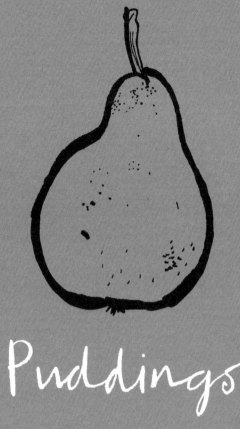

Puddings

I love puddings, and here are a few I make for friends and family that can be quickly knocked together with ingredients readily to hand.

Many involve fruit; whatever is seasonal and in fridge or fruit bowl. Rhubarb and gooseberries, figs, apples, pears and pineapples are all favourite pudding inspirations.

Nothing, though, beats the wow factor of a huge platter of prepared fruit at the end of a meal. Individual dipping bowls of something creamy or chocolate sauce make it extra special. Fruit purées are useful to have on standby in the fridge, ready to spoon over yoghurt, fromage frais or other creamy little puddings.

Sometimes I make comforting puddings like Chocolate Puddle Pudding, fruit tarts or a pudding cake, but trifle loaded with fruit always goes down well whatever the time of year.

FLAT WHITE PEACH MELBA

SERVES 6 | **PREP** 20 MINUTES | **COOK** 10 MINUTES

The sweet white flesh of doughnut peaches is particularly gorgeous when the fruit is poached or roasted. They are perfect for peach Melba, poached first in white wine, then perched over a scoop of vanilla ice cream and drenched in a thick raspberry sauce. It's an occasion to sieve the raspberries to get rid of their copious pips, but be sure to scrape under the sieve so that nothing is wasted. It's a usefully make-ahead, wow-factor pud, peaches and sauce chilled under clingfilm until you are ready to serve.

150g fresh or frozen
   raspberries
6 ripe doughnut/flat peaches
   or 3 ripe peaches or
   nectarines
4 tablespoons caster sugar
250ml white wine
500g vanilla ice cream

Boil the kettle. If using frozen raspberries, spread them out on a plate to defrost. Plunge the peaches or nectarines in the hot kettle water for 30 seconds. Peel away the skin. Halve regular peaches or nectarines round their middles, twist apart and discard the stone. Leave the stone in doughnut peaches.

Dissolve the sugar in the wine in a pan that can hold the fruit in a single layer over a medium heat and cook the peaches or nectarines, covered, for 5 minutes, turning halfway through. Scoop the fruit onto a plate to cool.

Place the raspberries in a sieve over a bowl, spoon 4 tablespoons of the hot sweet wine over the top and press through with the back of a spoon, scraping underneath to avoid wastage. (Set aside the remaining poaching liquid for future use or boil it down to make a syrup.)

Place a flat whole peach or upturned regular peach/nectarine over a scoop of ice cream and cover with raspberry sauce. Class.

CITRUS FRUIT SALAD WITH LEMON GRASS SYRUP

SERVES 6–8 | **PREP** 45 MINUTES, PLUS CHILLING | **COOK** 15 MINUTES

The ratio of oranges to other citrus fruit depends on what you have available, but the idea is to arrive at a pretty contrast of size, colour and taste. This is also good made with pineapple – quarter it lengthways, cut off the woody core, skin and remove all the hairy 'eyes' and slice very thinly across the width – either on its own, or with oranges, say, or a mix of citrus. Pineapple creates lots of liquid as it steeps, so bear that in mind. Save leftover juices for vodka cocktails.

1 red bird's eye chilli
2 lemon grass stalks
4 kaffir lime leaves (fresh,
   frozen or dried)
100g white sugar
5 large navel oranges
2 large lemons
3 limes
3 red grapefruit
1 pomelo

Split the chilli, scrape out the seeds and slice into skinny batons, then into tiny dice. Bruise the lemon grass. Place both in a pan with the lime leaves, sugar and 400ml cold water. Swirl the pan to melt the sugar as it comes to the boil, reduce the heat and simmer for 15 minutes. Leave to cool.

Slice the skin off the citrus fruit, removing all the white pith. Rotate each piece of fruit as you slice between the membrane to remove the skinless segments. Split any fat segments; you are after thin and dainty. Transfer to a glass serving bowl with all the juices. Discard the lemon grass and lime leaves, then pour the cooled syrup over the fruit salad. Mix, cover with clingfilm and chill before serving.

FRESH FRUIT PLATTER WITH VANILLA DIPPING CREAM

SERVES 6 | **PREP** 20 MINUTES

This is one of the simplest, most stunning puddings I know. Everyone loves it because it's healthy, informal and easy to eat and can be varied depending on what's in season and which fruits you favour. Any type of melon, so long as it is ripe, works. Instead of vanilla-flavoured crème fraîche, it could be served with whipped cream, chocolate sauce or cold custard from a carton.

1 ripe melon
500g strawberries
500g cherries
1 large ripe pineapple
few small mint sprigs
1 teaspoon vanilla extract
350ml crème fraîche
icing sugar for dusting

Quarter the melon, scrape out the seeds and cut off the skin. Use a melon-baller or cut into bite-sized pieces. Rinse the strawberries and cherries. Trim the pineapple, quarter lengthways and remove the skin and woody core. Slice across the pieces to make large bite-sized chunks.

Arrange the strawberries, cherries, pineapple and melon sequentially. Decorate with mint sprigs. Beat the vanilla extract into the crème fraîche and decant into 6 ramekins or similar. Chill until required. Serve the fruit platter with a dusting of icing sugar and the crème fraîche for dipping.

LEMON POSSET WITH PLUM COULIS

SERVES 6–8 | **PREP** 15 MINUTES, PLUS CHILLING | **COOK** 20 MINUTES

Creamy sweet-sour lemon posset is a favourite dinner party pudding because it's easy to shop for, takes five minutes to make and will sit happily in the fridge for a couple of days. It sets almost instantly but should be served chilled. I've winged it with 45 minutes, although a couple of hours is better. The only important point is using a large saucepan so that the cream and sugar can boil high without fear of accidents. This fluffy plum purée is a stunning, almost healthy counterbalance.

600ml double cream
200g caster sugar
2 lemons
400g plums

Tip the cream into a deep saucepan over a medium heat. Add 150g of the sugar, stirring until melted. Boil steadily for 3 minutes exactly. Remove from the heat.

Remove paper-thin, long strips of zest from half of one lemon and set aside. Squeeze the juice into a measuring jug; you want 100ml. Whisk the juice into the cooked cream, then pour back into the jug for easy decanting into pretty glasses or ramekins. Don't fill to the top; you want space for the coulis. Cool, cover with clingfilm and chill.

Place the lemon zest in a lidded pan with the plums sliced off the stones. Add the remaining sugar and 150ml water. Simmer, stirring until the sugar dissolves, cover and cook for about 15 minutes or until virtually disintegrating. Liquidize. Pass through a sieve into a bowl. Cool.

Skim the possets with cooled plum purée, as much or little as you fancy. Re-chill, covered, until required.

APRICOT AND ALMOND TART

SERVES 6 | **PREP** 30 MINUTES, PLUS CHILLING | **COOK** 40 MINUTES

Oh my, this looks so good; halved apricots in an almond paste that puffs and billows around them in thin, crisp, buttery shortcrust pastry. Dusted with icing sugar, this is a tart amongst tarts, a real show-stopper. It tastes pretty good, too, the creamy, eggy almond mix set into a soft fluffy paste, and the flavour and colour of the apricots concentrated beyond belief. Wonderful; serve alone, warm or cold, with or without crème fraîche.

125g plain flour plus extra
  for dusting
pinch of salt
75g butter plus extra
  for greasing
1 egg
icing sugar for dusting

For the frangipane
75g soft butter
75g caster sugar
2 eggs
75g ground almonds
15g plain flour
10 ripe apricots, about 400g

To make the pastry, sift the flour into a bowl with the salt. Cut the butter over the top and use fingertips to rub it into the flour until it resembles breadcrumbs. Whisk the egg and stir into the mixture, continuing as it comes together. Knead lightly whilst forming into a ball. Pop in a plastic bag and chill for 30 minutes.

Preheat the oven to 200°C, Gas Mark 6. Butter the inside of a 26cm loose-based tart tin. Add 1 tablespoon flour, letting it dust the butter, thus making the tin reliably non-stick. Roll the pastry to fit the tin.

For the frangipane, cream the butter with the sugar in a food processor or in a bowl with a wooden spoon until pale and fluffy. Mix in the eggs to make a smooth paste, then fold in the almonds. Sift the flour over the top and stir in gently. Spread the almond paste over the base of the pastry case. Halve and stone the apricots, then arrange, cut-side uppermost, on top.

Bake for 20 minutes, then reduce the heat to 180°C, Gas Mark 4 and continue for 20 minutes until the apricots are very soft and the paste risen around the pieces. Dust with icing sugar. Stand on a can to release the ring and then slip the tart onto a plate.

ORANGE FIG JAM WITH FROMAGE FRAIS

SERVES 6 | **PREP** 15 MINUTES, PLUS COOLING | **COOK** 20 MINUTES

Here's a cute way of serving those luscious black Bursa figs that sweep in from Turkey at the end of the summer at knockdown prices. Chopped and cooked with honey and fresh orange juice into a thick, fresh jam, they are very good spooned over anything creamy, from fromage frais to panna cotta. This combination is also good piled over baked puff pastry, either as a large tart or cut into squares, circles or slices.

8 black Bursa figs
2 tablespoons honey
2 juicing oranges
400g fromage frais

Trim and quarter the figs, slice each piece in half lengthways and then chop. Melt the honey in the orange juice in a spacious frying/sauté pan over a medium heat, stirring constantly for a couple of minutes. Stir in the figs and stir-simmer for 3–4 minutes until almost soft, the seeds floating free.

Tip the contents of the pan into a sieve over a bowl. Pour the juice back into the pan and simmer, stirring often, until reduced to 3 tablespoons syrup. Tip the figs into the bowl, pour over the syrup, agitate to disperse and leave to cool and thicken into jam. Serve over a generous scoop of fromage frais.

BANANA TOFFEE TARTS

SERVES 4 | **PREP** 15 MINUTES | **COOK** 25 MINUTES

I'm not mad about cooked banana, but these little tarts are an exception. When bananas are tossed in Angostura, piled over puff pastry and served hot with an Angostura and lime-flavoured toffee sauce they become irresistible.

flour for dusting
200g puff pastry
45g butter
4 medium bananas
4 tablespoons Angostura
    bitters
3 tablespoons demerera sugar
2 tablespoons golden syrup
1 tablespoon lime juice
300ml crème fraîche
1 egg

Preheat the oven to 200°C, Gas Mark 6. Dust a work surface with flour. Cut the pastry into 4 equal pieces and roll each approximately 14cm square. Leaving a 1cm border, make fork marks all over the pastry to stop it rising. Use 5g of the butter to smear a non-stick baking sheet and lay out the pastry squares without touching.

Peel and halve each banana and quarter lengthways. Toss the pieces in 2 tablespoons Angostura. Put the sugar, syrup and 15g butter in a pan together. Cook on a medium heat, stirring occasionally, until a good toffee colour. Remove from the heat and stir in the remaining Angostura, lime juice and 2 tablespoons of the crème fraîche.

Paint the border of the pastry with beaten egg, then snuggle the banana within the border. Paint the banana with the remaining 25g butter, melted. Bake in the middle of the oven for 15–20 minutes until the pastry border is puffy and golden. Allow to cool slightly, then pour over the warm sauce. Serve with a dollop of crème fraîche.

ORANGE POACHED PEARS WITH THYME

SERVES 6 | **PREP** 25 MINUTES, PLUS COOLING | **COOK** 30 MINUTES

One of my weekly treats through their season is a bargain bag of tiny pears from the apple and pear stall at my local farmers' market. Most are hard, but they ripen perfectly after a few days in my warm kitchen. Catching them before they turn, secretly bruising from the inside out, is the downside with pears, but any just-ripe pear is perfect for poaching.

This poaching liquid is a cocktail of white wine sweetened with honey, orange juice and zest, with a hint of lemon and thyme. I keep the pears whole, peeling them but leaving the stalk intact and cutting out the core in a pointed plug shape so that they sit nicely. They are eaten cold, the juice simmered for a few minutes to concentrate the flavours. Serve them with vanilla ice cream and a dollop of crème fraîche. Any leftover juices will lift your next fruit salad. Allow one or two pears, depending on size.

3 juicing oranges
1 lemon
2–3 tablespoons runny honey
750ml dry white wine
2 thyme sprigs
6–12 firm ripe pears

Remove 3 strips of paper-thin zest from one orange and a single strip from the lemon. Squeeze the juice from the oranges and half the lemon into a lidded pan that can comfortably hold all the pears, standing up or on their side. Add 2 tablespoons honey, the wine and thyme. Simmer gently, stirring until the honey melts, for 10 minutes, while you prepare the pears.

Peel the pears carefully, leaving the stalk intact. Cut out the core in a pointed plug shape. Smear with lemon juice as you finish each pear to avoid discolouring. Transfer the pears to the pan, cover and leave to cook for a further 10–15 minutes, turning a couple of times so that they cook evenly, until tender to the point of a knife.

Stand the pears in a glass or china bowl and simmer the liquid for a further 10 minutes. Taste and add extra honey if needed. Pour the liquid over the pears and leave to cool before serving.

GRILLED PINEAPPLE WITH RUM

SERVES 6 | **PREP** 20 MINUTES | **COOK** 10 MINUTES

I learnt to make this on a trip to Trinidad where Angostura bitters are made. The recipe is a well-guarded secret, but its aromatic, tangy flavour is definitely helped by rum. This pudding is unbelievably delicious, the pineapple very juicy with an alcoholic kick.

2 small ripe pineapples
4 tablespoons rum or
  2 tablespoons Angostura
  bitters
6 tablespoons soft dark
  brown sugar
vanilla ice cream or crème
  fraîche, to serve

Trim the pineapples and cut into quarters lengthways. Slice off the skin, cut off the woody core and slice each quarter lengthways into 3 chunky pieces. Cover the grill pan generously with foil and lay out the pieces.

About 10 minutes before you are ready for pudding, season the pineapple lavishly with the rum or Angostura bitters and then dredge with the sugar. Heat the grill to its highest setting and cook for 7–10 minutes, turning halfway through cooking, until the sugar has melted and the pineapple is very juicy. Serve with ice cream or crème fraîche.

RUSSIAN RASPBERRY PUDDING

SERVES 4–6 | **PREP** 10 MINUTES | **COOK** 55 MINUTES

I am very greedy when it comes to raspberries and love nothing better than raspberries and vanilla ice cream, but one of the best ways of making a little go a long way is Russian Raspberry Pudding. The recipe originates from one of my favourite cookbooks, Margaret Costa's *Four Seasons Cookery Book*, first published in 1970 but now available in a Grub Street edition. The recipe is related to clafoutis, but the combination of warming the raspberries in the oven and using soured cream with a very little flour in the egg mixture is slightly different. Do try it.

450g raspberries
3 tablespoons caster sugar
   plus extra to serve
2 eggs
300ml soured cream
1 tablespoon plain flour

Preheat the oven to 150°C, Gas Mark 2. Place the raspberries in a 1.5-litre oval gratin dish. Sprinkle with 2 tablespoons of the sugar. Place on a low shelf in the oven and leave for about 10 minutes until hot and juicy.

Lightly whisk the eggs, then mix in the soured cream and remaining 1 tablespoon sugar. Sift the flour over the top and mix thoroughly. Pour the custard over the raspberries, return to the oven on a middle shelf and cook for 30–45 minutes until puffed, firm but with a slight wobble and golden. Dust with a little extra sugar before serving hot, warm or cold.

CHOCOLATE PUDDLE PUDDING

SERVES 4–6 | **PREP** 20 MINUTES | **COOK** 40 MINUTES

Distantly related to Margaret Costa's equally sublime Lemon Surprise Pudding in her *Four Seasons Cookery Book*, this light chocolate sponge generates its own sauce. The recipe is foolproof, fills the house with wonderful aromas and is great with lemony fromage frais or crème fraîche.

100g soft butter plus extra
   for greasing
100g golden caster sugar
3 eggs
100g self-raising flour
25g cocoa powder
100ml milk
½ teaspoon vanilla bean
   paste or extract
salt

For the sauce
100g soft dark brown sugar
25g cocoa powder
fromage frais or crème
   fraîche, to serve

Preheat the oven to 180°C, Gas Mark 4. Butter a 1.5-litre pudding dish – mine was oval and 4cm deep.

Cream the butter and caster sugar until fluffy. Separate the eggs and fold in the yolks. Mix together the flour, cocoa, a pinch of salt and the vanilla, then fold into the creamed mixture, followed by the milk. Whisk the egg whites until they hold soft peaks. Gently but firmly fold into the mix. Spoon into the dish and gently smooth the top. Boil the kettle.

Mix the sauce ingredients with 300ml hot water from the kettle and ladle over the pudding. Bake in the centre of the oven for 40 minutes.

The pudding will swell through the sauce to make a moist sponge with a thin crust. The sauce will be thick and chocolately underneath. Serve immediately with fromage frais or crème fraîche.

APPLE, DATE AND WALNUT FLAT CAKE

SERVES 8–10 | **PREP** 20 MINUTES | **COOK** 1 HOUR

I can't bear the term tray bake, but that's what this extraordinarily good cake is. It's easy to make, laden with fruit and, because it's made with oil rather than butter, has a light and springy texture with crusty edges. The apple keeps the cake moist, the top attractively patchy where the final dusting of icing sugar melts against it. Great for pud with whipped cream, for al fresco and al desko, and it freezes.

200g light muscovado sugar
3 large eggs
200ml grapeseed oil
200g self-raising flour
1 teaspoon bicarbonate
  of soda
1 teaspoon ground cinnamon
½ teaspoon ground nutmeg
½ teaspoon salt
60g stoned dates
60g walnuts
15g butter or 1 tablespoon
  sunflower oil
2 Bramley apples, about 500g
1–2 tablespoons icing sugar

Preheat the oven to 180°C, Gas Mark 4. Use the butter or 1 tablespoon oil to smear a 30 × 22cm baking tray or round tin (I use a 26cm tarte Tatin tin and cut into wedges, not squares).

Whisk the muscovado sugar and eggs until thick, light and fluffy. Whisk in the grapeseed oil in a gradual, steady trickle. Sift together the flour, bicarb, cinnamon, nutmeg and salt. Stir thoroughly into the creamed mixture. Chop the dates – I like quite big pieces – and walnuts, then stir into the mix.

Quickly quarter, core, peel and thinly slice the apples across the quarters, then stir into the thick mixture. Spread in the prepared tin and bake for 45 minutes–1 hour until firm. Cool in the tin. Dust with the icing sugar and cut into squares.

STRAWBERRY ALMOND CRUMBLE

SERVES 6 | **PREP** 20 MINUTES | **COOK** 35 MINUTES

Is it criminal to cook strawberries? I used to think so, but urge you to try this strawberry crumble made with ground almonds. The strawberries will taste like very good jam and the topping like soft, crumbly almond shortcake. Totally gorgeous, particularly with clotted cream or Normandy crème fraîche.

800g English strawberries
25g fresh white breadcrumbs
75g caster sugar
100g plain flour
100g ground almonds
100g butter

Preheat the oven to 190°C, Gas Mark 5. Halve large strawberries and leave small ones whole. Tip into a mixing bowl and toss with the breadcrumbs. Pile the fruit into your favourite crumble dish – mine holds 2 litres, is earthenware, oblong and 8cm deep.

Mix the sugar, flour and almonds together in a bowl and cut the butter over the top. Quickly rub the butter into the dry ingredients until evenly crumbed. Spread over the strawberries and bake for 25–35 minutes until golden, checking after 20 minutes in case the crumble is colouring too quickly. If so, cover loosely with foil. Allow to rest for at least 10 minutes before serving so that the juices settle and the crumb won't burn your lips.

STRAWBERRY TRIFLE

SERVES 6 | **PREP** 30 MINUTES, PLUS COOLING | **COOK** 20 MINUTES

My childhood trifles always included jelly, canned fruit and a thick, hard layer of Bird's custard under the whipped cream. I remember the smell rather than the taste of sherry and it's that sweet boozy smell of custard, fruit and cake that is so evocative however the trifle is made. This one is made with pale yellow Madeira cake, a lot of sherry, quickly made fresh strawberry jam, supermarket fresh custard, whipped cream and freeze-dried strawberry sprinkles. Make it in sundae glasses or a glass bowl and pile the top with more strawberries, strings of redcurrants and raspberries.

400g strawberries
150g caster sugar
1 tablespoon thick balsamic vinegar such as Belazu or balsamic syrup
2 tablespoons lemon juice
6 slices of Madeira cake
100ml sweet sherry
500g luxury thick vanilla custard
250ml double or whipping cream
2 tablespoons icing sugar

To decorate
250g strawberries
100g raspberries
100g strings of redcurrants
small mint sprigs

To make the jam, rinse the strawberries and remove the stalks and leaves – quickly done with a small knife, cutting in a pointed plug shape, turning the strawberry rather than the knife. Quarter large ones, halve medium-sized fruit and leave small ones whole. Place in a medium-sized pan over a medium heat with the sugar, balsamic and lemon juice, stirring constantly until all the sugar has melted. Increase the heat and boil, stirring regularly in a figure of eight, for about 10 minutes until the jam looks thick and syrupy. Test by placing a teaspoonful on a saucer. Cool, then push with your finger. If it wrinkles, it's done. If not, continue boiling for a few more minutes. Remove from the heat and pour into a bowl to cool.

Cut the slices of cake to fit the base of sundae glasses or a glass trifle bowl. Pour over the sherry to saturate. Spoon the cooled jam over the top and add the custard to cover. Use a whisk to whip the cream with the icing sugar by hand until it holds firm peaks. Spoon it over the custard and decorate with a greedy pile up of halved strawberries, raspberries, strings of redcurrants and sprigs of mint.

ROAST RHUBARB AND ORANGE MARZIPAN TARTS

SERVES 8 | **PREP** 30 MINUTES | **COOK** 30 MINUTES

Roasting rhubarb renders it silky soft without altering its shape. For these tarts, lengths of rhubarb are lined up over a thin layer of marzipan on puff pastry, merging, as they bake, into a beguiling combo of molten almond paste, sweet orange and tart rhubarb on crisp, flaky puff pastry. And the tarts look amazing.

knob of butter
320g ready-rolled puff pastry
80g marzipan
icing sugar for dusting
800g rhubarb
1 egg
1 blood or juicing orange
1 tablespoon caster sugar
crème fraîche, to serve

Preheat the oven to 220°C, Gas Mark 7. Smear a heavy-duty roasting tray with butter. Cover with baking parchment and smear that, too. Lightly roll the unfurled pastry into a 40 × 24cm oblong. Divide into 8 equal pieces. Transfer, spaced apart, to the prepared tray. Etch a 1cm border, then fork all over within it.

Divide the marzipan into 10g pieces. Dust a work surface with icing sugar and roll the pieces very thinly to fit within the border – it doesn't have to fit exactly or neatly – lifting by working free with a palette knife. Cover with lengths of rhubarb (reserve the trimmings).

Whisk the egg and glaze the border. Dust the rhubarb with icing sugar. Roast for 20 minutes, checking after 15, until pastry is puffy and golden, the rhubarb tender. Transfer to a wire rack to cool and firm.

Finely slice the rhubarb trimmings and simmer for 8 minutes with the orange juice and caster sugar. Force through a sieve, scraping underneath. Stir. Use to glaze the rhubarb. Serve with crème fraîche.

MANGO AND LIME FOOL

SERVES 4–6 | **PREP** 10 MINUTES, PLUS CHILLING

So simple and so delicious.

2 ripe mangoes
1 juicy lime
150g double or whipping
   cream
150g natural yoghurt (I like
   sheep's milk yoghurt)

Peel the mangos over the bowl of a food processor (so that no juice is wasted), then slice the flesh directly into the bowl, discarding the stones. Add the lime juice. Blitz with a hand held electric blender until smooth.

Pour the cream into a mixing bowl and whisk until holding soft peaks. Stir in the yoghurt. Add the mango, folding it through the cream so that it makes thick streaky swirls.

Spoon into pretty glasses before chilling – it will thicken and set – for a couple of hours. If you can't wait, serve over raspberries.

WILD HONEY AND LEMON APPLE OPEN CRUMBLE

SERVES 6 | **PREP** 20 MINUTES, PLUS CHILLING | **COOK** 20 MINUTES

I'm slowly working through a jar of bright yellow, richly subtle Italian wild honey. It had a powerful effect on this simple, versatile apple purée, but any honey, preferably a set one, would suffice. I like the purée cold with hot porridge or over anything creamy though it is spectacular sandwiched between homemade lemon and almond biscuits with thick yoghurt. The crumbly biscuit mix is also perfect for this deconstructed crumble, a delicate standby pud to serve DIY-style – apple, yoghurt and crumble in separate dishes – or assembled in pretty glasses.

50g soft butter
30g caster sugar
75g plain flour
30g ground almonds
1 lemon
1 large Bramley apple,
   about 400g
1 juicing orange
1 tablespoon set honey
450g thick, creamy yoghurt

Cream the butter and sugar until pale and fluffy. Fold in the flour, almonds, 1 teaspoon fine lemon zest and 2 teaspoons juice. Knead into a ball, then chill in a plastic bag for 30 minutes.

Quarter, peel, core and chop the apple. Boil, covered, for 5–10 minutes with the remaining lemon juice, orange juice and 1 tablespoon water. Beat in the honey until the purée is fluffy, thick and smooth. Cool.

Preheat the oven to 200°C, Gas Mark 6. Briefly knead the biscuit dough until smooth and pliant, then crumble between your hands, encouraging different-sized pieces. Spread out on a greaseproof paper-lined baking sheet and bake for 10 minutes or until golden.

Serve the apple topped with the yoghurt strewn with hot or cold crumble.

INDEX

ACKNOWLEDGEMENTS

On April Fools' Day 2008, I was invited to lunch by Emma Tucker, the new editor of *T2*, *The Times'* arts supplement. I was already writing a weekly cookery page for the paper, but Emma asked if I would start a daily after-work recipe column similar to the one that I used to write for the *Evening Standard*. Within six months Emma was telling me that I should publish some of the recipes in a book, and now, eight years later, it's finally happening. Along the way, my agent Bruce Hunter retired and I segued into the care of his colleague Andrew Gordon, who introduced me to Stephanie Jackson, Publishing Director of Octopus Books. Stephanie promptly commissioned a *Dinner Tonight* book. The tentacles of her team have been all embracing and everyone so patient and helpful. I particularly want to thank Leanne Bryan, who wrestled the copy to fit, and Jaz Bahra's constantly evolving design, necessitated by my constant pleas to include more recipes. Special thanks, too, to copy editor Jane Bamforth, who was meticulous in making sure everything I wrote made sense. I've loved Lucinda Rogers' illustrations since her days drawing Chris Hirst's much-missed Weasel column for the *Inde*, so was delighted that Octopus could persuade her to be involved. We've ended up with a fabulously user-friendly book thanks to the commitment and support of everyone at Octopus, particularly Leanne and Jaz. Special thanks, though, to Emma Tucker, now Deputy Editor of *The Times*, without whom this book would never have happened.

www.lindseybareham.com

Publisher's acknowledgements

Publishing Director Stephanie Jackson
Senior Editor Leanne Bryan
Designer Jaz Bahra
Copy-editor Jane Bamforth
Illustrator Lucinda Rogers
Production Controller Meskerem Berhane